Applied Family Law in Islamic Courts

'This unique ethnography derives from patient observation of proceedings, enriched by the author's insider knowledge of the intricate social environments in which justice is constructed in Gaza. She dialogues with actors from multiple strata, showing sensitively and impartially how they interact in, behind, and beyond the court arena. The book is a valuable addition to our sociological understanding of (Islamic) law.'
—*Édouard Conte, Laboratoire d'anthropologie sociale, CNRS, Paris*

'Based on an in-depth investigation in Gaza courts, Nahda Shehada's book also relies on the most relevant and up-to-date academic sources and official archives. She shows how a sharia family court really works in one contemporary Arab society: a society that is peculiar in that it suffers from daily political confinement. In Gaza, women and judges interact in the search for a both negotiated and innovative law, the least unfavourable possible for both parties. All this is brilliantly illustrated by a stimulating book that was much needed and fills a gap in anthropology.'
—*Bernard Botiveau, Emeritus Director of Research at the CNRS, Paris*

Written from an ethnographic perspective, this book investigates the socio-legal aspects of Islamic jurisprudence in Gaza-Palestine. It examines the way judges, lawyers and litigants operate with respect to the law and with each other, particularly given their different positions in the power structure within the court and within society at large. The book aims at elucidating ambivalences in the codified statutes that allow the actors to find practical solutions to their (often) legally unresolved problems and to manipulate the law. The book demonstrates that present-day judges are not only confronted with novel questions they have to find an answer to, but, perhaps more importantly, they are also confronted with contradictions between the letter of codified law and their own notions of justice. The author reminds us that these notions of justice should not be set *a priori*; they are socially constructed in particular time and space.

Making a substantial contribution to a number of theoretical debates on family law and gender, the book will appeal to both academic and non-academic readers alike.

Nahda Shehada is Senior Lecturer in Gender, Culture and Development at the Institute of Social Studies (ISS), Erasmus University, Rotterdam, The Netherlands. Her major area of interest is anthropology of Islamic law, particularly in the MENA region. She has published widely in books and leading international academic journals focussing on Islamic law.

Islamic Law in Context
Series Editor:
Javaid Rehman, Brunel University, UK

The Islamic Law in Context series addresses key contemporary issues and theoretical debates related to the Sharia and Islamic law. The series focuses on research into the theory and practice of the law, and draws attention to the ways in which the law is operational within modern State practices. The volumes in this series are written for an international academic audience and are sensitive to the diversity of contexts in which Islamic law is taught and researched across various jurisdictions, as well as to the ways it is perceived and applied within general international law.

Changing God's Law
The Dynamics of Middle Eastern Family Law
Edited by Nadjma Yassari

Woman's Identity and Rethinking the Hadith
Nimat Hafez Barazangi

Applied Family Law in Islamic Courts
Shari'a Courts in Gaza
Nahda Shehada

www.routledge.com/Islamic-Law-in-Context/book-series/ISLAMLAWCXT

Applied Family Law in Islamic Courts
Shari'a Courts in Gaza

Nahda Shehada

LONDON AND NEW YORK

First published 2018
by Routledge

2 Park Square, Milton Park, Abingdon, Oxfordshire OX14 4RN
52 Vanderbilt Avenue, New York, NY 10017

Routledge is an imprint of the Taylor & Francis Group, an informa business

First issued in paperback 2020

Copyright © 2018 Nahda Shehada

The right of Nahda Shehada to be identified as author of this work has been asserted by her in accordance with sections 77 and 78 of the Copyright, Designs and Patents Act 1988.

All rights reserved. No part of this book may be reprinted or reproduced or utilised in any form or by any electronic, mechanical, or other means, now known or hereafter invented, including photocopying and recording, or in any information storage or retrieval system, without permission in writing from the publishers.

Notice:
Product or corporate names may be trademarks or registered trademarks, and are used only for identification and explanation without intent to infringe.

British Library Cataloguing-in-Publication Data
A catalogue record for this book is available from the British Library

Library of Congress Cataloging-in-Publication Data
Names: Shehada, Nahda Younis author.
Title: Applied family law in Islamic courts : shari'a courts in Gaza / Nahda Shehada.
Description: Abingdon, Oxon ; New York, NY : Routledge, 2017. | Series: Islamic law in context | Includes bibliographical references and index.
Identifiers: LCCN 2017053999 | ISBN 9781138194670 (hardback)
Subjects: LCSH: Domestic relations courts—Gaza Strip. | Islamic courts—Gaza Strip. | Domestic relations (Islamic law)—Gaza Strip.
Classification: LCC KMG187 .S52 2017 | DDC 346.5694/3015—dc23
LC record available at https://lccn.loc.gov/2017053999

ISBN: 978-1-138-19467-0 (hbk)
ISBN: 978-0-367-59184-7 (pbk)

Typeset in Galliard
by Apex CoVantage, LLC

To Lamar, Zyn, and Karim

Contents

List of tables   x
Acknowledgements   xi

1 **Introduction**   1
   1.1 Background 1
   1.2 Research questions 4
   1.3 Methodology 4
   1.4 Theoretical considerations 5
   1.5 Limitations of the study 9

2 **Islamic jurisprudence now and in the past**   12
   2.1 The Shari'a 12
   2.2 Methodologies of jurists 14
   2.3 Ijtihad 15
   2.4 Role of customary law in constructing the Shari'a 16
   2.5 Taqnin (codification) 18
   2.6 Contemporary Ijtihad 23
      2.6.1 Shaham (1999a) 23
      2.6.2 Botiveau (1997) 24
   2.7 Conclusion 25

3 **The Gaza Shari'a courts: an overview**   32
   3.1 Scribes: first point of contact 32
   3.2 Ushers: eyes and ears of the judges 32
   3.3 Archives 33
   3.4 Women's waiting room: forum for peer-to-peer advice 35
   3.5 The courtroom: arena for negotiation 38
   3.6 Gender in the legal profession 43
   3.7 Background of judges 43
      3.7.1 Procedure for appointing judges 44
      3.7.2 Internal relations in the Shari'a court 46
   3.8 Conclusion 48

4 The daily practice of judges: perception vs reality 50
4.1 Ethical stance of judges 50
4.2 Codified law and use of discretion by the judges 57
4.3 Conclusion 70

5 The sociology of Nafaqa (maintenance) 73
5.1 Social context 73
5.2 Legal framework 80
5.3 Judicial procedures 81
  5.3.1 Strategies of judges and lawyers 82
  5.3.2 Strategies of female litigants 83
5.4 Conclusion 93

6 Obedience, rebelliousness and agency 98
6.1 Roots of concept of obedience 98
6.2 Views of Madhahib 101
6.3 Contemporary legal text and practice 102
6.4 Viewpoints of practitioners 105
6.5 Legal practice in Gaza 107
6.6 Synthesis 110
6.7 Conclusion 114

7 The articulation of gendered parenthood: care vs guardianship 117
7.1 Legal text 117
7.2 Hadana in practice 126
7.3 Conclusion 136

8 Civil society, women's movement and family law reform 140
8.1 Background 140
8.2 Political context of the debate in Palestine 142
8.3 Model parliament for women and legislation 145
8.4 Conclusion 148

9 Change, a step at a time 154
9.1 Law, society and social change 155
9.2 Background: integrating the Shari'a with the PA 156
9.3 Deliberation within the women's movement 159
9.4 Draft of women's movement 161
9.5 Disagreement within the religious establishment 164
9.6 Al-timimi's draft 167

9.6.1 On the age of marriage 167
　　　9.6.2 On the wife's return to her husband's house 167
　　　9.6.3 On the role of the wali 167
　　　9.6.4 On consulting women 168
　　　9.6.5 On nafaqa 168
　　　9.6.6 On mukhala'a 168
　　　9.6.7 On compensation for arbitrary unilateral divorce 169
　　　9.6.8 On tafriq (judicial divorce) 169
　　　9.6.9 On hadana (care of children) 170
　　9.7 Gradual change in the new millennium 170
　　9.8 Conclusion 175

10 Epilogue   182

　Glossary   189
　Index   194

Tables

5.1	Nafaqa suits as percentage of total cases at Gaza Shari'a courts, 1993–2001	74
5.2	Marriages and divorces at Gaza Shari'a courts, 1993–2001	80
5.3	Tawabi' in marriage contracts at Gaza Shari'a courts, selected years between 1920 and 2000	85
5.4	Linkage of tawabi' and nafaqa in cases at Gaza Shari'a courts, 1998–2001	87
6.1	House of obedience petitions filed at Gaza Shari'a courts, selected years between 1927 and 2001	104

Acknowledgements

This work would not have been completed without the help of numerous friends and family members. My students at the Institute of Social Studies (ISS), in The Hague, were pivotal in sharpening my ideas and arguments, and I thank them all. My colleague, Edouard Conte, of Berne University in Switzerland was generous with his time and efforts to clarify many doubts during the writing process. Ron Shaham and Bernard Botiveau kindly gave me permission to use short excerpts from their work to argue my case in Chapter 2. I would also like to thank Zed Books for giving me permission to re-publish parts of my chapter, "Debating Islamic family law in Palestine", in this volume.

I am grateful to my friend Amin Kassam for editing the manuscript of this book and helping me to get it ready for submission to the publisher. My daughter Diana gave me constant loving support during the writing and kept me going when the work began to pile up. My eldest son Hani, his wife Walaa and my youngest son Karam were extremely helpful, not only with their constant technical support but also because of their daily love messages full of humour, which is one way to cope with life in their besieged Gaza. I am grateful that I have been blessed with such a wonderful family.

1 Introduction

This study examines two different articulations of Islamic family law, one expressed in the public sphere and the other implemented daily in the Shari'a court. The research was conducted in the Gaza Strip, one of the two areas comprising the Palestinian territories, which were occupied in 1967 by Israeli military forces. The occupation has made travel within and between the two areas both difficult and hazardous, especially due to multiple checkpoints and frequent Israeli raids on Palestinian towns and cities.[1] The restrictive measures imposed by Israel on travel between Gaza and the West Bank since 2007 have made it almost impossible for ordinary Palestinians to cross from one area to the other, so I had to confine my research to the Shari'a courts in Gaza. The research confronted me with the dynamics of law and social justice in a highly adverse developmental setting. The multi-layered application of law by judges and the innovative strategies of litigants inspired me to look in depth at the dialectics of law and justice, with special attention to the negotiations taking place inside the court arena. The result comprises the content of this book.

1.1 Background

In 2001, when I began my 14 months of fieldwork, the entire Gaza Strip, an area around 47 kilometres in length and 18 kilometres in width, was isolated from the rest of Palestine and the outside world. The Gaza Strip is considered to be the most densely populated part of the world; for example, in al-Shati' Camp, 84,077 refugees live crammed into an area of only 0.52 square kilometres.[2] More than three-quarters of Gazans are registered refugees from the Palestine of 1948.[3]

The conditions created by frequent Israeli raids have affected all aspects of Palestinian life, and thus also the Shari'a judicial system, as subsequent chapters will show. Whenever Israel invades a Palestinian city, inhabitants of other cities fear that they will be the next victims, so every family prepares for that eventuality by storing supplies of food, water in plastic containers and cooking gas in cylinders, to the extent that they can afford to do so. For Palestinians, contingency reserves have become an obsession, amid long and frequent electricity cuts and scarcity of clean water because of Israel's destruction of infrastructure and blocking of oil supplies to Gaza's power plant. Inevitably, these difficulties, as well as severe financial problems caused by the ongoing blockade, have had negative effects on family life in Gaza, which are reflected in many of the cases that end up in the Shari'a courts.

The seeds that led me to start investigating how Shari'a courts implement the family law in Gaza were planted in the second half of the 1990s, when I became involved in the women's movement campaign for family law reform.[4] That experience never left me, and in 2001, when I was in Gaza to carry out other research that turned out to be impracticable, I attended several court sessions. I was so fascinated by the proceedings that I spent hours listening to the daily encounters between the judges and litigants. The court proceedings made me realize that the Shari'a is not implemented as rigidly as is generally presumed. I then obtained permission from the qadi al-qudah (chief judge) to do research in the courts and started attending the hearings regularly. To try and blend in, I started wearing the headscarf and sat in the section reserved for the litigants' family and friends. The first days were difficult for me, and for the judges, since I had been highly critical of Shari'a courts during the campaign for family law reform, and some of them were suspicious about my motives. However, it helped that I had come to their place of work wearing a 'different hat' and with a different agenda. I was a student standing before the judge, asking him for clarification and explanation. Over time, their reserve began to melt. Lawyers accepted my presence right from the beginning, and I can recall hardly any tension with them.

In addition, I spent hours in the women's waiting room, listening to litigants' stories about their daily lives, their comments on politics and, most importantly, their perceptions of family law and their reasons for resorting to the Shari'a court. To understand their legal actions, I needed to know what had brought them to court, what their perceptions were and how their cases were being handled. I confirmed in practice that looking at the articulation of law through the eyes of women and litigants in general is essential for arriving at a more adequate analytical framework than a narrow legal perspective would provide (Dwyer 1990).

The daily visits to the Shari'a courts transformed my perceptions of family law. It was then that I understood the difference between the making of law from above and the dynamics of its remaking from below. The experience revealed the gulf between accounts of family law presented by different political groups and its actual implementation in court. I was also struck by the difference between the expression of desires and needs by political activists and those voiced by women in the courts. It was vivid corroboration that different positionalities of women (Moors 1995) and their different experiences influence their strategies, interests and needs. Another important aspect with regard to the construction of interests is the issue of audience. In the court, 'individual' women address their needs to an 'individual' judge, whereas the collective women's movement addresses quite a different political audience and claims to represent all Palestinian women's interests.

I was struck by the discrepancy between the judges' public discourse on family law reform and their practical, less ideologically charged, application of law. The encounters with the judges, lawyers and female litigants, as well as the process of continuous negotiation and bargaining inside the courtroom, led me to reexamine my biases and assumptions. After a few weeks, it became obvious to me that the social construction of law differs significantly from the law in the books.

I was particularly struck by the flexibility of the judges. Contrary to the stereotypical view of Shari'a court judges, they play a considerable role in protecting women from abuse by their male relatives. They show sympathy and consideration and do not hesitate to reprimand men for treating their wives badly, citing Quranic verses that call for women to be treated with respect and compassion. In their daily interaction with litigants, judges often refer to the general principles of the Shari'a or to community welfare. I had to acknowledge that judges are not mere implementers of the law; they are community members working in a particularly paradoxical framework, seeking to protect the weaker members of the community while preserving the existing social order. When ruling on cases, judges sometimes emphasize the text of family law. At other times, they refer to broader values of justice and humane treatment to remind the litigants of the importance of love and compassion in their relations. This moving back and forth between different frames of reference demonstrates that the application of family law is neither rigid nor sacred as ideologists claim.

The interplay of customary practice, codified law and the multiple references of the judges convinced me that the purported boundaries between these aspects of law have been devised for ideological reasons. Codified law is not universally applicable jurisprudence. It has less weight than I had originally assumed. Moreover, codified family law is not an homogeneous set of rules; although intertwined with gender bias, cultural symbols, religious ethos and political sentiments, it is also a product of historical process and bears traces of all the controversies and contradictions that came up during the development of its constitutive elements.

As I analysed the family law debate for this volume, it became clear that much of the rest of the content would not deal with the codified law or Shari'a, nor would it concentrate on the strategies of the women's movement. It would also not solely focus on the discrepancy between theory and practice. Rather, it would be dedicated to analysis of the court as a fragmented world with temporal unity in which people interact, define and defend their interests and world views. In this sense, the court is an arena of negotiation, bargaining, conciliation and manipulation; an arena in which the judge plays a major role, but, surprisingly, has received the least scholarly attention. Therefore, the judges' multiple identities and frameworks, their dilemmas and action as well as their exercise of 'ijtihad' (independent reasoning) will be subjects of analysis in various chapters of this volume.

The main issue that needed to be explored, once I had become convinced of the importance of analysing the application of family law, was the dynamics of the legal arena in which the implementation takes place. The power imbalance between the actors is most evident when negotiations over interests and world views are conducted through the specific medium of the Shari'a court. Comaroff and Roberts (1981) argue that in judicial tribunals, rules do not always rule (see also Moore 2005). Within the same universe of litigation, they contend, rules and social relations of litigants intertwine with the actors' interests. In view of this, who are the actors in the arena, and what are their motivations and strategies? Particularly important was the need to examine the role and motivation of the ultimate arbiter in that arena: the judge. Among the many questions that this study needed to answer were: how is it possible for the judges to provide solutions without destabilizing the existing order based on gender asymmetry? How do they arrive at judicial decisions when several references are at hand, and how do they move back and forth between them?

Thus, the research journey was not linear. The research questions, methodology and analysis were subject to major change and adjustment and were tailored and sharpened during my fieldwork and in the course of writing. There is no one way to write up research findings. Certain materials were excluded and others included for reasons related to proper presentation and consistency of argumentation, as well as for reasons related to the ethics of research, in the hope of encouraging readers to engage in the discussion.

1.2 Research questions

The research focuses on the following major sets of questions:

1   *Public debate and political contestation*
    - Who have been the participants in the debates about family law in terms of political and social affiliation? What positions have they adopted? What are the major differentiations along lines of gender, political affiliation and class? How do they conceptualize the desired nature of Palestinian family law, including its procedures and institutional organization?

2   *Legal practice in the courts*
    - How do judges, lawyers, litigants and other actors in the court operate with respect to the codified family law?
    - What sorts of ambivalences in codified law allow these actors to negotiate their positions?
    - What are the intersections and impacts of social differentiation of litigants and judges on the application of family law?
    - What is the impact of codification on the application of the Shari'a-inspired family law?

1.3 Methodology

Methodological 'recipes' do not exist (Patton 2002) and should not be developed. This research distances itself from positivist methods based on sole recourse to a 'tool-box' of techniques, hypothesis-testing and the isolation of 'determinants' of social behaviour. Instead, a partially open-ended ethnographic approach is adopted. As a reflexive process, ethnography is 'about seeing, hearing, noticing' and understanding meaning (Law 1994: 50), which denotes following the logic of practice (Neuman 1997). This implies that fieldwork and analysis are conducted simultaneously, with, at each stage, evidence and theory shaping each other (Bertaux 1980).

The research combined this method with semi-structured interviews with judges, lawyers, litigants and court personnel as well as community figures and social-justice activists. The interviews were carried out in the form of 'conversations', which best convey the flavour and context of utterances and gestures embedded within the routine enactment of focused encounters. Litigants' life histories (see Bertaux 1980; Gluck and Patai 1991; Fisher 1991) and those of relevant other actors were collected in order to gain more insight into the backgrounds and positions of those concerned. In particular, while processing the cases, I constructed some individual life histories, recorded ideological positions, investigated occupational or economic circumstances, composed the dispute history and gathered information on norms relating to specific actions. The qualitative data were combined with analysis of the text of family law and its various interpretations.

As the aim of the study was not to develop an overview, but to gain insight into negotiations between various actors in the courts, and because the political as well as military conditions in Palestine made travel between cities and towns difficult and hazardous, the research was conducted only in the Gaza Strip Shari'a courts.

I visited the courts every day and took detailed notes on the dialogues, conversations and other interactions between the various actors. I built up a rapport with judges and court clerks. The female litigants were the easiest to talk to, as we could interact in the waiting room. In some cases, I took the addresses of women and visited them at home. I used conversation as a means of entering and engaging with their everyday life-worlds. My identity as an Arab, and a Palestinian by choice, facilitated the conversations with women, court clerks and judges.

Observation of court cases and conversations with the court attendees and clerks were my entry point for understanding the application of family law. They helped me to select a number of court cases relating to specific articles in the legal text in order to understand the universe of the Shari'a court and to record the circumstances in which they were embedded. Having done so, I conducted quantitative research in the court archives in order to determine how the application of Islamic family law had developed in the twentieth century. I was able to trace the historical process of generation and consolidation as well as the ongoing shaping of the application of family law in specific types of cases. I identified certain trends and the socio-economic and cultural variables associated with them. I ascertained the domains of social action as well as other internal and external factors that contribute to the shifts in certain applications.

1.4 Theoretical considerations

Transformations of family law at the macro level may be studied by comparing successive statutes (in the Gaza Strip, the *Book of Personal Status Rulings* of 1875 and the *Gaza Law of Family Rights* of 1954). However, such a focus does not by itself enable a researcher to understand the social construction of law as a whole. For that, we need to take into account people's counter- or consensual actions as well as their needs, including the ways in which the communication between the state and citizens is mediated, through, for instance, court personnel (Griffiths 1992). Palestinian society is plural, between as well as within communities; judges, lawyers, police and litigants (male and female) view family law through different spectacles.

Griffiths (1992: 153) distinguishes two approaches towards law. The first is the instrumental one, which perceives law as an 'instrument for social engineering'. The advocates of this approach are concerned with the 'effectiveness' of law. The second approach, sociology of law, has 'devoted its attention instead to things like dispute processing'. The points of departure of the instrumentalist approach are threefold: first, society comprises isolated individuals, whose social connections are unimportant; second, the communication between law and individuals is perfect and people understand and comprehend the command of law; and finally, the state has a normative monopoly over regulation, as if there were no other norms or structures but state law. These assumptions lead advocates of this approach to look for 'the recalcitrant self-interest or "deviant" character of the individual as the prime suspect in the case of non-compliance,' instead of acknowledging multiple structures and regulations.

Instead of adopting this narrow approach, Griffiths (1992: 155) suggests a sociological frame of analysis. The first entry point is the importance of appreciating individuals as fundamentally social beings, 'people who together compose a society as all their individual or collective activities are "social through and through".' In this context, the state plays 'at most a distant and indirect role'. Second, the communication between 'legislative and individual is almost never unmediated'. And third, the plurality of the legal realm: '[t]he state organization is but one of the many arenas in society where regulatory activities take place.' This approach towards law puts the social life instead of the intention of the legislators at centre stage (ibid.: 157). Griffiths' theoretical position thus looks not at the law's 'effectiveness' but at its 'social working'. This study employs Griffiths' frame of analysis, which, as he acknowledges, is inspired by the seminal work of Moore (1978).

Moore (1978) contends that in studying law and society one should consider the role of ideology, action, continuity and change. This framework takes into account how law is ideologically conceptualized by different political groups, how it is implemented in real life, why it continues to exist through time and space and how it is gradually and historically modified. According to Moore, law goes through two major social processes: order and change. Between these two processes, there is space for indeterminacy. Order always exists in some way, but it never takes over. It always leaves gaps, which require adjustment, that is, change. The interplay between order and change offers space for thinking of social processes as not fully determinate. Determinacy (order) exists due to the rule and role of culture and particular social relationships at specific times and in specific spaces. However, culture and social relations are full of inconsistencies, ambiguities and discontinuities. They are not fixed; rather, their temporality is essential, which entails that indeterminacy exists as a pervasive quality of social and cultural order. Thus, people's behaviour might be interpreted in two ways. On the one hand, they try their best to control their lives by furthering the rule of order and working to fix and crystallize social reality. Such attempts at 'social regularizations' would ultimately produce what Moore calls 'conscious models', which are meant to organize and systematize people's 'customs and symbols and rituals and categories and seek to make them durable' (Moore 1978: 50). This fixed model has its own merits; it allows people to live in relative stability and predictability, thus enabling them to plan their lives and interact with others on the basis of reasonable expectations of behaviour.

However, when the 'conscious model' becomes unbearable, people tend to search for indeterminacies or ambiguities in the model in order to achieve their objectives. They may even generate such indeterminacies to accommodate the new challenges of life. They engage thus in 'processes of adjustment'. The ambiguous area between the previous order and the new adjustment is the area in which indeterminacies occur. I found that this is the area where Palestinian women who go to the Shari'a court play out their interests. They often search for such gaps of indeterminacy, ambiguity or uncertainty in the interplay of codified law, social customs and the multi-referential framework of judges to find space to express and materialize their needs and interests. In the course of their attempts to obtain justice, women often manœuvre and manipulate these structures and sometimes succeed in turning them to their benefit.

Moreover, Moore's framework does not regard the determinate and indeterminate as fixed states, but rather as ever-changing processes. What is fixed is only the continuous renewal. If 'situational adjustment' is adopted, repeated and becomes a pattern in people's lives, then it is likely to be part of the processes of regularization; this implies that each process 'contains within itself the possibility of becoming its schematic opposite' (Moore 1978: 51).

Moore concludes that the complex relationship between social life and cultural representation is difficult to handle unless we take into account these three elements of regularization, adjustment and indeterminacy. Law is one major factor in these activities (ibid. 1978: 52–3). Understanding of how law works as a social phenomenon provides a window into how family law operates in real life. For example, family law ensures the right of women to maintenance and links it with their obedience, but in practice women are able to adjust this provision to meet their objectives, which often do not match the intentions of the law. It is in this ambivalent area between fixity and indeterminacy that women claim their rights and materialize their interests.

Moore also stresses the importance of investigating the context within which the law operates, and thus within which familial disputes are resolved. The source of the law used in dispute settlement does not matter analytically as much as the context within which the process of 'amalgamation' takes place (Moore 1978). Dwyer (1990) cites Joseph (1990) as emphasizing the importance of 'personal ties' that set the parameters of the outcome of legal action during dispute settlement in Lebanon, while Rosen (1989), who studied the operation of Islamic courts in Morocco, stresses the 'open-textured' nature of concepts relating to social relationships, which allows individuals to define and redefine their relationships within their context.

Moreover, the judges and litigants operate in what Gluckman (1955: 20–1) calls 'multiplex relationships'. These relationships 'endure through the lives of individuals and even generations.' Each relationship is part of a complex network of multiple bonds. Chapters 5, 6 and 7 demonstrate that the implications of any dispute between spouses reach far beyond their 'private' life, in the sense that the social relations between their respective families are heavily involved. What makes the picture more complicated is the fact that these familial relationships (between the spouses' families) are also part of the larger social setting of Gaza, in which the boundaries between kinship, politics and economy are very much blurred. The consequence of any disruption in one aspect of these multiplex relationships is equivalent or greater disruption in a series of other relationships. Therefore, it is often observed that the judges not only investigate the particular dispute beforehand but also expand their investigation to reach out to other ties that embrace many interests 'which may endure into the future' (ibid.). It is in this light that this study analyses the judges' sincere attempts to avoid, for example, a breakdown of the marriage relationship because, in their view, the respective families and the community in general should be able to live peacefully in the future (see Chapter 4 on the conduct of judges, Chapter 5 on nafaqa (maintenance) and Chapter 7 on guardian rights). Consequently, in such cases judges tend to make their rulings more in line with solutions based on reconciliation and compromise.

In the context of Islamic family law, the duality of customary practice and codified law raises the question of how we should define law, or, what law is. Moore (1978) points out that we should not apply the term 'law' only to those binding rules enforced by governments or states. For sociologists, law is better seen as a social phenomenon (Pospisil 1971) that indicates 'every form of rule pertaining to an organized group in any society' (Moore 1978: 18). In particular, any form of rule that has authority, intention of universal application, obligation and sanction should be called law (Pospisil 1971). In Moore's view, the dichotomy between codified law and 'other' laws is made to serve a particular ideological point of view. In reality, there is no such division. She observes that even in industrial societies, where a presumed 'rational' state law is applied, one can point to occasions when rational law is sidelined in practice. Thus, in complex as well as 'simple' societies, formal laws can work only partially; they have never controlled (and perhaps never will be able to control) every activity or action.

Customary practices or customs are the usual practices, and they entail ethical values (Gluckman 1955: 236). They are defined by anthropologists as describing 'patterns of behaviour of a particular group' (ibid.). Codified law and customary practice are different, but they are closely related. Their relation is akin to the relation between religion and culture; they arise from different sources, but the dialogue between them has always been intact throughout history. Culture embraces religion and religion accommodates cultural practices. Rights and obligations in the context of Islamic family law thus become subject to both. In daily life, there is no clear-cut division between customary practice and codified law. To accomplish their goals, people may exploit the fixity of the codified law on one occasion or emphasize the indeterminacy and flexibility of customs on another (Moore 1978).

In the Shari'a court, the identifiable legal concepts are those related to maslaha (public interest), istihsan (seeking the most equitable solution), social customs, accepted social behaviour and the community's general morality. These flexible concepts are put together with the family law to enable judges to find leeway when the codified law does not provide justice. This study will demonstrate how judges use these flexible, permeable, unspecific, non-written concepts to manipulate the codified law and surmount situations in which paradoxes between the written law and its objective are inevitable. Hence, the flexibility of judges is generated from this 'vagueness of and conflicts between principles, the multiplicity of principles, the combinations of precise and imprecise principles [which] give the [applied] law the quality of flexibility that enables it to work and makes it applicable to the unbelievable variety of contingencies involved in human affairs' (Moore 2000: 145).

1.5 Limitations of the study

Due to the Israeli military obstacles to travelling from Gaza to the West Bank, as well as political factors, which were outlined in section 1.2, the research for this study was restricted to two courtrooms in the Gaza Shari'a courts building. My analysis is principally based on the 14 months I spent in those courtrooms, observing the proceedings every day, as well as in the waiting room for women, where I talked to litigants about the circumstances that had led to their court action and how their cases were going. I was also able to speak on the phone with the qadi al-qudah in the West Bank to get his views on issues related to family law and its reform. Hence, while judges affirmed to me that their colleagues in West Bank Shari'a courts also apply family law flexibly, I cannot personally vouch for the extent to which my findings reflect the proceedings there.

On a different register, it must be stressed that neither the theory of Islamic law nor its practice is a unified whole. Even in the Gaza courts, practice is not unified, nor is it consistent. Individual interpretations, world views and personal engagements were involved in every case, and therefore the cases may represent fragmented realities.

Finally, the definition of Islamic law is problematic. If we dare to exclude the theological viewpoint, there are opinions derived from a legal perspective and others from the sociology or anthropology of Islamic law. The 'ultimate truth' on Islamic law, to the extent that it exists, is beyond the scope of this study as it falls in the domain of belief, denominations and perhaps politics.

Notes

1 According to the Israeli human rights organization Btselem, 'as of 31 Jan. 2017 there were 98 fixed checkpoints in the West Bank, including 59 internal checkpoints located well within the West Bank. In addition, the military erects hundreds of surprise "flying" checkpoints along West Bank roads. In April 2015, the UN Office for the Coordination of Humanitarian Affairs (OCHA) counted 361 flying checkpoints, as compared with 456 in December 2014, 256 in December 2013, and 65 from September 2008 through March 2009.' <www.btselem.org/freedom_of_movement/checkpoints_and_forbidden_roads>, accessed 17 August 2017.
2 This statistic is from the United Nations Relief and Works Agency. <www.unrwa.org/where-we-work/gaza-strip/beach-camp>, accessed 17 August 2017.
3 These statistics are from <www.us-israel.org/UN/unwa6.html>, accessed 24 August 2017.
4 I was particularly active in the Model Parliament for Women and Legislation (1997–99), which will be discussed further in Chapter 8.

Bibliography

Bertaux, D. (1980) 'From the Life-History Approach to the Transformation of Sociological Practice', in D. Bertaux (ed.) *Biography and Society: The Life History Approach in the Social Sciences*, pp. 29–46. Beverley Hills: Sage.

Comaroff, J. L. and S. Roberts (1981) *Rules and Processes: The Cultural Logic of Dispute in an African Context*. Chicago and London: University of Chicago Press.

Dwyer, D. H. (1990) 'Law and Islam in the Middle East: An Introduction', in D. H. Dwyer (ed.) *Law and Islam in the Middle East*, pp. 1–15. New York: Bergin & Garvey.

Fisher, M. (1991) 'The Uses of Life History', *Anthropological Humanist Quarterly* 16(1): 24–7.

Gluck, S. and D. Patai (1991) *Women's Words: The Feminist Practice of Oral History*. New York and London: Routledge.

Gluckman, M. (1955) *The Judicial Process Among the Barotse of Northern Rhodesia*. Manchester: Manchester University Press.

Griffiths, J. (1992) 'Legal Pluralism and the Social Working of Law', in B. Brouwer, T. Hol, A. Soeteman and A. de Wild (eds.) *Coherence and Conflict in Law: Proceedings of the 3rd Benelux-Scandinavian Symposium in Legal Theory*, pp. 151–76. Amsterdam and Deventer: Kluwer Law and Taxation Publisher.

Joseph, S. (1990) 'Working the Law: A Lebanese Working-Class Case', in D. H. Dwyer (ed.) *Law and Islam in the Middle East*, pp. 143–61. New York: Bergin and Garvey.

Law, J. (1994) *Organizing Modernity*. Oxford and Cambridge, MA: Blackwell.

Moore, S. F. (1978) *Law as Process: An Anthropological Approach*. London: Routledge & Kegan Paul.

Moore, S. F. (2000) *Law as Process: An Anthropological Approach (1978): New Introduction by Martin Chanock* (2nd ed.). Hamburg: LIT Verlag and James Currey.

Moore, S. F. (2005) 'Certainties Undone: Fifty Turbulent Years of Legal Anthropology, 1949–1999', in S. F. Moore (ed.) *Law and Anthropology: A Reader*, pp. 347–67. Malden, Oxford and Victoria: Blackwell.

Moors, A. (1995) *Women, Property and Islam: Palestinian Experiences 1920–1990*. Cambridge: Cambridge University Press.

Neuman, W. L. (1997) *Social Research Methods: Qualitative and Quantitative Approaches.* Boston, MA: Allyn and Bacon.
Patton, M. Q. (2002) *Qualitative Research and Evaluation Methods.* London and New Delhi: Sage Publications.
Pospisil, L. (1971) *Anthropology of Law: A Comparative Theory.* New York: Harper & Row.
Rosen, L. (1989) *The Anthropology of Justice: Law as Culture in Islamic Society.* Cambridge: Cambridge University Press.

2 Islamic jurisprudence now and in the past

This chapter presents a brief overview of the literature on issues related to the Shari'a and fiqh, with the purpose of clarifying certain boundaries between the original sources (the Quran and sunna)[1] and the human construction of Islamic jurisprudence (fiqh).[2] It sketches some elements related to the evolution of fiqh and exercise of ijtihad (independent reasoning) and explores the debate on the 'gates of ijtihad'. The chapter also traces the incorporation of urf (customs, norms, social traditions) into Islamic jurisprudence and examines whether this tradition still bears on the application of codified law in contemporary Shari'a courts. Finally, it presents an outline of a sociological analysis of the process of codification.[3]

2.1 The Shari'a

For Muslims in Palestine, the legal elements of relations inside the institution of the family are regulated by personal status law, which is implemented by Shari'a courts. These courts rule on issues such as marriage, divorce, inheritance, custody and so on. Family law is regulated according to the Shari'a and codified by the 1954 *Gaza Law of Family Rights* with regular reference to the *Book of Personal Status Rulings According to the School of Abu Hanifa* compiled by Qadri Pasha.[4] The public perceives the Shari'a court as a religious institution for two reasons: first, family law is derived from the Islamic Shari'a; and second, the judges are graduates of Islamic schools.

The literal meaning of the Shari'a has often been confused with its sources and methodologies. As Vikør (2000) observes, most of the controversy about the Shari'a stems from the fact that there is no clear idea about what it comprises. In his view, it has never been defined or compiled in a systematic manner or in a single body of written work. The Shari'a is best understood as a set of shared representations of Muslim society, based on a literature that is broad but not necessarily consistent or approved by any single authority. Vikør points out that this situation contrasts with the legal systems of the contemporary world, in which law is defined as a systematic set of stipulations written into a code and authorized by a specific elected body. The Shari'a does not have such a specific form; hence, it is known as an uncodified set of laws.

Literally, the word 'shari'a' means 'a waterhole where animals gather daily to drink' (Philips 1990: 1). Al-Yaffi (1983) compares the importance of water in the lives of creatures to the role of the Shari'a in the lives of believers, playing a vital function in their legal and religious life (cited in Botiveau 1997: 59).[5] The Sufis, for their part, define Shari'a as derived from the Arabic root shara'a, 'to introduce' or 'prescribe'. For them, the Shari'a is 'the canonical law of Islam as put forth in the Quran and the sunna and elaborated by the analytical principles of the Sunni and Shi'a schools of law (madhahib)' (Kianfar 2003).

When Islam emerged in Arabia, it appeared in a community which had its own pre-established laws, customs and traditions. Some of those were rejected by the new religion, whereas others were incorporated into the 'prescribed path' (the Shari'a). It is crucial to note that the Quran and sunna did not cancel all older laws in the Arabian peninsula; only those pre-Islamic norms that were explicitly forbidden by the Quran and sunna were labelled 'un-Islamic'.

From this perspective, referring to the Shari'a as simply 'Islamic law' is not fully correct because only part of it is derived from the Revelation, and the rest stems from other sources. Ramadan (1970: 25) suggests that the

> very term 'Islamic law' reflects, in the first instance, an idea far from the common concept of the nature and function of law. Religion is generally conceived to be a spiritual sphere of supra-human connotation that cannot be identified with 'law', which is basically a secular concern. A vast background of legendary notions, sacerdotal build-up and political history has contributed to the estrangement of law and religion.

Being subject to human reasoning and life circumstances, law is changeable. Religion, in contrast, purports to remain constant (ibid.). At least for believers, it is fixed by the very fact that it was revealed by God. There are two major differences between law and religion. The first pertains to their distinct development and the second to their sources. Law, although religiously motivated, is subject to human needs, aspirations and the power distribution in society; religion is based on the ordinances of God (Ramadan 1970: 26). Brohi (1970: 15) points out that it would be incorrect to foreclose any possibility of Islamic law changing to meet the evolving conditions of Muslim societies. Islamic law is neither divine nor immutable. In the Quran and the sunna, only a few passages stipulate principles of legislation; the rest are left open to humans to decide according to place, time and circumstance.

Moreover, the Shari'a is not an exclusive invention of Muslims; it incorporates elements of many non-Muslim juridical systems, such as pre-Islamic Bedouin law, commercial law from Mecca and agrarian law from Madina.[6] During the first phase of the development of fiqh, jurists did not hesitate to use local legal conceptions, such as the customary practices of conquered lands, in their reasoning. Roman-Byzantine and Jewish laws were smoothly incorporated into the fiqh provided they did not contradict the Quran and sunna (Botiveau 1997: 40). The incorporation of various customs, social norms and laws was clearly articulated by Imam Malik, founder of one of the major Sunni schools, when Caliph Harun al-Rashid wanted to establish Malik's *al-Muwatta* as a uniform code to be followed by all Muslims in the Abbasid empire.[7] He went so far as to suggest hanging Malik's book in the Ka'aba' in Mecca.[8] Imam Malik dissuaded him, saying: 'O leader of the believers! The Companions of the Prophet went here and there carrying with them what they had heard and seen during the lifetime of the Prophet. They also carried with them different opinions on many details' (quoted in Ramadan 1970: 88).

There are two things to note in Malik's response: the first is that no comprehensive knowledge of sunna was available to any single Companion; the second is Malik's reference to the Prophet's Companions going 'here and there', which indicates acknowledgement of the influence of local cultures and customs on the jurists' reasoning. To display his book as the main legal source for Muslims would have, in Malik's opinion, deprived the Shari'a of its main glory: 'Difference among Muslim scholars is but a divine mercy for this nation. Each of them follows what he considers to be right, each of them has his argument, and all of them sincerely strive in the way of God' (ibid.).

Thus, the Shari'a derives from the Quran and the sunna; it incorporates laws from pre-Islamic society; it also accommodates laws and customs from conquered societies. Finally, it has been framed and elaborated by Muslim jurists from different madhahib. Let us now move on to a more controversial issue in the debate around the Shari'a, namely the methodologies used by Muslim scholars to interpret God's will.

2.2 Methodologies of jurists

Ijtihad is an intellectual exercise that consists of interpreting the Quran and sunna by applying different methodologies: analogical reasoning (qiyas), the consensus of the community (ijma'),[9] the principles of istihsan (seeking the most equitable solution) and the principles of istislah or masalih mursala (seeking the solution that will best serve the public interest) (Dwyer 1990: 2). In addition, familiarity with customary law (urf) is considered a crucial qualification for a Muslim to be a competent jurist (Abu Husayn al-Basri [d. 436/1044], quoted in Hallaq 1984: 189).[10]

The difference in methodologies adopted by various jurists is the major explanation for the emergence of different schools of law in Islamic jurisprudence (Botiveau 1997: 63). Whereas the Quran and the sunna set high moral ideals for people to follow, the role of the jurists is to use interpretative tools to arrive at correct judgments (ahkam). To arrive at ahkam shar'iyya (Islamically legitimate judgments), jurists have either to go back to the nass (the text of the Quran or sunna) or to deduce the judgment by using certain methodologies. 'Abd al-'Ati (1977: 14–15) stresses the importance of delineating the boundaries of the Shari'a and fiqh:

> Much of the confusion can probably be avoided if the analytical distinction between the Shari'a and fiqh is borne in mind and if it is realized that Islamic law is held by Muslims to encompass two basic elements: the divine, which

is unequivocally commanded by God or His Messenger and is designated as Shari'a in the strict sense of the word; and the human, which is based on and aimed at the interpretation and/or application of the Shari'a and is designated as fiqh or applied Shari'a.

Judge Musa points out that Muslim jurists often displayed differences in opinion over time: it is 'common for one of them to say something today and say something else the day after' (Musa 1958: 15). Imam Shafi'i, for example, changed his opinion on several issues after he moved from Iraq to Egypt (Ramadan 1970: 93). This indicates the relevance of context for the reasoning of fuqaha' (grand thinkers). Therefore, judge Musa (1958: 15) argues that it is not wise to say that the jurists' opinions are the Shari'a itself. Significantly, as fiqh was developing, no single jurist claimed his reasoning to be the correct one. More importantly, the schools of law did not exist during the lifetime of the grand thinkers; what we know now as the Hanbalite, Shafi'ite, Hanafite and Malikite schools were only established by the followers after the death of the fuqaha' (Ramadan 1970: 91).

2.3 Ijtihad

There are at least two viewpoints regarding the continuing use of ijtihad. One says that ijtihad was restricted after the third century of the hijra (about 900 A.D.),[11] and the other maintains the contrary.[12] According to the feminist jurist Qudsia Mirza (2000: 196), 'the closing of the gates of ijtihad [. . .] and the restricted use of ra'y (reasonable interpretation), the two key hermeneutic methods by which reinterpretations of Islamic law took place, have led directly to this reduction in progressive interpretations.'[13] This viewpoint is probably derived from Schacht (1964: 70–1), who argued that by

> the beginning of the fourth century of the hijra the point had been reached when the scholars of all schools felt that all essential questions had been thoroughly discussed and finally settled, and a consensus gradually established itself to the effect that from that time onwards no one might be deemed to have the necessary qualifications for independent reasoning in law, and that all future activity would have to be confined to the explanation, application, and, at the most, interpretation of the doctrine as it had been laid down once and for all.

Gerber and Hallaq, who scrutinized the work of Muslim jurists during the centuries following the fourth century of hijra, challenge this opinion. Gerber (1999: 112), in his study of Islamic law and culture between 1600 and 1840, gives examples of the fatwas of Ibn Abidin and Al-Ramli to show that the gates of ijtihad had not closed and, if anything, that saying they have closed fosters an unacceptable essentialism.[14]

Hallaq (1984), a chronological study, also provides evidence that the gates of ijtihad have not been closed. Hallaq traces the writings of Muslim mujtihidin (particularly after the fourth century) to disprove this widespread, 'baseless and inaccurate' claim (1984: 4), which has played a significant role in interpretation and construction of Islamic history. He argues that mujtahids and ijtihad have existed throughout, as proved by the ample material available from that period. Hallaq demonstrates that the notion of closing the gates of ijtihad appeared only at the beginning of the sixth/twelfth century. Questions relating to who is allowed to exercise ijtihad and in what areas, although veiled by methodological concepts, are far from technical; they are at the heart of the political debate and conflict in Muslim countries, between those who still occupy the seats of power and thus preserve their interests and those who challenge them.

2.4 Role of customary law in constructing the Shari'a

The role of customary law has received considerable attention from Muslim jurists. Abu Husayn al-Basri (d. 436/1044) was not the only jurist to acknowledge the importance of urf in constructing the Shari'a. Others, such as al-Sarakhsi (d. 490/1097), implicitly associate urf with consensus of the community, citing the following hadiths as justification for recognizing custom: 'my community will not agree on error' and 'everything the Muslims regard as good is good in God's eyes' (cited in Libson 1997: 147). Blurring the boundaries between urf and ijma' (consensus of the Madinese during the time of Prophet Mohammad) was perhaps a manoeuvring strategy to accommodate distinct customs and forms of urf in different contexts.

Latter-day jurists such as Ibn Abidin (d. 1836) have also stressed the importance of customary law. Gerber quotes Ibn Abidin as saying that not all the Shari'a comes from the Revelation; the madhahib 'took much of the law from the field rather than from hadith or Quran' (Gerber 1999: 111). In other words, 'urf overpowers the books of the madhahib, but it is illegal [only] if it counters the nass [text of the Quran or sunna]' (Gerber 1999: 112). Gerber strongly opposes the idea that customary law has been engaged in a struggle against textual Islamic law; the secularization of Islamic law has been going on throughout Islamic history without 'changing the formal framework of sanctity [. . .] urf was in fact a built-in legal mechanism within the fiqh, not an external force attacking it from without' (Gerber 1999: 115).[15]

Masud (2001: 13) believes that in order to translate Shari'a into an operative system of law, jurists had to dig deep into social representations to establish a normative basis. He does not think that legal norms can be realized if they are not founded on social ones. My observation of the workings of the Shari'a courts in Gaza confirm that, even with the codification of family law, urf is still of great practical importance. Rosen (1989) contends that in Islamic history the law was not in conflict with people's norms, customs or morals; on the contrary, Islamic law has always been embedded in the social context. His observation of the proceedings in a Shari'a court in Morocco confirms that the judges do not operate according to the rigid text of Islamic law; rather, they process the text through the prevailing societal norms.

As early as Umayyad times, customs were actively incorporated into the verdicts of judges. Esposito (1982: 127) shows that during that period the judge would refer to the Quran and the sunna, and if he could not find relevant passages there, he would resort to the customs of his community. For example, customs such as dividing the mahr (dower) into two parts, prompt and deferred, had been practised in pre-Islamic societies and were not enjoined in the Quran and sunna; yet they were invoked in the application of personal status issues and legalized by codified family law. Customs were thus incorporated into Islamic law by recognizing some pre-Islamic traditions and by incorporating the usages of Umayyad and Abbasid communities in which the first fuqaha' lived. Other references to customs can be discerned by going through the fatwas of muftis, which were opinions regarding what was acceptable or forbidden in a given context, throughout Islamic history (Esposito 1982: 128–9).

Judge Anis Abu Salman, whom I interviewed on 2 March 2002, shed light on the significance of urf in the daily practice of the contemporary Shari'a court:

> We all act in accordance with our customs and traditions. I prefer customary conflict resolution more than the court because it saves people's face, while the use of 'formal' mechanisms like the law and courts (even if it is the Shari'a court) always has elements of coercion and authoritarianism, and perhaps police interference. In any case, customary law provides a better outcome in terms of maintaining family ties, so why not use it? People feel that their pride and dignity are preserved, the structures maintained and their positions within the wider community protected. When applying customary law, the mediator is somebody who is chosen according to the weight of the implicated families. Class and social status are crucial for preserving the 'face' of the parties involved. The mediator should have the symbolic authority derived from his reputation, social status and moral power. The mediator always takes into account the context of the conflict and accordingly devises the relevant mediation strategy.

The judge was stressing a methodology of balancing alternatives: what could be done to achieve the objective without people losing face? In other words, if istislah is motivated by promoting public good, which in this case means easing the situation and saving people's face, then why not use it? Familiarity with, and appreciation of, the actual inequalities in their communities guide the judges towards finding practical solutions. Ultimately, they do not advocate social change; rather, they try to keep the social order intact. The second issue stressed by the judge was the process of mediation. Strict rules have to be respected in this process. If mediation takes place outside the court (that is, in the mag'ad),[16] the main condition is full acceptance by the parties of the mediator's decision, regardless of its nature. The most influential element here is the authority of the mediator, which is generated from various power resources, but above all his ability to execute his decision. For example, when the mediator decides that one party should pay a sum of money to the other, he pays the amount from his own pocket during the very session in which the negotiation is taking place. Then the person who has to pay the money no longer has any say or power of negotiation and has to reimburse the mediator later.[17]

2.5 Taqnin (codification)

In contrast to their predecessors, contemporary judges deal with different texts; it is no longer the Quran, sunna and books of fiqh that they have to reflect on to rule on cases, it is the codified text of family law. The focus is on Ottoman and Egyptian codification because they set the precedent for codification in other Islamic countries.

The codification of personal status laws was a complex historical process derived from the interplay of social, political and religious elements, which necessitated the integration of often contradictory frames of reference. This process involved, on the one hand, a strong articulation of state hegemony remarkably attenuated by the complete neglect of its own legitimacy and, on the other, a particular recognition of the social change underway at the turn of the twentieth century (Botiveau 1997).[18] Codification also involved an acknowledgement of certain customs, in the sense that legislators selected certain practices and customs to be defined as *the* Islamic customs. Its intention was to transform the Shari'a into a written and binding law that claimed to be comprehensive, accessible and applicable to all Muslim citizens. All these elements had to be cautiously projected into the new law. Codification thus became a process of integrating different madhahib (though inconsistently presented and legalized) as well as a means of exercising independent reasoning.

The first attempt to codify the Shari'a in Islamic history took place as early as 1534, when the Ottoman Sultan Sulayman al-Qanuni had criminal laws compiled and set down in writing (Botiveau 1997: 156). In fact, his name (al-Qanuni: the legislator) refers to his being the first legislator of a system subsequently identified as a corpus of law as distinct from the Shari'a (ibid.). This step introduced two major shifts in the legal system of the Ottoman Empire. First, instead of being determined by the Quran, the sunna and different madhahib, the law was derived from, *inter alia*, Ottoman customs. The second was that the new law was solely determined by the state. Three centuries later, the Ottomans introduced commercial and civil laws in a process known as Tanzimat through adoption of codification based on the European model. Later, the *Majalla* appeared (1869–76) as a compilation of Hanafi rules on civil law (Welchman 2000).[19] The significance of the *Majalla* is that it was the first attempt at codification from within fiqh sources to be promulgated as legislation by a political authority.[20] The Hanafi principles continue to be applied by Shari'a courts, but now on the basis of codification (ibid.).

Modernity affected all aspects of life, including family relations, that required the legislators' attention. It is not clear, though, whether codification of personal status law was a tool for modernization or a response to it. Some scholars regard it as a legal response to the modernization of society and the family. For example, Esposito (1982: 91) defines the process of codification as reinforcement of a particular shift of emphasis from 'the extended to the nuclear family which has been slowly taking place in modern Muslim society'. In his view, this process suggests that legislators had genuinely aspired to 'improve' the status of women and children.[21]

At the beginning of the twentieth century, ten years after restoration of the 1908 Constitution, the Ottomans introduced the first personal status code of its kind, known as *The Ottoman Law of Family Rights*, for application in the Shari'a courts (Welchman 2000). With regard to Palestine, Welchman points out that this law was promulgated on 17 November 1917, only one month before the British military conquest of Palestine. It is ironic that the Ottomans who promulgated this law never had the chance to implement it; it was the British who applied it (Welchman 2000).[22]

For centuries, the Shari'a was the exclusive field of Muslim jurists, who developed and delineated particular methodologies to arrive at legitimate judgments. They established particular schools of law, and thus multi-referential Islamic literature and sources were compiled. The process of codifying the Shari'a involved elevating some legitimate measures to formal legality and debasing others despite their legitimacy.

Two main approaches towards codification are identified by Botiveau (1997). The first is the policy defined as 'talfiq' (fabrication) in which legislators devised a method of articulating shar'i (legitimate) answers from the legacy of the different madhahib into binding laws. The legislators carefully used pieces from different Sunni madhhab in order to claim thereafter that the views of each Muslim community (that is, following a particular madhhab) had been taken into account in formulating state-codified law.

The talfiq venture can be seen clearly in the following measures: (a) giving women the right to set conditions in the marriage contract, which is derived from the Hanbali madhab; (b) specifying the exact ages when children can be placed in the custody of fathers and mothers, which is taken from the Malikite madhhab (Botiveau 1997: 220); and (c) the kafa'a (parity or equivalence of status) of the groom, which is derived from the Hanafi madhhab.[23] This methodology of 'fabrication' became a legacy and was used by most Arab nation-states when new codification (reform) was on the agenda.

Botiveau identifies three levels (or methods) of talfiq. First, there is a complicated process of bringing together the four madhahib into a single piece of legislation and writing the text in such a way as to make it applicable. The second method is internal talfiq, whereby the legislators choose certain rules and measures from each of the four madhahib and synthesize them into a single law. The third is a combination of internal and external talfiq, whereby the legislators take rules from the four madhahib and add elements from legal dispositions foreign to the Shari'a.[24]

The policy of talfiq found popularity among a number of jurists, who justified it either by highlighting the need to unify the nation under a single law or by stressing the rigidity of the Hanafi madhhab. For example, in Egypt in 1936, the famous jurist al-Sanhuri called for personal status issues to be dealt with under a single code applicable to all Egyptians without strict adherence to any particular madhhab. In his words, 'We can choose among the four madhahib which corresponds most to the modern life.' Al-Sanhuri used the Ottoman *Majalla* as the precedent for codifying and writing up the Islamic fiqh (al-Sanhuri 1936, cited in Botiveau 1997: 165).

In 1880, the Ottomans decreed that the judges of Shari'a courts should base their judgments solely on Hanafi doctrine (Botiveau 1997: 215). Indeed, Muhammad Qadri Pasha's compilation of personal status rulings was derived solely from Hanafi sources. In Egypt at the beginning of the twentieth century, the introduction of measures from other madhahib was objected to by groups loyal to the policy and madhhab of the Ottomans. For instance, Musa (1958: 31) refers to the following as an example of the battle for change and reform in Egypt during the early years of the twentieth century. In 1914, a committee, comprising the Shaykh al-Azhar, the mufti and prominent Egyptian jurists, was established to review personal status norms and integrate measures from different Islamic schools instead of relying only on the Hanafi madhhab.[25] The committee worked on the reform (islah) project for two years. It even prepared a memorandum announcing a new personal status code. At the last minute, however, their document was rejected by the conservative 'ulama' of al-Azhar, who described the proposal as talfiq. In their view, any talfiq was void.

However, that was just a minor obstacle; the thrust for reform continued as its advocates learned how to handle the politics of the issue.[26] First, the reformists dealt with the negative connotation of the term 'talfiq'. Henceforth, they spoke of takhayyur (selection) instead. This designates a more inclusive and receptive process of selection, connoting freedom of choice. Selection means that the legislators are dedicated to choosing the measures that best respond to the needs of Muslims from within the established schools.[27] Second, legislators employed various original, yet instrumental, strategies to avoid objections from the conservative clerical circles in the religious establishment. For example, the new Egyptian personal status code of 1923 (Law No. 56) did not change the age of marriage, but it forbade the judges from ruling on cases of couples younger than 16 years and 18 years for girls and boys, respectively. Couples younger than the specified ages could conclude their marriage contracts but had no legal right to file cases before the Shari'a court judge (Abu Zahra 1950). This amounted to a ban on early marriage.

Botiveau (1997: 216) describes the reduction of the judges' authority and of the freedom they had enjoyed as 'the strategy of deception'. This approach was particularly successful because classical Islamic fiqh does not specify the judges' mandate (ibid.). Egyptian legislators further limited the freedom of the judges through amendments introduced in 1931. This step demonstrated the growing role of the state in organizing family relations through denial of particular social practices, regardless of their religious legitimacy.

The second approach towards codification identified by Botiveau is renovation (tajdid), which aimed at abandoning certain measures that did not suit contemporary conditions. An example of this is the legal treatment of divorce. Before codification, the husband could terminate the marriage bond (irrevocably) by saying the word 'talaq' three times on the same occasion (Abu Zahra 1950: 302). The 1917 Ottoman law as well as the 1929 Egyptian *Law of Family Rights* changed this: while the effect of a talaq accompanied by a number in word or sign is a divorce, it does not amount to a threefold immediate irrevocable divorce; each declaration of talaq counts as a single instance, no matter how many times the husband utters it.

Two major methods of tajdid were followed. The first referred to peripheral opinions that were hardly considered in the classical works on fiqh. This implied that marginal views were no longer necessarily minor; they could be incorporated into codified law. The Ottoman decision to set the age of marriage at 17 years for girls and 18 years for boys is an example of this; the measure was based on a marginal opinion of the Hanafite jurist Ibn Shibrima (Botiveau 1997: 250; see also Abu Zahra 1950: 8). The second method was derived from a general norm of fiqh that allows the ruler to intervene in judges' affairs. That measure, known as siyasa shar'iyya (in this context it may be translated as governmental policy) provided legislators with a religious justification for legal reforms. Esposito (1982: 94) points out that this approach

> grants the political authority the prerogative power, whenever he sees fit, to take administrative steps in the public interest in order to ensure a society is ruled according to the Shari'a. Thus, full judicial power rested in the sovereign's hands so that he could determine the organs of legal administration as well as the extent of their jurisdiction.

The process of codification presupposed that only the state was entitled to determine what was shar'i (legitimate) and what was not, irrespective of its own legitimacy (Botiveau 1997). Codification also involved another major shift related to the introduction of rules and procedures not clearly identified in the Shari'a (ibid.). The post-colonial state had to subject all of its Muslim citizens to the law. That had not been so with fiqh, according to which every group of Muslims was dealt with in accordance with its own madhhab and thus had its own fiqh. For example, it was common in pre-modern Egypt to have four judges, one from each Sunni madhahib (Sonbol 1996), using different approaches and methodologies for each constituency. To establish binding rules, the state stipulated a version of fiqh as national fiqh, and thus some measures became binding even for non-Muslim citizens. One example of this is the Muslim law of inheritance, extended to Muslim and non-Muslim citizens alike (Botiveau 1997: 355).

It is clear that codification did not consist of collecting scattered rules and texts or abruptly introducing new measures; rather, it presupposed a process of decision-making about fundamental standards set out in the Quran (ibid.: 160–1). For example, the legislators' first attempt to intervene in issues relating to divorce was in 1917 with the *Ottoman Law of Family Rights*, which was followed by the Egyptian Law of 1920 (Botiveau 1997: 244).

22 *Islamic jurisprudence now and in the past*

The justifications for the new measures are clearly presented by judge Musa, dean of the Shari'a College of 'Ayn Shams University in Cairo, in his book, published in 1958, a few years after the Egyptian revolution. Judge Musa points out that the reform in the first years of the twentieth century, and thus the incorporation of different measures from different madhahib, was attributable to the rigid positions of the Hanafi madhhab and its incompatibility with 'modern life' (Musa 1958: 30). He lists three examples of such incompatibility:

1   Continuation of nafaqa for divorced women even after the end of their 'idda (three menstruations, a period equivalent to three months); some women continued to receive nafaqa even 30 years after their divorce.[28]
2   According to Hanafi doctrine, denial of judicial divorce to the wife of a man who had disappeared (for example, at times of war or while travelling).
3   In the Hanafi school, denial of judicial divorce to women whose husbands had a biological defect ('ayb) such as the inability to consummate the marriage.

Esposito (1982: 91) regards extending the grounds upon which women may sue for judicial divorce, restricting polygyny and child marriage, as but a few examples of the legislators' aspiration to reinforce particular structures and relations within the 'modern' family. The process of introducing judicial divorce required legislators to establish measures enabling women to request a judge to pronounce such a divorce. In this regard, the legislators were to distinguish three situations.

The first was divorce due to the disappearance of the husband. The First World War, which resulted in many wives being uncertain as to their marital status due to their husbands' disappearance, led legislators to consider this problem. Since the Hanafi school offered no solution, the 1917 *Ottoman Law of Family Rights* (*OLFR*) granted wives dissolution after their husbands had been missing for a reasonable period. Legislators here recurred to the Malikite madhhab (Abu Zahra 1950; Samara 1987; Welchman 2000) but then referred to the Hanbali madhhab in order to include tafriq (judicial divorce) for disappearance in the wider framework of divorce for injury (Welchman 2000). The effect of granting women the right to seek judicial divorce for absence is indicated by the number of such cases filed by women at the Gaza Shari'a courts. In 1920, the percentage of such divorce applications constituted 30% of all cases submitted. The reasons advanced by the wives were all the same: their husbands had joined (or had been forced to join) the Turkish army and had not returned. The reasons for the husbands' not showing up again were not specified in the case descriptions, but presumably they had either died in combat or had preferred to continue living in the countries where they served. This type of suit again became frequent in 1971 and 1972, after a number of Palestinians who had joined the battle against the Jordanian army in the Black September crisis of 1970 did not return. Here, too, the percentage of divorce cases on the ground of absence was high: 27% of all cases filed.

The second ground on which women may claim judicial divorce is when the husband fails or refuses to pay nafaqa. Here, also, the legislators did not follow the Hanafi school but relied mainly on the Malikite, Hanbalite and Shafi'ite' madhahib (Welchman 2000: 299). The introduction of judicial divorce was gradual. The 1917 *OLFR* and the 1920 Egyptian Law (EL) introduced less controversial measures such as the right to divorce for women whose husbands were missing (mafqud) and those whose husbands had a physical defect that prevented the couple from having a normal sexual life. Subsequently, the EL of 1929 included the right of wives to seek divorce for 'strife and discord' (niza' wa shiqaq), an ambiguous concept that made the addition difficult to implement. Botiveau (1997: 244) considers this step as the first clear conceptualization of divorce for injury (talaq lil darar). The reasoning was that discord and strife bring harm (darar) to the wife and thus entitle her to judicial repudiation if she provides the judge with proof that she has been injured (Welchman 2000: 284). This judicial route for seeking repudiation is another step taken by the legislators towards reforming the law through talfiq. The Malikite rather than the Hanafite school permits women to divorce for discord and strife. The Hanafite school is the most restrictive in granting divorce rights to women.

2.6 Contemporary Ijtihad

This section gives an overview of two relevant studies that analyse the struggles of contemporary judges with the new legal system, their room for manœuvre and how these new circumstances remodel the concept of ijtihad.

2.6.1 Shaham (1999a)

In his study of 24 cases brought before a twentieth-century Egyptian judge, Shaham concludes that the judge exercised independent reasoning and used the term 'ijtihad' in a novel way.[29] He views this shift in meaning as the product of the legal changes that occurred during the twentieth century. The conventional meaning of judges' ijtihad was to arrive at hukm (judgment) on issues where no relevant opinion had been given by fuqaha' and jurists. Therefore, they had to devise and use particular methodologies. In contrast, the role of modern judges is to exercise independent interpretation, not of the original sources (the Quran and sunna) but of codified law, particularly in cases where the latter is most ambiguous. Shaham compares the practice of ijtihad during the first and second centuries of the hijra with modern ijtihad. During the first century, the individual judges occupied a central role in deciding the cases brought before them. This was attributable to the lack of consensual methodology in applying the law. The fact that the corpus of legal literature was relatively restricted during the early days of Islam also left much leeway to judges, which in turn allowed their creativity to flourish. Under such circumstances, judges had to pull together not only the text of the Quran and sunna, but also 'a variety of surrounding legal influences' (ibid.: 451). With

24 Islamic jurisprudence now and in the past

the emergence of fiqh in the second hijri century, judges gradually lost their creative role and came to rely mainly on the works of fuqaha' (ibid.). Shaham (1999a: 451) concludes:

> Modern circumstances have perhaps demanded that qadis demonstrate a higher degree of legal creativity than they have demonstrated during most of Islamic history. The restriction of the shari'a courts' jurisdiction, the creation of civil courts, the absence of clear-cut definition by the state as to the status of the shari'a vis-à-vis the sovereignty of statutory legislation – all these have created a situation of legal ambiguity and uncertainty. In the absence of a clear legal methodology appropriate to the new situation, and in a situation in which al-Azhar's establishment has cooperated with the government's demands and has not manifested its creativity in adjusting the law to the modern circumstances, a vacuum has developed in the legal system. The qadis [...] have had to fill this vacuum. Their need to pass decisions in concrete cases submitted to their courts has obliged them to search for a legal methodology to guide them in the new reality that has been forced on them.

Shaham informs us about the dilemma of Shari'a judges in modern circumstances. The shifting meaning of ijtihad is quite telling in terms of how it was used by enlightened judges and how it is generally used by Orientalists and modernists. Ambiguity and uncertainty, the state's hegemonic role and the gradual, however firm, restriction of their room for manœuvre forced them to adapt to the new circumstances by continuously shifting the terms of reference between the codified laws and their old informing legal system (the Shari'a). Some questions that still need to be answered are those related to the comparison of the new methodology and dilemmas of contemporary judges with those of the old fuqaha'. What is the conceptual reasoning of the contemporary judges? How do they justify their rulings? These questions were at the heart of Botiveau's study of the relation between the Shari'a and law in Arab societies.

2.6.2 Botiveau (1997)

In his study of jurisprudence in Arab societies, Botiveau (1997) observes that the judges in modern-day Egypt are still loyal to the principles of the Shari'a, and they are still struggling to find solutions that protect the legally weak party. In order to do so, judges have to overcome the restrictions imposed by codified law and contain the tensions resulting from the new economic and social policies of the state. Two routes are available to them: to resort to the principle of fairness (which is loosely defined) or to rely on the principle of maslaha (public interest).

In this sense, employing ijtihad does not entail revisiting the Quran and sunna; rather, as Botiveau concludes, it entails engaging in 'tafsir' (exegesis, explanation, interpretation) of codified law on the basis of fiqh (ibid.: 356). This reformist enterprise may bring about positive change in areas related to banking and insurance, but when it comes to personal status and criminal law, tafsir can develop into a battlefield for opposed perspectives reflecting distinct political, economic and social interests. Tafsir entails a return to a legal culture that views fiqh as the cornerstone of application and main reference for judges. Due to its rich historical development, Islamic legal theory can offer wide-ranging answers on how to conceptualize a new fiqh that can support the legitimacy of law, on the one hand, and prove compatible with modern life on the other (ibid.).

Let us see how these processes develop in Egyptian courts and how judges practically yet innovatively deal with the new legal system. Which strategies do they follow? And how do they sometimes articulate their judgments with reference to Quranic verses and on other occasions to principles of the Shari'a, interpreting codified law so as to justify their final verdicts? The following exposition is intended to situate my own observation in the Gaza Shari'a court in the context of the ongoing practice of contemporary ijtihad.

In his study of the strategies of judges in Egyptian courts of personal status, Botiveau indicates that they strive to provide both legitimate and legal bases upon which to act. In justifying their judgments, judges systematically use a methodology of gradual citation, referring to articles from the codified law. However, they also often refer to a broader and less-binding paradigm such as 'the accepted measures of certain madhhab', just as they may refer to an even more general framework such as the 'principles of the Shari'a'. For example, judges' verdicts often mention the 'dominant opinion in the Hanafi school' or the 'established principles of fiqh'. This is particularly so when a case involves a decision regarding the obligatory nature of nafaqa. Interestingly, when the judges wish to add legitimacy to their judgments, they support their verdicts with some 'general principles of the Shari'a'.

Yet another significant strategy observed by Botiveau is how judges employ and operationalize Quranic verses and sunna on different occasions. When the case requires emphasis on love and compassion in marriage, the judge quotes the well-known sura that stresses these qualities (al-rum: 21). If, however, love and compassion no longer exist, the judge uses this fact to justify his ruling on separation. When he accepts the wife's request for tafriq because of darar (repudiation due to injury), he quotes the hadith, 'No one should be injured' (la darar wala dirar) to validate his ruling. On some occasions, the judge resorts to all the sources available to him (codified law, sunna, ijma' and the rulings of old Islamic courts) in an attempt to justify his verdict. This notably occurs in nafaqa suits when judges refer to the importance of estimating the amount of nafaqa in relation to the man's financial means. The frequent alternation between fiqh and codified law indicates that these references do not enjoy the same status in the course of validation. The practice apparently reflects the fear that judgments may lose some of their value if legitimacy is not founded on shara'i grounds (Botiveau 1997: 242).

2.7 Conclusion

Botiveau's and Shaham's studies provide a clear picture of the status, mandate and behaviour of contemporary judges. When fiqh was first codified, the intention was to provide a coherent interpretation of the Shari'a in the context of personal status issues. Codified law was conceived as the main source for judges to use in their judgments. Botiveau and Shaham show, however, that codification falls short of providing answers to social problems in societies undergoing profound change, particularly in gender relations. Yet, fiqh and the Shari'a, perhaps due to the very suppleness of their defining principles, remain relevant sources for judges.

Shaham and Botiveau demonstrate that despite persistent attempts to deprive the judges of their subjectivity, codification has failed to do so. When judges feel that codified law does not provide a 'just' answer, they refer to sources such as Hanafi fiqh, principles of the Shari'a or the Quran. A vacuum is created in the legal system by the constraints imposed on Shari'a courts. These include transferral of the mandate of Shari'a courts to civil courts, ambiguity of legal framework(s), lack of a well-defined methodology to deal with new circumstances, and political concerns of religious-legal authorities that preclude social and legal issues. Under the circumstances, the judges exercise independent reasoning in order to resolve the problems posed by an awkward legal system.

We have reviewed two studies concerning the subjectivity of judges, one by an historian specializing in Islamic studies and the other by a jurist studying the political economy of law. Both conclude that judges have maintained their subjectivity and that they often work outside the strict framework of the law. Shaham views this as a revival of ijtihad, while Botiveau interprets the behaviour of judges in terms of their reliance on principles of fairness and justice. The authors have not conducted ethnographic research, but they have observed the similarities in practice by studying cases in the archives or by analysing judgments (ahkam) pronounced in family law courts.

The daily proceedings I witnessed in the Gaza courts show that the judges are confronted with cases that often need to be considered on their own merits. I believe that the judges practise ijtihad with a lower-case 'i', while muftis practise ijtihad with an upper-case 'I'.[30] Muftis tend to relate their fatwas to schools of fiqh, while judges relate their judgments to the immediate public interest. Judges are always confronted with cases that compel them to make choices: how can the social order be preserved while the weak party is protected through their rulings?

Law often overlooks the richness and contradictions reflected in the problems of everyday life. When the codified law, namely the 1954 Egyptian *Law of Family Rights*, is 'deaf', judges shift their frame of reference in quite a subtle way back to the principles of the Shari'a, which appreciate and accommodate people's practices. Ultimately, they arrive at a solution in keeping with the spirit of the Shari'a, to protect the weak and preserve community welfare.

Moreover, judges do not consider themselves to be scholars qualified to exercise independent reasoning, nor do people perceive them as such. When I asked judge al-Ansari whether he considered his flexibility and dedication to finding a 'just' solution on the basis of multi-referential sources to be a form of ijtihad, he looked at me astonished and said, 'We are very far from being mujtihidin; this requires 'ilm (knowledge) that we do not have.' The response showed that the normative definition of mujtihidin and ijtihad influences even the perceptions of its practitioners. When I asked another judge about his views on ijtihad, he answered: 'Why are you so much concerned by these questions? We are trying to give haqq [right] to the people who deserve it, no more, no less [...] we are much simpler than you think!'

Furthermore, the Gaza judge is not trained in a law school; his background is simply in the Shari'a, fiqh and usul al-din [theology]. In religious schools, as Asad (2001: 14) observes, students get more knowledge of ibadat (devotions) and less of mu'amalat (law), which 'presupposes an entire range of moral and spiritual disciplines'. Reviewing the work of Egyptian reformist Muhammad Abdu, Asad (2001: 13) notices that there is 'a ritual cultivation' in the religious schools 'to be a moral pre-requisite for the acquisition of certain intellectual virtues by the judge'.

When appointed as judge, his first intellectual confrontation is with the codified law. Instead of applying what he learned in the Shari'a school, he has to restrict himself to the parameters of the already delimited codified law. He has to find a way out of the contradictions between the morally inspired Shari'a and the restricted tool at his disposal. This triggers another problem: how can he provide justice by using the text of the law and abandoning the rich resources of the Shari'a? This dilemma, which I often observed, is overcome by shifting to a wider frame of reference that helps him to make justice prevail. During my fieldwork, I often heard judges say that religion is meant to facilitate life rather than to create hardships (dinuna din taysir, la ta'sir). When confronted with cases that exceed their capacity as state judges, they act as community leaders. In one hearing I attended, the judge succeeded in restoring a woman to her home after she had been expelled by her husband. Another case involved a judge's intervention to save a woman from harming herself and her fœtus. In an extreme demonstration of authority and subjectivity in another case, a judge intervened to return children to their widowed mother after their uncle, exercising his shar'i and customary right, had taken them from her. The judge in this particular case violated not only the codified law but also the established norms of the major Sunni schools.

In the chapters that follow, this study will focus on the actors and factors in and outside of the courtroom that influence the judgments of judges.

Notes

1 There is a difference between the Revelation (the Quran) and the words and actions of Prophet Muhammad (sunna). For discussion of this, see Libson (1997).
2 The literal meaning of fiqh is 'the true understanding of what is intended'. Fiqh also refers to 'the science of deducing Islamic laws from evidence found in the sources of Islamic law. By extension it also means the body of Islamic laws deduced' (Philips 1990: 1).
3 There is ongoing debate on Shari'a and codification in various Muslim countries. It revolves around the status of the Shari'a as *the* source (as opposed to a source) of legislation, and thus its viability to meet the challenges of 'modern' life.

28 *Islamic jurisprudence now and in the past*

4 The 1976 Jordanian *Law of Personal Status* is applied in the West Bank.
5 The word also means 'path', the path that Muslims should follow to accomplish God's will. To quote the Quran: 'then we gave you a shari'a in religion; follow it, and do not follow the lust of those who do not know' (XLV: 18).
6 *Encyclopædia of the Orient*: http://i-cias.com/e.o/index.htm, accessed 12 August 2017.
7 The desire of the Abbasid caliph is strikingly analogous to the persistent attempts by modern post-colonial nation-states to establish a unified legal system for all their citizens.
8 The most sacred place in Mecca, known as the House of God.
9 In practice, ijma' designates the consensus of the 'ulama' (religious scholars). Reference to ijma' is another source of contention among Muslim jurists; some refer to consensus as the ijma' of the Medinese (people of Medina during the time of Muhammad); others refer to it as the consensus of legal scholars. There are also jurists who regard it as the consensus of the entire Islamic world (see Libson 1997).
10 According to Al-Basri, for an Islamic jurist to be considered a mujtahid (scholar qualified to exercise independent reasoning), he must have knowledge of the Quran, the sunna, and principles of inference and qiyas, all of which requires familiarity with the Arabic language. In addition, the jurist must acquaint himself with God's attributes and should have the confidence of the Muslim community (Hallaq 1984: 289).
11 For example, Schacht (1964) and Lewis (1982).
12 For example, Hallaq (1964) and Gerber (1999).
13 Bernard Lewis wrote in the early 1980s that ijtihad ended during the Ottoman period, when 'all the questions had been answered; in the traditional formulation, the "gate of ijtihad was closed" and henceforth no further exercise of independent judgement was required or permitted. All the answers were already there, and all that was needed was to follow and obey' (Lewis 1982: 229–30).
14 Gerber further argues that the reasons for the decline of scientific thought in Islam must be sought in historical developments rather than in a 'genetic flaw' within Islam. Hallaq reaches the same conclusion as Gerber, namely that the reasons for the decline of Muslim societies have to be sought in other areas than the legal sphere. The jurists' writings about the 'disintegration' of Muslim life demonstrate that the 'shari'a had not been in the centre of criticism as had been the political and socioeconomic situation as a whole' (Hallaq 1984: 18).
15 Gerber (1999: 112) says that even this latter statement expresses an ideological position rather than the daily practice of jurists. He gives many examples of ijtihad that do not comply with the nass (text), but these examples are related to other sections of Islamic law than those being considered in this volume (for instance, transactions).
16 The common house of the extended family (or hamula) where mediation takes place. See section 7.2 of Chapter 7 for more on customary law mechanisms.
17 The information on customary law mechanisms is taken from several informants.
18 What Botiveau means by the 'complete neglect of its own legitimacy' is that the state was not chosen or elected on a basis corresponding to Islamic rules or more contemporary democratic legislation.
19 'Majalla' means 'digest'. The full name is *Majallat al-ahkam al-'adliyya* (*Book of Rules of Justice*).
20 Personal communication with Welchman (May 2005).
21 Recent studies have challenged this stereotypical view of the pre-modern family being predominantly an extended one. See, for example, Doumani (2003).
22 Welchman (2000: 36–7) says that the *Majalla* faced the same fate; it was applied as an absolute civil code only after the collapse the Ottoman Empire, when the British endorsed it under Article 46 of the Palestine Order-in-Council 1922.

23 According to Esposito (1982: 128), 'the Hanafi doctrine of marriage equality (kafa'a) which required that the husband be the equal of his wife in a number of respects, among them lineage, financial standing, and profession, is peculiar to the Hanafi school and reflects the practice of a more socially stratified, class-conscious society than Madina.' In particular, when Abu Hanifa settled in al-Kufa (Iraq), he was responsive to the social composition and norms of that city.

24 Judge Musa (1958: 32) notes that Egyptian Personal Status Law No. 25 of 1929 drew some of its dispositions from the four madhahib and some from different sources unrelated to the madhahib altogether.

25 Abu Zahra (1950: 9) notes that the committee consisted of shaykhs from the four Sunni schools.

26 For more discussion on the struggle between reformists and conservatives, see Abu Zahra (1950), especially his introduction (pp. 1–15). He states that in 1926, reformists formed a committee which drafted a law fully inspired by the opinion of the reformist Mohammad Abdu. The draft not only integrated measures from the four schools of fiqh but went so far as to exercise ijtihad in the classical sense; that is, by reinterpreting the Quran and sunna without reference to the four Sunni schools. For example, the committee proposed that divorce be invalidated if the husband did not obtain permission from the qadi. Conservatives at al-Azhar were outraged by these measures. The result was that 'the proposal slept in the archives of the Ministry of Justice until 1929' (ibid.: 14). Thus, another committee was formed in 1929 to draft a new law, from which Abdu's proposal was left out.

27 The policy of takhayyur became popular even among feminists in Egypt. According to Shaham (1999b: 461), a proposal for inserting stipulations in the marriage contract was initiated and promoted by Egyptian feminists in 1995. The proposal was meant to insert nine stipulations in the official form of the marriage contract, most of which would support the wife's interests. Feminists who were searching for shar'i (justification for their proposal) appealed to the 'principles of selection (takhayyur), which had been adopted by Egyptian legislators as early as the 1920s'. They called for the 'adoption of the Hanbali opinion, which considers any stipulation in a marriage contract as valid and binding as long as it does not contradict a binding shar'i text (nass)' (Shaham 1999b: 476).

28 The application of 'modern' measures, as conceptualized by judge Musa, shows the degree to which modernization can reduce women's ability to bargain with their husbands. This is in comparison with the pre-modern Hanafi school, which gave women the right to deny (truthfully or otherwise) that they had experienced the three cycles of menstruation; on the basis of this provision, women could continue to be entitled to maintenance for extended periods (communication with Lynn Welchman, May 2005).

29 The judge in Shaham's study is Shakir (1892–1958).

30 Hallaq makes a similar point. He argues that by virtue of their particular nature (juz'i), judges' decisions do not accede beyond the parties involved in a dispute. In his view, the mufti's 'fatwa is universal (kulli) and applicable to all similar cases that may arise in the future' (1997: 154). Nevertheless, the application of law as a social process is focusing on these particular decisions.

Bibliography

'Abd al-'Ati, H. (1977) *The Family Structure in Islam*. Indianapolis: American Trust Publications.

Abu Zahra, M. (1950) *Al-Ahwal al-shakhsiyya: qism al-zawaj [Personal Status: Marriage]*. Cairo: Arab Thought Publishing House (Daar al-Fikr Al-Arabi).

Asad, T. (2001) *Thinking About Secularism and Law in Egypt*. Leiden: ISIM.

Al-Yaffi, A. (1983) 'Makanat al-shari'a wa sha'wuha al-ijtima'i' ['The Status of Shari'a and Its Social Position'], *Al-turath al-'arabi* 11–12: 7–16. Damascus. < http://archive.sakhrit.co/newPreview.aspx?PID=1931373&ISSUEID=16103& AID=361974>, accessed 25 December 2017.

Botiveau, B. (1997) *Al-shari'a al-islamiyya wa al-qanun fi al-mujtama'at al-'arabiyya. [The Islamic Shari'a and Law in Arab Societies]*. Cairo: Sienna.

Brohi, A.K. (1970) 'Introduction', in S. Ramadan (ed.) *Islamic Law: Its Scope and Equity*, pp. 11–20. Lahore: Shirkat Press.

Doumani, B. (ed.) (2003) 'Introduction', in *Family History in the Middle East: Household, Property, and Gender*, pp. 1–23. Albany: State University of New York Press.

Dwyer, D.H. (1990) 'Law and Islam in the Middle East: An Introduction', in D.H. Dwyer (ed.), *Law and Islam in the Middle East*, pp. 1–15. New York: Bergin & Garvey.

Esposito, J. (1982) *Women in Muslim Family Law*. New York: Syracuse University Press.

Gerber, H. (1999) *Islamic Law and Culture 1600-1840*. Leiden: Brill.

Hallaq, W. (1984) 'Was the Gate of Ijtihad Closed?', *International Journal of Middle East Studies* 16: 3–41. Also in I. Edge (ed.) (1996) *Islamic Law and Legal Theory: The International Library of Essays in Law & Legal Theory*, pp. 287–325. Adershot: Dartmouth.

Kianfar, S. (2003) *Shari'a, Tariqa & Haqiqa: A Survey of Sufi Philosophy and Islamic Law*, Part 2. <http://www.sufismjournal.org/history/historysharia2.html>, accessed 22 November 2003.

Lewis, B. (1982) *The Muslim Discovery of Europe*. London: Weidenfeld and Nicolson.

Libson, G. (1997) 'On the Development of Customs as a Source of Law in Islamic Law: *al-rujuu ila al-urfi ahadu al-qawaidi al-khamsi allati yatabanna alayha al-fiqhu*', *Islamic Law and Society* 4(2): 131–55.

Masud, M.K. (2001) *Muslim Jurists' Quest for the Normative Basis of Shari'a*. Leiden: ISIM Publication.

Mirza, Q. (2000) 'Islamic Feminism and the Exemplary Past', in J. Richardson and R. Sandland (eds.), *Feminist Perspectives on Law & Theory*, pp. 187–209. London: Cavendish.

Moore, S.F. (1978) *Law as Process: An Anthropological Approach*. London: Routledge & Kegan Paul.

Musa, M.Y. (1958) *Ahkam al-ahwal al-shakhsiyya fi al-fiqh al-islami [Measures of Personal Status in Islamic Jurisprudence]*. Cairo: Dar al-Kitab al-'Arabi.

Philips, A. (1990) *The Evolution of Fiqh: Islamic law & The Madh-habs*. Riyadh: International Islamic Publication House.

Ramadan, S. (1970) *Islamic Law: Its Scope and Equity*. Lahore: Shirkat Press.

Rosen, L. (1989) *The Anthropology of Justice: Law as Culture in Islamic Society*. Cambridge: Cambridge University Press.

Samara, M. (1987) *Ahkam wa athar al-zawjiyya: sharh muqaran li-qanun al-ahwal al-shakhsiyya [Rules and Consequences of Marriage: Comparative Commentary on the Law of Personal Status]*. Jerusalem. (no publisher).

Schacht, J. (1964) *An Introduction to Islamic Law*. Oxford: Clarendon Press.

Shaham, R. (1999a) 'An Egyptian Judge in a Period of Change: Qadi Ahmad Muhammad Shakir, 1892-1958', *Journal of the American Oriental Society* 119(3): 440–56.

Shaham, R. (1999b) 'State, Feminists and Islamists: The Debate over Stipulations in Marriage Contracts in Egypt', *Bulletin of the School of Oriental and African Studies* 62(3): 462–83.

Sonbol, A. (1996) 'Adults and Minors in Ottoman Shari'a Courts and Modern Law', in A. Sonbol (ed.) *Women, the Family and Divorce Laws in Islamic History*, pp. 236–59. Syracuse: Syracuse University Press.

Vikør, K. (2000) 'The Sharia and the Nation State: Who Can Codify the Divine Law?', in Bjørn Olav Utvik and Knut S. Vikør (eds.) *The Middle East in a Globalized World*, pp. 220–50. Bergen: Bergen University.

Welchman, L. (2000) *Beyond the Code: Muslim Family Law and the Shar'i Judiciary in the Palestinian West Bank*. The Hague: Kluwer Law International.

3 The Gaza Shari'a courts
An overview

This chapter provides a brief overview of the Gaza Shari'a courts from an ethnographic perspective. It highlights the specific context of the courts, their operation, traditions, culture and institutional arrangements. The chapter also analyses the roles played by each of the actors in the court. Most of the data were generated through discussion and interviews with the court actors and from information obtained from records in the archives. The structure of the chapter reflects the experience of litigants when they go to the courts building.

3.1 Scribes: first point of contact

Scribes are an important initial point of contact for litigants. Self-employed and allowed to work only with the permission of the court, they transform a litigant's fragmented story of alleged injustice into a legal plea for help. They fill out the proper application form for each litigant. When the case is too complex to be presented fully by answering the questions on the form, the scribe composes a long, hand-written description of it in the format of a letter addressed to the judge and attaches it to the form. Most of the time, the letters are written in a way that corresponds to the judge's world view, invoking verses from the Quran or framing the litigants' case in a manner that portrays them as victims of their spouses. Some litigants are so pleased with the scribes' work that they exclaim they would never have been able to present their cases so well themselves. The scribes also act as informal advisers to the litigants. They volunteer information on the length of time the case can be expected to take and what costs it might entail. In addition, they recommend lawyers whom they consider suitable for specific cases. The scribes are permitted to store their desks inside the court building after the working day is over.

3.2 Ushers: eyes and ears of the judges

Men and women are segregated physically in the building. The ground floor comprises a big hall in the centre, in which males wait, surrounded by two courtrooms and several administrative offices. The women's waiting room is slightly hidden; it is located directly in front of the courtrooms, and males are not allowed to enter it. This layout enables an usher to summon a woman to the courtroom without calling out her name for all to hear. Men, in contrast, are summoned by their names being called out loudly. The building's floors, too, represent a hierarchical separation. The ground floor is reserved for the offices of the clerks and the Shari'a courtrooms, the first floor for the office of the deputy qadi al-qudah and the Court of Appeal. There is also a small mosque on the first floor, reflecting the importance of prayers. This building was constructed after the establishment of the Palestinian Authority (1994) and the appointment of Abu Sardana as the first qadi al-qudah in Palestine.

The usher is more than just a doorman. The judges use him to find out what litigants are saying about their cases outside the courtroom. Over time, he becomes familiar with the proceedings of the Shari'a courts and sometimes intervenes in cases before they reach the judge. He listens to and advises the litigants. He volunteers to persuade lawyers to represent poor women without a fee. He offers advice to any woman who asks for counsel. Women tend to trust him because he treats them with respect. An indication of the influence wielded by ushers was given to me when I heard one consoling a woman who had lost her case, telling her that he would 'speak' about her suit to a member of the Court of Appeal and advising her to approach a specific judge. Thus, ushers have a calming effect on the female litigants, many of whom are nervous about appearing before a judge for the first time as a party in an adversarial suit. Their advice can influence the way a case is presented by a litigant.

One usher, Abu 'Ali, who had worked in the courts for 25 years, was particularly helpful to me, informing me about the dates of what he considered to be 'important' cases. He frequently sought me out to ask me to hurry to a courtroom where a particularly interesting case was being heard. Each morning, Abu 'Ali would provide me with a cup of tea and brief me about the day's cases; sometimes he would tell me, 'You had better sit with the women in the waiting room today. Don't attend the sessions because all of today's cases are boring, nothing interesting.' He often volunteered to take me to the house of a litigant whose case was of interest to me. He also vouched for me, telling litigants that I could be trusted with personal information.

3.3 Archives

The archives, which are situated in the basement of the court building, are a storage place for court records (sijillat) as well as the venue where some marriage contracts are concluded. The court's administrative manager (who is also a judge) realized the historical importance of the records in the year 2000 and started classifying and binding the court documents, contracts and sijillat. Some valuable documents still need to be catalogued, and I saw some lying on the floor, covered with dust. Some had even been burned in the past due to lack of space. In addition to filing the records, the archivist is also responsible for copying marriage, divorce, inheritance and other documents at the request of members of the public.

Researchers can access the archives easily. I obtained permission from the deputy qadi al-qudah, started my research immediately and spent a long time gathering data from the archives as well as witnessing marriage contract ceremonies. Some university students also received permission to use the archived material for their term papers. During the long hours spent in the archives, I engaged in discussion with several clerks, who offered me their opinions about the approach and procedures of the Shari'a courts.

Unfortunately, Gaza court sijillat only date back to 1918. Historian Salim al-Mubayyid, who teaches at the Islamic University in Gaza, told me that the Gaza court had lost its older records because it had never been a central court; all the pre-1918 sijillat had been posted to the Jerusalem or Haifa courts. Furthermore, when the British invaded Gaza during the First World War,[1] people fled north (to Haifa, Jaffa, Aleppo, Damascus, Beirut and other places). Some court clerks then tried to save their sijillat, taking them to wherever they fled. A sijil from Gaza has been found in Damascus, where a paper on it has been written by Abdul-Karim Rafeq (Rogan 1989: 173).[2]

At one level, the sijillat can be used to document the political history of the Gaza Strip. For example, the stamps used in the marriage contracts of 1921 were trilingual. The name of the country (Palestine) was written in English, Arabic and Hebrew. It was in that year that these stamps replaced the Ottoman stamps (which were used in the sijillat of 1918, 1919 and 1920) on the orders of the British. On 28 May 1948, only two weeks after the first Arab-Israeli war, Egyptian stamps began to be apposed on the contracts. Sijillat can also be read discursively. They endorse certain 'facts', which do not necessarily correspond to the 'details' collected from people's narratives. For instance, there is an obvious difference between the age of marriage given by informants and that recorded in the sijillat between 1920 and 1970. Before 1926, some marriage contracts specified the bride's age as 10, 11 or 12 years, but early marriage 'disappeared' suddenly after 1926, with no brides appearing to be less than 15 years old, as if people had realized the disadvantages of early marriage. However, it is reasonable to assume that, after 1926, Gazans became aware of the British regulation concerning age of marriage and started inflating the age of brides to avoid problems. Some judges informed me that the ma'dhun (marriage notary) used to note the bride's age arbitrarily in order to conform to British Mandate law (compare with Moors 1995).

How did the judges treat women from different social strata in those days? The names of women of higher standing used to be preceded by the honorific 'hanim' or 'khanum'. In the 1930s, those women used to go to court to appoint a proxy (wakil) to run their business or to manage their waqf (endowment). In such instances, some of them apposed their signatures to the sijil, an indication of their literacy, whereas others used personal stamps to specify their names. Some judges used to go to the élite women's houses to conclude a wikala (proxy document) for a lawyer or shaykh to run their business or to represent them in court cases. Poor women, who usually petitioned for nafaqa, were called hurma and signed the documents with a thumbprint, indicating their illiteracy. They used to go to the courts either accompanied by a wakil or alone. I was unable to verify whether or not the wakil's presence was compulsory, but in some cases a wakil's name appears as representing a female or a male, and in some others the petitioners appear alone regardless of their gender.

The archivist has to be a graduate of a Shari'a college or have a degree in Arabic Literature. The court demands that all clerks be transferred to a new department every six months so that they can acquire skills in all aspects of the court's work. The court employees prefer to pray together. Often, the deputy qadi al-qudah acts as imam. After the midday prayer, the clerks often do not do any further public work. They wrap up their daily tasks and write up cases in formal sijillat for the next day. Some judges sit and discuss their cases with the deputy qadi al-qudah on the first floor while the rest prepare cases and files for the next day.

3.4 Women's waiting room: forum for peer-to-peer advice

The waiting room is a microcosm of the poorer section of Gazan society. The majority of the women (and men) who go to court are from low- and middle-income groups. Some do not even have the money to pay for transportation to and from the court. The majority of the court staff are from the same class background. Most staff members are of refugee origin, and the rest are from Shija'iyya and Zaytun, where most residents belong to the lower-income strata. It is therefore not surprising to see friendly relations develop between the staff and litigants.

Most of the female litigants are 'housewives', but women factory workers, informal-sector traders, low-ranking government employees and others also turn to the court. Although most wear the jilbab,[3] there are differences in the quality of the cloth, style of the garment, shoes, quality and quantity of gold ornaments and so on. The traditional 21-carat bracelet worn by poor women is a way of carrying their wealth with them; upper-class women prefer 18-carat gold jewellery, the value of which is determined by factors such as design rather than the quality or quantity of the gold. The negative connotation attached to the intervention of the formal legal system deters the better-off families from taking their disputes to court. When they do need to approach the court, they prefer to do so through a lawyer and not to attend the hearings.

The women's waiting room is where the female litigants develop networks on the basis of geographical location and shared experiences. Such networks are a vital resource for information and knowledge, sustained as they are by shared norms and location. The interactions often occur spontaneously, and women quickly establish a rapport with each other. If one has brought her child with her, the others start playing with the child and offer sweets. Most of the time, talking about children breaks the ice. If a woman has been coming to the court for a while, the others ask how her case is going. During their conversations, women give ideas to each other, which may encourage or deter them from implementing certain actions. Such detailed discussions enable each litigant to analyse and reflect upon her case.

In summer, the waiting room is full of beautiful teenage girls who have come to sign their marriage contracts. They often wear clothes that are designed for older women, such as high-heeled shoes and fancy jalabib (sg. jilbab), and wear rather heavy make-up. When the bride is younger than the minimum age of marriage (15), her family dress her like an older woman to convince the judge that she is nubile. Most of the brides-to-be are younger than 20, but a few postpone marriage until they finish their university studies. In Gaza, it is commonly assumed that women older than 20 will find it difficult to get a husband.

Women rarely come to court alone; they are accompanied by at least one family member. When a male accompanies his female relative, he sits in the hall with the other men. If he needs to talk to his female relative, he approaches the waiting room with bowed head as a sign of respect and decency. He then whispers to his relative to approach him. Men are not allowed to enter the women's waiting room, although there is no door to close it off from the corridor.

Older women usually come with their daughters, sons, nephews and sometimes neighbours or friends. Often, they are the ones who lead the conversations in the waiting room. This is perhaps because they are not directly involved in the cases and thus stay seated longer than the others do. In this way, they express the authority conferred on them by age. When an older woman sees a bride coming to sign her marriage contract, she volunteers lengthy advice: be good to your mother-in-law; obey her; she will be your mother. Sometimes, the advice is more specific; for example, when advising an 'angry' (hardana) woman to present her case wisely, telling her not to be too aggressive because in the end she will have no one but her husband to look after her. Conversations in the waiting room also include discussions about the ability to handle certain cases of this or that lawyer.

The importance of this interaction among women in the waiting room lies in the significance of information exchange in women's legal initiatives. In a different context, Long (1979: 125) points out that the ability of a person to succeed in realizing his/her objectives is influenced by the nature and breadth of his/her personal network. Networks provide access to essential information, resources and social support. Social networks are distinctly divided into those based on 'strong' and 'weak' ties (Granovetter 1973). According to Granovetter, information disseminates more quickly if it passes through weak ties that link groups of relatively dense relationships. Moreover, 'the more weak ties a person has, the more information he is likely to receive' (Long 1979: 123–58).

These findings are relevant to the study of women's legal initiatives. In the first place, women's legal initiatives are associated with the process of information flow and processing. Secondly, one can assume that a woman's initiatives towards various objectives are largely affected by the knowledge she obtains through her networks. In this respect, court personnel (particularly scribes and ushers) and peer women in the waiting room may represent such weak ties, while their familial network may be assumed to reflect strong ties that provide her with a vague understanding of how legal settlements are handled. Legal information is needed only when one is implicated in such settlements, and thus one cannot assume everyone to be a legal 'expert'. Thirdly, the differential and complex personal strong and weak ties lead to variation in information and thus to different interpretations being received by different women, which then contribute differently to generating initiatives.

Much knowledge comes from practice, and the waiting room shows this, with women who have a long history of litigation advising new litigants. If the adviser seems to be doing well in her own suit, other women tend to act on her advice. Thus, the information exchange in the waiting room can play a significant role in women's legal actions. I saw some women deciding which strategy to use or which lawyer to approach after receiving information from other women in the waiting room. Some advice relates to how peer litigants should approach the judge, what vocabulary they should use and how they should construct their stories. The 'experts' (that is, those who have a long history in the court) also give advice on which facts to hide or highlight when in the courtroom.

The transmission of knowledge extends to the point where 'expert' women advise 'new' female litigants on how to approach different judges. For example, a woman whose case had lasted long enough to be examined by two judges at different times provided her analysis to another litigant. She told her:

> If your case is with this judge [pointing to one courtroom], he will need you to describe every detail of your story and repeat that at every session. So, prepare yourself, remember your story and do not say something today and contradict yourself at the next session. But if your case is with that judge [pointing to the other courtroom], he will finish it soon; he does not like blabbers. Here you should also be careful, because he is very skilful. He may decide your case without allowing you to manœuvre. In any case, if you are dissatisfied, you can always go to the first floor, to qadi Salama [the deputy qadi al-qudah] and explain your case to him. He loves to listen to women. When you approach him, you had better shed some tears while describing your story, he will be most attentive. Also, do not display the gold you wear, for – in that case – his sympathy will decrease.

The interaction and exchange of knowledge draw our attention not only to the importance of such instantly established ties but also to a particular meaning of agency. Agency, if considered as the person's ability to make a difference in his or her life, is embedded in social relations and only becomes effective through them (Long 2001: 17). The ability to improve one's own choices or make a difference in one's own life does not, in this context, depend on one's wealth, personal charisma, or the like, but on how one 'translates' objectives into concrete actions (ibid.).

Other recommendations relate to how to handle the case within the family. Some women give lengthy 'lectures' to others about the way they should treat their husbands or in-laws. These suggestions are not always in conformity with the ideological portrayal of gender roles and relations espoused within the family. Some are profound enough to reveal the deep contradiction between the ideological representation of gender and the day-to-day contestation. Furthermore, the political awareness of women shown in their comments about Israeli attacks and the class orientation of the newly established Palestinian Authority (PA), refer not only to women's particular 'political knowledge' but also to their socially embedded and empirically validated criticism.

Chapters 5, 6 and 7 will show how effective female litigants' strategies and tactics can be in specific types of cases. For now, let us continue with this overview of the Shari'a courtroom and focus on how the judges and lawyers work together to ensure justice.

3.5 The courtroom: arena for negotiation

From the beginning, it is made clear to the litigants that they are only supplicants in the court building. The courtroom doors carry signs giving strict instructions on how members of the public are expected to behave: for example, warning them that smoking is forbidden in the courtroom and that they are expected to be quiet and to switch off their mobile phones. They are also confronted with Quranic verses about justice and the heavy burden placed on the judges.[4]

The judges usually arrive at their offices at around 8 a.m. and review the day's cases for an hour before hearing them between 9 a.m. and 11:30 a.m. Then, they join the court staff for the midday prayer. In the afternoon, they often hear only cases concerning marriage contracts because those do not require much time.

In each courtroom, the judge's desk dominates the room. On it rest a telephone, the official stamp, a number of books relating to family law, interpretation (tafsir) or fiqh, and a big copy of the Quran. The Holy Book is used frequently by the judge when he asks witnesses to take the oath. For simple issues (for example, when testimony is being given in a marriage ceremony), this is sufficient. In serious cases, however (for example, when a witness is about to testify in a divorce case about having heard the husband pronounce the talaq to his wife), the judge may also question the witness about his background. Rosen (1989: 53) points out that these combined methods are meant to make the truest assessment possible. The judge intends to understand the state of mind of the witness through 'occurrences that draw together the qualities of nature, background and biography to make an inner state "obvious".'

A rectangular table is set at right angles to the judge's desk, with four or more chairs for the litigants and their lawyers. One chair is reserved for the katib (court recorder). Relatives or supporters of the litigants sit on a bench against one wall. During my early visits, I used to sit on this bench, but after a few weeks the judges invited me to sit nearer to them on a chair reserved for closer consultation with lawyers.

Although there are no dress regulations for judges and lawyers in Shari'a courts, the judges always wear a jubba (ceremonial robe) and a turban; these symbolic garments reflect a certain image of authenticity and adherence to Islamic discourse and give their presence a strong religious meaning. Even in the heat of summer, judges never conduct a hearing without a turban.

In a few cases, either because the judge considers it necessary to exclude the public or because a litigant requests it, hearings are held *in camera*. During my fieldwork, I never saw a judge refuse such a request, regardless of the litigant's gender. Normally in such cases, only the litigants and katib are allowed to stay, although sometimes women request the judge to send everyone away, including the katib. I was privileged to attend such hearings; on one occasion, the judge presented me as a member of the court.

In this context, it is worth noting how the nineteenth-century reformist Muhammad Abdu perceived the power of Shari'a courts. According to Abdu, the court 'intervenes between husband and wife, father and son, between brothers as well as between a guardian and his ward. There is no right relating to near or distant kin over which these courts do not have jurisdiction' (Asad 2001: 9). Asad observes that

> the Shari'a court judges look into matters that are very private and listen to what others are not allowed to hear. For even as they provide the framework of justice, they also act as a depository for every kind of family secret. In other words, the courts are expected both to guard the privacy and to work through the sentiments on which "society" ultimately depends.
>
> (ibid.)

Holding some hearings *in camera* is therefore a way of guarding the privacy of litigants when necessary.

The katib does not record court proceedings as they are going on. Instead, the judge periodically dictates a summary to him. In this way, the proceedings, conducted in dialectal Arabic ('ammiyya), are recorded in classical Arabic (fus-ha). At the end of the hearing, the litigants and the judge sign the document, which then becomes part of the case file. Each file consists of these summaries, the original application and the written defences of the lawyers. Later, the katib writes a summary of the hearing to be included in the sijil, which is well organized, coded, dated, numbered and indexed. He does this in beautiful Arabic calligraphy, which is an essential qualification for a katib. The judge's signature and stamp (if available) appear on the sijillat in addition to the signatures of the judges of the Court of Appeal if the case has gone to them. When there are witnesses in a case and the lawyers have presented lengthy arguments, the summary might fill a page or so. If not, which is generally the case, it does not take up more than half a page. If the case requires several hearings, a summary is written for each hearing. At the end of each sijil, there is an index. Thus, the sijil is a summarized 'rendering' of the proceedings rather than an exact reflection of what was really said and negotiated.

All the sijillat are stored in the archives. However, some cases are dealt with outside the courtroom; some litigants are advised to withdraw their suit because, in the judge's opinion, they may get a better deal if customary law is applied. A major part of the court negotiation and bargaining are not included in the sijil. The fact that judges have the authority to dictate the written record allows them to decide on the exclusion or inclusion of certain material: oral negotiations, the devices of certain judgments, out-of-court solutions, in-court propositions and the like appear nowhere in the court record. There is no way to reconstitute the entire picture unless we adopt an appropriate methodology based on close observation of daily proceedings.

The judges listen carefully to the litigants and their lawyers. Sometimes, they interrupt to remonstrate or give advice. I have sometimes heard a judge reprimand a man for using violent and improper words to describe his wife's behaviour. The judges use Quranic verses to advise litigants to be compassionate to their family members; usually they refer to the verse about the responsibilities of the man or the woman as wali (guardian) of the family. While providing this advice, the judge stresses that he is only trying to reach a better solution and that his words should not be taken as an indication that he wants to dismiss the litigant's claim. Sometimes, to try to persuade litigants to withdraw a case that he feels can be settled within the family, a judge tells them that their cases will probably take longer than other avenues. However, when a case involves a serious issue, judges insist on following it up on their own.

Sometimes, men accuse judges of favouring women. Asked about this, judges told me that whenever they provide true justice to women, some men view them as pawns used by women against men's interests. Some women do receive attention and sympathy from judges, but this also depends on the women's conduct in court; those who appear totally victimized and wear highly conservative clothing receive sympathy from the judges.

When addressing the judge, women often use particular language to present their case. They may appeal to the judge's religious beliefs by saying, 'How will you meet Allah in the next life without giving me justice?' or praise him as 'the father of Muslims'. Men, however, do not employ this resource. They may appeal to the judge's religious beliefs, but the vocabulary they use is different, so their interaction with the judges rests on a different kind of communication. They may tell a judge, 'You are not following the Shari'a, you are influenced by the soft voice of women', which is the best way to upset a Shari'a court judge.

When litigants appear in court, the judge first asks them their name, age and address. He also insists on seeing the litigants' and witnesses' identification cards. If the litigant gives an address that is different from his or her place of origin, the judge insists on being told the place of origin. In Gaza, knowing where litigants dwell is not enough; they have to reveal their village or town of 'origin'. There are three reasons for this request. The first is administrative; in the court application forms, litigants must fill in two spaces: one for their current address and the other for their place of origin. The second relates to the judge's role as an active member of the community. By knowing where the litigants come from and whom they know, the judges can view others through geographic, political and social lenses. Another important reason for the query is that most judges are refugees, and for refugees the places of origin, the pre-1948 villages, are still significant markers of identification. Thirdly, the place of origin gives the judge a general impression of the power balance between the disputants. Knowing the place of origin puts the judge in a better position to determine the larger context of the dispute.

I once attended a hearing that involved a man working for the Palestinian Authority whose family had taken refuge in Lebanon in 1948 and who thus had no clan relationship with Gazans. As soon as the judge heard that, he stopped trying to ascertain the man's exact place of origin since he was not familiar with its relevance to the development of the case. Instead, he focused on another marker, the governmental agency employing the man, because that could provide a clue as to his connections.

The Shari'a court is a socio-legal institution whose purpose is to resolve familial problems. It is an arena for negotiation and legitimization of certain interests and needs. It is also an arena where the world views of judges, litigants, lawyers and clerks interact. In the process, the nature of the dispute is clarified; shared or divided expectations emerge; and interests are justified and rationalized. The parties to familial conflicts, having access to unequal sources of power, mobilize social relations and 'deploy discursive and other cultural means' to attain specific ends, including that of perhaps simply remaining in the exercise (Long 2001: 59).

For example, when the case involves claims about maintenance, each partner composes a story that emphasizes severe economic hardship. Women display their inability to meet living costs. They often bring to the fore religious and economic justifications. Men, in contrast, use more politically charged language, citing the Israeli closure and ensuing unemployment. As for the judges, they enforce their role as positive mediators at the expense of their falsely perceived detachment and neutrality. When a husband claims economic hardship, they often ask questions that place most of the blame on him: 'If your wife were still in your house, wouldn't you feed her? Pay her medical fees? Buy her clothes? If you want to minimize your costs, find a way to bring her back to you peacefully.'

The judges have their own world views and prejudices, especially about issues relating to gender. Women wearing make-up, even if dressed in jilbab and headscarf, do not get as much respect and attention as do conservative women. One judge even ordered a woman with make-up on her face to go home and remove it before coming to the court. Thus, the gender conduct of women determines whether or not judges perceive them as fragile.[5] Meaning related to gender conduct is maintained by some actors that perceive themselves as representatives of a larger, united community, albeit one created and manipulated for particular and not necessarily shared purposes. It is important to recognize such 'multiple realities' (Long 2001) when analysing Shari'a courts.

For example, I witnessed the case of Asil, a women's movement activist, who went to court with her husband to conclude a mutually agreed divorce (mukhala'a). The husband had not wanted the divorce, but after years of conflict and disagreement had agreed to it in exchange for ibra' (renouncing of financial rights). Usually in such cases, the judge attempts to find a solution that could reconcile the spouses, but since the couple appeared to have made up their minds, he decided to proceed without delay. After asking both parties to confirm their agreement to divorce, he told them to repeat the divorce formula after him. Then he declared them divorced. After the procedure had been completed, he ordered the husband to finalize the administrative work as it was his responsibility to 'run around' the court offices to assemble all the papers for signing by the judge. Once that had been done, the judge handed a copy of the papers to the wife, who was standing silently next to her father. This gendered division of labour reflects the particular world view of judges, according to which, even immediately after divorce, the man is expected to serve as a public agent for his former wife.

The man explained to the judge that he had agreed to the divorce because of his wife's active role in the women's movement: 'Before she started working with those evil women, we were living in peace and tranquillity. Since she joined them, we have not been able to spend a day without conflict. Those women are the reason for the destruction of my home.' The judge consoled him without commenting on his remark on the women's movement.

After the couple had left, the judge and the lawyers present started discussing the women's movement and its role in destabilizing families. One lawyer said, 'The women's movement, instead of inciting wives against their husbands, should teach them values related to the importance of family peace and well-being.' The judge replied, 'That is why Allah does not allow women the right to decide on divorce. If they had this right, half the families would fall apart. Look at the women in America; they got the right to divorce and what happened? Within less than half a century, they succeeded in ruining the vast majority of families. No family structure is left. Women are emotional in nature and this constitutes their weakness and strength at the same time.'

Then he turned to me with a smile on his face: 'I know that you do not like what I said, daughter. Don't think that all women are educated; they have small minds and limited knowledge.' I smiled in response, not wanting to start an argument with him about nature/culture, difference/sameness. I let it go even though I knew the woman involved in the divorce case. She had been married for 12 years, during which she had tried her best to become pregnant. Her husband had a problem with his sperm count, and she had gone with him to Jordan several times to try artificial insemination. She used to save her salary to go to Jordan every summer for that purpose. Recurrent failure had created constant discord and misery in the couple's relationship. Finally, at the age of 32 years, feeling that she was running out of time to experience motherhood, she had decided on divorce. This was the version of the story that the judge and lawyers had not heard.

In most cases, litigants are represented by lawyers, but sometimes the judges prefer to hear the litigants give their own version of the facts even if they have lawyers present. Lawyers do not limit themselves to the letter of the law; they also use the Shari'a and cultural norms as reference points while presenting their cases. For example, in a case where a father was trying to obtain custody of his daughter, the mother's lawyer employed religious and cultural norms to disqualify him as a suitable custodian. He produced witnesses to an incident when the father had quarrelled with his daughter in the street, beating her and tearing off her headscarf. The humiliation caused by the public beating would not have been sufficient to disqualify the father, but since the headscarf is considered to be an essential aspect of women's public appearance, the judge rejected the father's application.

3.6 Gender in the legal profession

Lawyers have to sit for an examination before being allowed to plead in Shari'a courts. Under Israeli rule, women were allowed to be lawyers in civil courts, but no attempt was made by women to do so in the Shari'a courts. After the establishment of the PA, female lawyers asked the newly appointed qadi al-qudah to allow them to take the same examination as their male counterparts. Since then, four female lawyers have started practising as Shari'a lawyers. One practises only in the Shari'a courts and thus is well known among the judges and litigants, while the others alternate between Shari'a courts and civil courts.

While attending the court sessions, I heard the judges and court clerks advising women who could not afford to pay lawyers' fees to approach Hala Anwar, a famous female lawyer appointed by the Palestinian Centre for Human Rights to defend poor women free of charge. I often heard the judges exchanging jokes and softly conversing with Hala Anwar, telling her that her services had been extremely useful to poor women. Sometimes they teased the male lawyers that Hala Anwar had taken clients from them. Qadi al-Karmi told me once that he and his colleagues prefer Hala Anwar to take women's cases because women can easily relate their private problems to a female lawyer:

> It is better to get the real story from a female lawyer than to puzzle over what is behind the filing of a case. A female lawyer can understand and work according to the agenda of her female client. Her job is similar to that of the female doctor; women can discuss their problems more easily with a female gynæcologist than with a male one.

This portrayal of litigation as a symptom of illness may indicate the judges' perception of the court as a space in which illness is diagnosed and treated, which reflects their conception of the court as a social 'hospital' rather than a detached legal institution. The attitude towards employment of women in the Shari'a court has undergone a profound change since the establishment of the PA, and they have become more visible and competitive professionals. Chapter 9 explores the growing presence of women in Shari'a courts since the beginning of the new millennium.

3.7 Background of judges

In contrast with the judges in Palestine under the British Mandate, the judges in Gaza today are less likely to be from prominent or rich families. Between 1930 and 1960, the opportunity to obtain a diploma in religious studies at Al-Azhar

University in Cairo was the privilege of families that could afford the fees. Social representations and symbols of social status changed over time. Unlike the situation today, when graduates from the religious schools are disdainful of a qualification from Al-Azhar University, such a diploma then provided graduates with respect that added to their already established rank in society.

In the early 1960s, Egyptian President 'Abd al-Nasir made university education free for Palestinians. This enabled thousands of students from poor families, especially refugees, to obtain higher degrees, including in theology studies at Al-Azhar. However, after the 1978 Camp David agreement, Egyptian President Anwar Sadat suspended this privilege, and Palestinians once again had to pay fees.

The period of free education coincided with the Gulf countries' economic boom of the 1960s and 1970s and their growing demand for teachers, engineers and doctors, which led students to graduate in those fields. Who, then, pursued religious studies? It is probable that, since good secondary school marks were required for other subjects, only those who did not receive high marks were attracted to religious studies. Of course, a number of students would have opted for theology, but since job opportunities depended on technical qualifications, religious studies were not the first choice of most students. It is also probable that this field did not attract many students because the dominant political discourse in the two decades following the nakba was influenced by the slogans of 'Abd al-Nasir, who expressed national aspirations in secular terms.[6] Religion and religious discourse became influential only in the 1970s.

Nowadays, most judges have a refugee background. They are graduates of Shari'a colleges or have graduated in theology (usul al-din) from the Islamic University. These institutions do not charge fees; on the contrary, they provide fellowships in the form of books and living allowances to poor students. Religious institutions are thus for the poorest students and for those who are unable to qualify academically for university. During the Model Parliament campaign, in which the Shari'a court judges and other religious figures in society opposed proposals by the women's movement for family law reform, political activists tended to link the conservative views of judges with their religious and social background.

Palestinian society is socially, economically, culturally and politically heterogeneous. This heterogeneity affects the perceptions and evaluations of the court's conduct and representation. The negative exchange between modern civil society organizations and the representatives of the religious establishment reflects not only the multiplicity of views regarding the role and qualifications of judges, but also oppositional views regarding the present state of affairs and the future of Shari'a courts with respect to their authority in the field of family law.

3.7.1 Procedure for appointing judges

Before the establishment of the PA, judges were trained as court recorders and then elevated to the rank of Shari'a court judges. A judge needs more than legal knowledge; he has to have knowledge of court administration, knowledge about the life of his community, and above all he needs to have a high moral stance that should guide all his actions.[7] While working as a katib, the judge learns how to operate administratively and legally. On the legal side, the judge learns the procedures for handling cases. The administrative task is rather different; it involves registering contracts (hijaj) of marriage, divorce, inheritance and wikalat.[8]

Civil court judges undergo different training. They train and practise as lawyers, after which they are appointed as judges in the court of first instance. Subsequently, they climb up the professional ladder. Civil lawyers, even though allowed to practise in both civil and Shari'a courts, are not allowed to become Shari'a court judges. Until recently, lawyers who graduated from Shari'a colleges could become Shari'a court judges only if they first worked as court recorders.

A new procedure was introduced in 2003. Deputy qadi al-qudah Mahmud Salama explained it to me during an interview on 27 December 2003:

> Now the court announces vacancies in the local newspaper, specifying the geographical area where the qadi is needed. The applicants must have a first degree in the Shari'a or usul al-din. They also have to sit for oral and written exams. Nowadays we prefer those who have an MA or PhD in Shari'a Studies from a prominent university, but if Shari'a college graduates or court recorders prove their competence, we take them.
>
> When the applicants sit for the oral exam, I ask them a standard set of questions: 'You are going to pray in the mosque. Suddenly you see a big crowd of people in your way. Obviously, there has been a quarrel. What should you do? Continue to the mosque so that you can pray on time, or intervene? And if you intervened, what would you say? What values would you emphasize when talking to them?'

The questions posed by deputy qadi al-qudah sum up important requirements for the position of qadi: the ability to lead the community, to be an advisor to the people and to guide them to peaceful solutions. The judge should be a peacekeeper and a community leader. He should be articulate and have the ability to express himself and to intervene in disputes orally. The answers to the questions provide clues as to the personality of the applicant, his vocabulary, his world view, his approach, and above all the way he projects himself. The deputy qadi al-qudah then explained to me the reasons for posing such questions:

> I want to know whether the applicant is able to give a speech, whether he is familiar with the community's daily problems and whether he is concerned about participating in solving these problems. Judges are not expected to sit behind the bench and only follow the book; that qualification is tested by the written exam. They are expected to be active in people's daily life and deliver the message of Islam. Islam means that we are one body; when an organ suffers from an illness, the whole body feels the pain and fever. Another important issue is the fact that it is usually poor women who have recourse to the Shari'a court. Judges should be sensitive and empathetic when dealing with poor people and should have a genuine sense of morality in communicating with them. The economic background of our judges and

their religious studies should enable them to fulfil such a task. They should respect our Islamic and oriental traditions.

The change in how judges are appointed is probably due to the growing number of qualified Shari'a graduates over the last few years as a result of the establishment of the Islamic University of Gaza. However, these changes have drawn criticism. According to lawyer Hasan al-Masri, the new qadi al-qudah tends to appoint judges who are newly graduated, which means, in his view, that they do not have the experience needed for the position.

3.7.2 Internal relations in the Shari'a court

This section describes the relations within the court and how they affect the judges' rulings. In classical Islamic law, as Rosen (1989) observes, no court has higher authority (and thus a higher moral claim) than another. Thus, there should be no hierarchy among judges. The Shari'a courts in Gaza, like all Shari'a courts in Palestine, are organized in a hierarchy; the qadi al-qudah represents the highest authority,[9] followed by the members of the Court of Appeal, and then the judges of the court of first instance. Judges are expected to be well acquainted with the written rules and regulations that organize their hierarchical relations. These hierarchical relations cause conflicts between the court members over whose views are legitimate and religiously correct. The court, as a social institution, is not a neutral space; there is always struggle over power and authority going on between its members, reflecting diverse interests and world views. The judges' rulings are subject to review by the Court of Appeal, and they do their best to leave no loopholes. This is illustrated by the way judges and lawyers co-operate in estimating the amount of nafaqa.

Husbands often go to the Court of Appeal when the amount of nafaqa set by the judge does not suit them. To discourage this, the judges arrange the amount of nafaqa with the wife's lawyer and then make sure that the sijil specifies the husband's commitment to paying that amount. Since the husband signs the case record in the sijil, he cannot later appeal the ruling. (This will be discussed again when the collaboration between judge and lawyer is explored.) When the judges are sure that their decisions are in conformity with codified law and unlikely to be reviewed by the Court of Appeal, they do not hesitate to inform the litigants that they do have the right to appeal to the higher authority.

The appeal procedure is not formal. Litigants go to the first floor of the court building and tell the Court of Appeal judges why they think the ruling is unfair. If their argument is convincing, they are asked to fill out the relevant form for the case to be reviewed by the members of the Court of Appeal and then sent back to the judge of the lower court. When litigants have some sort of connection with members of the Court of Appeal, the members either recommend 'special' treatment of the case by the judge or make their own ruling.

The court is not an isolated institution, it is part of the Gazan sociopolitical scene, which influences (and in turn is influenced by) the shifting power structure in Palestinian society. The pressures from different power groups with their respective resources affect the conduct of the court. This requires judges to review and negotiate their views and judgments constantly in the light of their environment. The judges (including the deputy qadi al-qudah and members of the Court of Appeal) respond to often-conflicting demands and expectations. They have to rule on cases with full acknowledgement not only of codified law but also of customary practices and the interests of diverse groups in society.

The judges cannot enforce their judgments. Gerber (1999) cites Schacht (1964), Nielsen (1985) and Coulson (1964) as all underlining that, unlike criminal court judges, Shari'a court judges have never had the authority to implement their decisions. In Gaza, the Shari'a courts rely on the implementation office (da'irat al-tanfith) to execute their judgments. This frees the judges to some extent from possible pressure by powerful parties involved in disputes. To quote qadi Muhammad al-Ansari (discussion on 3 August 2002), 'It is easier to prevent the implementation of a court decision by bribing a police officer than to prevent the qadi from pronouncing the verdict itself.'

Judges are not ideal justice providers; sometimes their personal interests become implicated in the struggle for power and control. Particularly in post-Oslo Palestine, the Shari'a court as an institution consists of active political agents who strengthen their institutional and discursive power, which supports the construction of Palestinian identity as essentially Islamic. This has impacted on the struggle for power and legitimacy between various actors in the wider political scene.

Some judges find it difficult to satisfy so many different demands, which leaves them with few options. In particular, they have to walk a fine line between the politics of the deputy qadi al-qudah, the politics of the Court of Appeal, codified family law and their own notion of justice. Confronted with all these requirements, some judges may make compromises that minimize their vulnerability, such as complying with the demands of the deputy qadi al-qudah or responding to the requests of the Court of Appeal. However, some judges prefer to go their own way and pay the price for their integrity and independence. Qadi al-Karmi, who has a PhD in Islamic Studies, is an example. He was active during the debate on family law reform in the late 1990s. He used to attend meetings, give talks, participate in workshops and write articles in the daily press. After he participated in the discussions of the Model Parliament in early 1998, the deputy qadi al-qudah forbade him from speaking publicly in the name of the Shari'a court. Qadi al-Karmi had not abandoned the overall position of the Shari'a court regarding family law reform, so the ban on public speeches had to be related to the internal politics of the court rather than his approach towards reform.

These examples show that the judges work in a complex context, in which multiple demands, views and interests have to be considered. In addition to the difficulties that arise from the application of codified law, judges also have to keep in mind the power games within the court and operate within the shifting power structure of Palestinian society in the period that followed the Oslo Accords, during which new dominant figures and groups appeared in the political and social arenas. In addition, they have to continue to deal with their communities, where customs do not change as easily and rapidly as the structure of political power.

48 *The Gaza Shari'a courts*

The court, as an administrative body, is an arena of competing interests and power struggle over whose interests should be served and whose voice should be heard.

3.8 Conclusion

This chapter has provided an introduction to the Shari'a court. It has shown how the various actors affect the litigants' decisions and strategy as well as the court's ultimate verdict. From a general point of view, the court community is socially, economically, culturally, administratively and politically heterogeneous.

Patterns of internal stratification divide the legal administration (judges) hierarchically, with the qadi al-qudah at the top, the Court of Appeal in the middle and judges of first instance at the bottom. Of the other influential actors, scribes, ushers and lawyers come next, followed by the male and female litigants. Although shared social origin (for example, refugee background) can have a strong impact on the interaction of the actors, differences emerge in the positions that litigants (men and women) and judges take in managing their encounters. All the actors possess power or have the potential to initiate change, and by doing so they may affect the cases of other actors. In this sense, we can speak of agency.

Judges, scribes, ushers and litigants encounter each other at the nodes or interfaces of the legal process. It is there that they influence each other's actions and internalize and integrate the outcomes into their own actions. This is also a way to enrol or be enrolled. People are both drawn into others' projects (for example, the usher's assurance to various women that he will talk about their cases to members of the Court of Appeal) and draw others into their projects (for example, the attempts of female litigants to influence judges through their choice of words).

In practice, women's legal actions are facilitated, and often supported, by judges. In some cases, women and their lawyers organize their own strategies for action. In other cases, judges and lawyers plot joint strategies to ensure that men carry out their responsibilities. Intervention from the judges' side plays a considerable role in protecting women from abuse by their male relatives, so as to promote 'Islamic justice' as the judges view it. Elements related to the judges' sense of justice, protecting the weak, membership of the community and the overall gender ideology can be viewed as the framework within which their conduct is to be interpreted. This will be the focus of the next chapter.

Notes

1 In 1917, Gaza was taken from Turkey by British forces under General Edmund Henry Hynman Allenby. <www.britannica.com/biography/Edmund-Henry-Hynman-Allenby-1st-Viscount-Allenby>, accessed 20 August 2017.
2 Abd al-Karim Rafiq, 'Ghazza: Dirasa 'umraniya wa ijtima'iya wa iqtisadiya min khilal al-watha'iq al-shar'iya, 1273–77/1857–61,' published paper from the Third International Conference of Bilad al-Sham, Amman, cited in Rogan (1989).
3 The jilbab is a long-sleeved, ankle-length garment worn over women's clothes.
4 One wall poster reads: 'The mountains refused to take up the responsibility that is on the qadi's shoulders.' The heavy responsibility of the judges is often referred to through a story about Abu Hanifa, the founder of the Hanafi school of fiqh. The Abbasid Caliph imprisoned him because he refused to be a judge. Abu Hanifa's

refusal was based on the knowledge of the huge responsibility of not only knowing the text of the law but also applying it in a way that would ensure God's justice. The judges of the Gaza Shari'a courts often refer to their job as a burden so heavy that even a great jurist like Abu Hanifa refused to take it up.
5 Bridges and Steen (1998) reach the same conclusion in a different context, which demonstrates that differences in how litigants are perceived engender different treatment.
6 'Nakba' is the Arabic word for the catastrophe of 1948, when the state of Israel was established on the land of Palestine, forcing hundreds of thousands of Palestinians to leave their lands to become refugees either in other parts of Palestine now known as Israel, or in the remnants of Palestine, now known as the West Bank and Gaza Strip, or in the Arab countries, where they still suffer from discrimination despite having lived there for 50 years. A considerable amount of literature is available on the impact of the nakba on the structure of Palestinian society. The nakba also impacted on the future of the entire Middle East.
7 Interview with deputy qadi al-qudah Mahmud Salama, 27 December 2003.
8 Wikalat (sg. wikala) is when a person gives another person authority to act on his behalf.
9 During my fieldwork, the qadi al-qudah was represented in Gaza by the deputy qadi al-qudah, Mahmud Salama.

Bibliography

Asad, T. (2001) *Thinking About Secularism and Law in Egypt*. Leiden: ISIM.

Bridges, G. and S. Steen (1998) 'Racial Disparities in Official Assessments of Juvenile Offenders: Attributional Stereotypes as Meditating Mechanisms', *American Sociological Review* 63(4): 554–70.

Coulson, N. J. (1964) *A History of Islamic Law*. Edinburgh: Edinburgh University Press.

Gerber, H. (1994) *State, Society, and Law in Islam: Ottoman Law in Comparative Perspective*. Albany: State University of New York.

Granovetter, M. (1973) 'The Strength of Weak Ties', *American Journal of Sociology* 78: 1360–80.

Long, N. (1979) 'Multiple Enterprise in the Central Highlands of Peru', in S. N. Greenfield et al. (eds) *Entrepreneurs in Cultural Context*. Albuquerque: University of New Mexico Press.

Long, N. (1992) 'From Paradigm Lost to Paradigm Regained', in N. Long and A. Long (eds) *Battlefields of Knowledge: The Interlocking of Theory and Practice in Social Research and Development*, pp. 16–47. London and New York: Routledge.

Long, N. (2001) *Development Sociology: Actor Perspective*. London and New York: Routledge.

Moors, A. (1995) *Women, Property and Islam: Palestinian Experiences 1920–1990*. Cambridge: Cambridge University Press.

Nielsen, J. S. (1985) *Secular Justice in an Islamic State: Mazalim Under the Bahri Mamluks, 662/1264–789/1387*. Istanbul: Nederlands Historisch-Archaeologisch Instituut.

Rogan, E. L. (1989) 'Archival Resources and Research Institutions in Jordan', *Review of Middle East Studies* 23(2): 169–79.

Rosen, L. (1989) *The Anthropology of Justice: Law as Culture in Islamic Society*. Cambridge: Cambridge University Press.

Schacht, J. (1964) *An Introduction to Islamic Law*. Oxford: Clarendon Press.

4 The daily practice of judges
Perception vs reality

This chapter analyses the judges' work in the Gaza Shari'a courts in greater detail. Contrary to the stereotypical view often held of them, judges play a significant role in protecting women and ensuring that they receive the rights due to them. Judges' decisions are informed by their understanding of the Shari'a as a set of ethical principles that aim at, on the one hand, protecting the weaker members of the community, and on the other, preserving the social order. Judges exercise a degree of discretion informed by their self-perception as members of their community rather than as mere implementers of the law. Membership of the community, as Antoun (1989: 58) points out, does not proceed automatically from shared residence in a given locality; rather, 'it comes about by the gradual accumulation of interests each constituting an additional strand to a relationship that becomes increasingly "multiplex".' In this context, judges do not only share the locality of their litigants; they are positioned, and thus operate, in the same power structure. Moreover, judges are well informed about 'who is who' in the community and have strong contacts with the makhatir (sg. mukhtar: extended family or community leader) and other influential social and political figures. Judges' decisions depend not only on the history of the cases brought to the Shari'a court but, more importantly, on the potential consequences of their judgments on the individual litigants and the larger community behind them (Rosen 1989).

This chapter begins by putting Leila Ahmed's perspective on the ethical and technical voices in Islam to the test by examining the ethical stance of judges in the light of their actual practice in the Gaza Shari'a courts. Then, it analyses whether the views of Sonbol (1996), Sanadjian (1996) and Tucker (1998) on how codification has affected the implementation of family law in contemporary Shari'a courts correspond to the judges' handling of the cases that are brought before them. The final section outlines the conclusions that arise from the chapter.

4.1 Ethical stance of judges

Leila Ahmed (1992) draws a sharp distinction between two voices in Islam: the technical voice and the ethical voice. She argues that the technical (orthodox and androcentric) voice has dominated the legal and institutional realms throughout

Islamic history, while the ethical voice of Islam has been widespread among laypeople. Furthermore,

> establishment Islam (institutional and legal Islam) articulates a different Islam from the ethical message that the layperson justifiably hears or reads in Quran, and unfortunately, that Islam, intolerant of all understandings of the religion except its own, which is authoritarian, implacably androcentric, and hostile to women, has been and continues to be the established version of Islam, the Islam of the politically powerful. These profoundly different meanings of Islam both exist simultaneously, the personal meaning as a source of ethical and spiritual comfort for those raised within traditional backgrounds and the political and historical meaning as the system of law and government imposed by the politically dominant.
> (Ahmed 1992: 225–6)

If Ahmed was referring to a legal text, her analysis would not be contested here, but it is difficult to accept her sharp distinction in the context of social processes. In contrast to textual analysis, the study of social processes reveals diversity, multiplicity and complexity rather than mere dichotomy. My observations in the Gaza Shari'a court show that judges, who represent the legal institution and are thus considered by Ahmed as androcentric and orthodox, act as 'protectors' of the female litigants, shielding them from the harm their male kin might inflict upon them. In this context, they frequently refer to fairness, love, compassion, care, peace and humane treatment to enforce the ethical message of Islam.

Empirical evidence does not support a dichotomy between two distinct groups in Muslim society. The fieldwork for this study showed that the boundaries between the two voices and those who articulate them are rather blurred. This is not to say that the protective behaviour of judges is informed by a desire to compensate for gender asymmetry. Like all members of society, judges are influenced by the dominant gender discourse in Gaza, which legitimizes the unequal division of rights and duties within the family. However, judges' daily encounters with the unfairness, oppression and injustice inflicted on women by their kinsmen enhance their sensitivity towards women's plight.

Moore (1978) observes that what is important is not so much the source of law as the context within which it is implemented. In the Shari'a courts, the context is the desire of the judges to protect the weak as much as possible, given the constraints under which they operate. For example, a qadi once scolded a husband who said he could not pay more than JD 30 as monthly nafaqa (alimony) to his wife. The qadi asked him: 'Is JD 30 enough for you to feed yourself for a whole month? To pay for the electricity? To pay the rent? To buy detergent for washing your clothes? To buy cooking gas?' Then he added, 'All men are the same. When they propose marriage to a woman, they present themselves as if they would sacrifice their lives for her, but when we require them to comply with their obligations, they flee.'

The standards according to which the judge assesses 'rightness' or 'wrongness' in each case depend on the context within which the dispute transpires (see Gluckman 1955). The qadi assesses the wrongdoing of the man against what is defined by society as 'ordinary' behaviour. As the qadi's remarks above demonstrate, the husband is customarily (not only legally) responsible for the maintenance of his family. When the man failed to fulfil this responsibility, the judge did not refer to the legal implications of his failure; rather, he invoked concepts related to what society, religion and general morality consider acceptable behaviour. This appears to be the yardstick used by the judges to assess the variety of cases brought before them.

Various strategies are used by judges to help female litigants. In one case, a woman who sued for nafaqa did not appear in court for the hearing. The qadi could have postponed the hearing or dismissed the case, but instead he asked the usher to phone her and remind her of the hearing. The husband, who was present in the courtroom, asked the qadi to postpone the case because of his wife's absence, but the qadi told him gently: 'Your wife must be busy preparing your children for school.' He took up another case until the woman arrived about an hour later; then, after urging her to respect the court's schedule in future, he started hearing her case. In contrast, in another case, when a man who was petitioning for custody over his children arrived only five minutes late, the qadi postponed the hearing, telling him that he should respect the court's schedule.

Judges also help women who come before them by advising them on how to handle their lawsuits. One case involved a woman who had married a Palestinian living in Bahrain. She lived with him for two months and then returned to Gaza because he mistreated her. She filed a case for nafaqa, although she knew that it would be very difficult to have the payment enforced. However, she hoped that she would then be able to get a divorce on the ground that he was not paying the nafaqa. When she came before the qadi, he asked her, 'What do you want? If you want nafaqa, you know there is little possibility of obtaining it because he does not live here, and it is unlikely that we can oblige him to pay as long as he lives abroad. But if you have a different intention, let me know because in that case I can help you.' She told him she wanted to get divorced as soon as possible. He then advised her to file for divorce on the grounds of the husband's absence (talaq li al-ghiyab). Later, when I asked qadi Muhammad al-Ansari why he had given her that advice, he replied: 'If she asks for a divorce because she has not received nafaqa, that will take time, much longer than a divorce on the ground of absence. I wanted to make the case easier and quicker for her.'

Although judges stress the importance of keeping families together, when they feel that a newly formed family is unlikely to preserve its unity, they help women to arrive at the easiest solution. This can also be seen in cases related to divorce before consummation of the marriage (talaq qabla al-dukhul), which mainly involve young couples. While judges regret the breaking up of a marriage, they acknowledge that in such cases it is better to secure the future of the girl than to attempt to preserve the marriage. Divorce before consummation gives girls a better chance of remarriage than divorce after consummation.

Judges always keep in mind that they are operating in the context of what Long (2001) calls 'multiple realities'. They understand the challenges of a society living under severe economic restrictions, and that is a factor influencing their judgments in cases involving economic issues. For instance, family law makes women's work outside the house conditional on the husband's approval, and men sometimes petition for a 'house of obedience' order on the ground that the wife is engaged in wage labour outside the home and refuses to stop doing so. However, the judges check if the wife was already working when the marriage took place; if so, they deem that the husband effectively accepted that situation and should not expect the court to support his subsequent refusal to let his wife continue working. Some men, astonishingly, answer that they were experiencing economic difficulties when they accepted the wife's employment, but since their situation has improved they no longer need her income. That can draw a harsh admonition; in one case, I heard a judge tell the husband, 'So you think that the law is at your disposal; one day you want to enforce it and the next day you forget it.' In such cases, the judge may advise the husband to reveal the real reason underlying his petition instead of hiding it behind his wife's employment.

In one case, a husband, who said he was a manager at one of the top hotels in Gaza and did not need his wife's salary, filed for divorce because his wife refused to obey his demand to stop working. When I talked to the wife, she said the real reason for her husband's suit was that he wanted to divorce her without accepting the financial consequences of that decision. Indeed, her deferred dower and tawabi' (value of wife's furniture) amounted to JD 6,000 each. The qadi dismissed the case in the presence of the wife, telling the husband that he had not provided sufficient reason for divorce on the ground of nushuz (disobedience). Later, the qadi told me that he suspected the man had wanted to have his wife declared nashiz (disobedient) so that he could divorce her without financial consequences.

Judges try to ensure that litigants are not exploited by their lawyers. I was often told by lawyers that judges want them to be honest and professional and to serve the public (particularly women) well. Once, a qadi scolded a lawyer for what he regarded as unprofessional behaviour: 'I want you to take this case without charging the woman, because she is poor. You have been selfish and have taken high fees from other women.'

The judges in the Gaza Shari'a courts are well informed about the actions of community-based organizations. They build up and maintain a good rapport with those that provide social services, especially in matters related to family conflict. This, as well as the judges' concern for the family life of litigants, was demonstrated in a discussion between qadi al-Karmi and a lawyer representing a non-governmental organization (NGO) that provides a meeting place for divorced parents who do not have custody of their children to interact with them. The Shari'a court ensures that divorced parents are able to do this once a week at a neutral venue, even though neither the 1954 *Law of Family Rights* nor the *Book of Personal Status Rulings* makes any such provision. However, article 163 of the *Jordanian Law of Family Rights* (1976) stipulates that 'the father, mother and grandfather on the father's side have equal entitlement to see the child when he or she is in the hands of the other.' The routine practice is for children to be visited (mushahada) by the parent at a police station, because, as one qadi told me, it is 'the only neutral space available'. It also provides official proof that the custodian is obeying the judgment regarding visiting rights.

In the discussion with the lawyer, the qadi made several suggestions for improving the conditions in the alternative premises provided by the NGO. He pointed out that if facilities were made available where children could play and enjoy themselves, it would be a much friendlier venue. Food could be served to the parents and their children so that they could eat together, because 'having meals together may remind the couple of their good days. Allah may restore peace in their hearts.' A TV and a video player could be installed to show parents films about other comparable cases, which might bring them together again. Al-Karmi also suggested that the NGO could set up a hotline to provide advice on raising children in general and on marital problems in particular. 'We are going through very difficult times. The family is the only thing that people can fall back on. Providing support to families is crucial not only at the social and political levels, it is also a moral and religious duty,' he observed.

Later, in December 2003, I had a discussion with qadi al-Karmi regarding his project to establish a department in the Shari'a court dedicated solely to providing social counselling. He told me: 'Israel can demolish thousands of houses. We can build them again. Yet, when a home [a family] is destroyed, that is a real sign of destruction. We should not allow it to happen.'

Judges are genuinely sensitive to the emotional aspects of the disputes brought before them. In one case, a qadi was asked to declare a couple divorced before they had consummated their marriage. The woman had brought to court her prompt dower in addition to the gifts she had received. The qadi checked to make sure they were all there and then handed them over to the husband. A divorce before consummation is irrevocable, and the woman is not obliged to respect the idda period (three months, during which a divorced woman is not allowed to marry again). The couple have the right to get together again by contracting a new marriage with a new dower. This type of divorce is called talaq ba'n baynuna sughra (divorce with lesser finality), as opposed to talaq ba'n baynuna kubra (divorce with greater finality), in which the couple cannot marry again until the wife has experienced consummation in another marriage, been divorced and has finished her idda.

When divorce takes place before consummation, there are two ways to settle the financial issues. If the wife demands the divorce, she is obliged to return the full dower in addition to all the gifts and presents she has received. Some men go so far as to demand reimbursement of costs such as transportation to and from the wife's house or meals in restaurants. If the husband is the one demanding divorce, his wife has the legal right to keep half of her dower.

Preserving the family is all-important. In divorce cases, judges do their best to reconcile couples. The man is entitled to divorce at will, whenever and wherever he wishes. He does not need court approval; all he must do is register his divorce so that the number of repudiations (talqat, sg. talaq) pronounced appears in the record. However, when a man tells the qadi that he wants to divorce (he has a niyyah: will), the qadi asks him to return with his wife the next day. If the couple return the following day, the qadi takes on the role of a social counsellor, advising them to rethink the situation. He also asks them to bring their families to the next session so that he can understand the situation better. He may ask them to send their family's mukhtar to assist in the mediation process. Advice along the lines of 'think about your children, what will happen to them, their lives will be ruined' is frequent. In this way, the qadi always searches for the ambiguities referred to by Yngvesson (1993: 10) that can be used to change the situation.

Sometimes the qadi gives moral advice and admonishes the man: 'Women are not toys to play with and to discard at will. They are the source of our existence.' Or he might draw the man's attention to the effect that divorce would have on his reputation: 'Who will accept a divorced man for marriage? Your decision will affect you most.' The qadi may also remind the man of the precepts of religion: 'Although Allah provided you with this haqq [right], you should remember that this is the vilest of permitted things thing in the eyes of God (abghad al-halal 'inda Allah al-talaq).' Often, the qadi will remind the man of the economic price of his decision: 'This will cost you a lot. We are going through crises in every sense, so why don't you save your white penny for a black day?' Even if the divorce is of the khul' type, the qadi still reminds the man that divorce is costly: 'You will marry again and that will cost you a fortune, so why don't you save your money for a better purpose? You should spend what you have on your children's education.'

Alternatively, the qadi may invite a lawyer who happens to be present in the courtroom to discuss the case with the couple. Lawyers are always willing to intervene and may take the man outside and initiate a discussion with him about the possibilities of solving the problem. On such occasions, Abu 'Ali, the usher, brings them tea and pitches in to convince the man that he would regret his action: 'Believe me, I have been working here for 25 years. I have seen men coming to the court full of anger and unwilling to listen to the qadi's advice. They divorce their wives but then come back the next day to ask the qadi for help. You should curse Satan and pray to Allah for calmness'. A lawyer may invite a couple to his office, only a few metres from the court, to help them settle their dispute. He can furthermore invite the couple's families to his office. The intervention might even involve a few visits to the couple's house to establish a relation of friendship with the family.

Another alternative for the qadi is an NGO established in 2000 for family counselling. A member of this NGO is in direct contact with the judges. If he is present during a divorce case, the qadi asks him to visit the family (after obtaining the husband's permission) and help work out a solution. I once heard a qadi tell the NGO representative jocularly, 'Don't just listen to the cases. Move on and do something to justify your salary,' which showed the rapport between the two. These initiatives can bring about postponement of the divorce or settlement of the dispute between the couple, if the man agrees. However, if he has already pronounced divorce and insists that he is in court only to register the number of talqat, no impediment is placed in his way. On the contrary, the qadi urges him to register his divorce.

The tactics used by judges to persuade husbands to rethink divorce are exemplified by the following case. A man came to court, saying that he wanted a divorce. The qadi asked him to return the next day with his wife to conclude the procedure. When the couple stood before him, the qadi asked them the reason for their dispute. The wife said, 'I do not have any problem with him. He wants to divorce me without telling me the reason.' The qadi turned to the husband and asked him, 'Why do you want to do the worst thing a Muslim could do? Have you not read the hadith: la'ana Allahu al-mutathawiqin wa al-mutathawiqat.' ['God curses fickle men and women,' that is, those who treat the marriage institution as if it is a dish of food to be thrown away when it is not to their taste.] The man answered, 'I just want to end this, I want to divorce her.' The qadi responded, 'Is it Islamic for a man to divorce whenever he wishes? This is against the will of God.' However, the man insisted on his decision, which made the qadi angry. He then said:

> All right, I will grant you a divorce once you bring me your wife's nafaqat al-idda and deferred dower in cash, here, on my desk [the qadi was looking the man in the eye and jabbing his finger on his desk. His tone was strong and affirmative, as if he would tolerate no argument]. Otherwise, there is no divorce. You have to bring JD 1,000 deferred dower and JD 250 for nafaqat al-idda immediately.

The man protested, 'I cannot pay now. I want the court to divide it into several instalments.' Then the qadi tried another strategy: 'Don't you have a respectable person in your family? In your neighbourhood? In your circle? You should have found somebody to mediate between you. You are still young and need help and wisdom.'

However, all the qadi's attempts were fruitless; the man would not budge. The woman had been crying all the while. The qadi asked the man to go and bring some official documents, apparently because he wanted to have a private talk with the wife. After the man left the courtroom, the qadi addressed her:

> Look, daughter, your husband has the full right to divorce you when he wants; this is the right given to him by Allah. Your nafaqa and deferred dower are your rights, but the mechanism of the court does not allow me to get them from him immediately. I was just threatening him to make him change his mind. This is a revocable divorce (talaq raj'i) which does not end the marriage completely. Perhaps Allah will show him the right way within the months of idda, so then he will take you back.

Then he asked her:

> Can't you tell me the real reason for your misfortune? No one gets up in the morning with such a decision in mind unless he had some major problem.

Tell me and I may find some way to convince him to change his mind. Did his eye fall upon another woman? Do you have a problem with your mother-in-law? Is it between your family and his?

The wife kept silent with her eyes full of tears. When the man returned with the documents, the qadi told him, 'We will postpone this session to give both of you the opportunity to rethink the situation.' The man said, 'I do not want any postponement. I want the divorce now.' The qadi looked at him with disapproval and asked him, 'Is anybody forcing you to divorce?' The man replied, 'No, it is my decision and I want to finish this now.' Left with no other option, the qadi then declared the couple divorced. As for the nafaqa al-idda and deferred dower, the qadi decided that the man should pay them in monthly instalments of JD 50.

The family law and the Shari'a encourage judges to try and rescue the marriage before starting the divorce procedure. Judges are supposed to try to understand the conflict, propose practical solutions or get the couple's families involved to the extent that is helpful. However, in the aforementioned case, the qadi not only tried his best to bridge the gap between the spouses but even went beyond what was required of him. He was not obliged to use the nafaqa al-idda and deferred dower as leverage, nor was he required to reprimand the husband for wanting a divorce. His actions can only be interpreted in the light of his moral duty to save the marriage, especially when it became clear that the wife did not want the divorce.

4.2 Codified law and use of discretion by the judges

This section reviews the work of three authors (Sonbol 1996; Sanadjian 1996; Tucker 1998), who focus on the effects of codification on the gendered distribution of rights and responsibilities in contemporary Muslim societies. The three scholars develop their arguments in the context of the prevailing trend in the literature that acknowledges the role of the 'modern' state in enhancing women's rights. The legal system in the pre-modern period is portrayed as more oppressive towards women than supposedly modern legislation. The work of these historians has revealed the richness of the application of Islamic law in the Ottoman period, which was not captured by earlier mainstream literature. Their work has advanced our understanding of the ways in which gender, as a symbol and as a concrete social relationship, was negotiated by lay people and handled by jurists and judges. Without their valuable contribution, we might have been still influenced by the ahistorical and static representation of Islamic law and application. However, in their attempts to develop refined arguments against the dominant view regarding the virtues of modernity, they have unfortunately overlooked the complexity of contemporary applications of codified law.

The three authors observe that the codification of Islamic family law has established the state as a main player in interpreting the Shari'a. The process of exclusion and inclusion depends upon many elements, primarily the world view of legislators, their power and the level of socio-economic development of society itself. Codification after the establishment of the nation-state is intended to impose a specific interpretation, which implies standardization of the Shari'a and minimization of judges' subjectivity. The codification of family law signifies a 'fixation' of specific gender roles and relations. The three authors believe that this implies that the application of the Shari'a in modern times is no longer flexible, in contrast to pre-modern times, when a plural legal system is supposed to have obtained.

Sonbol (1996) uses the marriage and divorce cases of minors to illustrate the flexibility of Islamic courts during the Ottoman period. Different madhahib prevailed in different parts of Egypt, that diversity providing people with flexible application of the Shari'a. Sonbol argues that, with the establishment of the nation-state and the advent of modernity, codified law moved society from dependence on flexible interpretations of the Shari'a by different madhahib and different social norms towards a situation in which the state constructs social relations. At the heart of codification was the definition of gender relations through legislation. In Sonbol's view, codified law retained only a partial interpretation of the Shari'a, ignoring that in the past there had been space for madhahib to differ.

Sanadjian (1996) is also negative about the process of codification. She argues that the codification of people's norms into rigid articles of law, whether these laws were codified by the nation-state or by colonizers, has brought about a selective process of exclusion and inclusion of custom. What to exclude or include depends upon many elements, including the world view of the legislators, their power and the level of socio-economic development of a community or society. In general, people observe Islamic norms, but when these are codified, they become rigid due to the tendency of Islamic scholars to draw strict lines between what is licit and what is illicit (halal and haram), a tendency that contradicts the Quranic verses defining all practices that are not specifically prohibited as being permissible. This has rendered the application of the Shari'a less flexible as regards interaction between the community and its environment. Therefore, in Sanadjian's view, codification has been a means of excluding many 'positive' practices that were permitted earlier.

In her work on the fatwas and decisions of judges in Syria and Palestine during the seventeenth and eighteenth centuries, Tucker (1998) emphasizes that the application of the Shari'a was flexible and incorporated social norms. She argues that the flexibility and fluidity of the Shari'a resulted from judges' ability to apply the appropriate solution from among those advocated by different madhahib for social problems. She adds that this flexibility is nowhere to be seen today due to, *inter alia*, the codification of family law. Tucker believes that the Islamic Shari'a (defined as a set of flexible rules and fluid regulations) and the nature of Islamic law (as uncodified and subject to the qadi's discretion and mufti's subjectivity) were helpful to women. Judges and muftis were attentive to the customs and norms of their communities; thus, gender rights and duties were subject to modifications within certain limits to suit the world views of the jurists concerning what constituted justice. Tucker concludes that the codification was meant to 'fix' a definitive interpretation of the Shari'a, thus standardizing it and minimizing judges' subjectivity. Codification, therefore, was a way to stipulate gender roles and relations: 'as soon as the law is codified, gendered rights and gendered duties become incontrovertible points of law, brooking no adjustments or modifications except from on high' (Tucker 1998: 185). Moreover, in Tucker's view, codification no longer allows judges to exercise discretion and muftis to interpret the Shari'a, which, in the context of gender analysis, entails relegation of women's rights.

> The ability of any individual woman to seek a legal judgment tailored to the specifics of her case is greatly reduced in the context of, on the one hand, impersonal codes and courts that are charged with strict and accurate application of the law, and, on the other hand, the obsolescence of the institution of the community-based mufti.
>
> (ibid.: 185)

This study agrees with Sonbol, Sanadjian and Tucker that codification has made the state a main player in interpreting the Shari'a. It also agrees with them that most implementation of the Shari'a regulations, past and present, refers to social norms. However, even after codification, judges, lawyers and other people in general still rely on social norms to solve contemporary social problems. Hence, in the context of the Gaza Shari'a courts, judges and lawyers (as representatives of the legal and religious institutions) and other people (as active social agents who seek to protect their interests), in their search for gaps and room in which to manoeuvre, prefer either to alternate or to intermesh the codified and uncodified laws.

This study argues, on the basis of fieldwork, that even after codification the Shari'a does not operate in a vacuum; it is bound by the context in which the judges' world view, state structure and people's agency together affect the perception and implementation of Islamic family law. Highlighting one element (in this case, the role of the state) and downplaying others (the judges and people's agency) does not provide an adequate understanding of what is really going on in contemporary Shari'a courts. We need to look at how these factors and actors interact, and when and how in the course of their interaction they come to construct a particular social reality. What sorts of knowledge/power/discourse exist, and under which circumstances do actors (including the judges) downplay codified law and bring social norms to the fore? What are the enabling factors that allow the judges to shift smoothly between codified law and social norms and yet claim that they do not exceed the limits of the Shari'a? And what are the wider social ramifications of such processes?

Understanding the application of laws concerning domestic disputes requires asking *what people do in the court* and not *whether people obey the law* (Griffiths 1992: 157). This requires adoption of a suitable methodology that allows the researcher to observe the process personally and involves understanding how family law is actually applied: what is included, what is excluded and how the actors interact. This may give us some insight into the complex process of the implementation of law and enable us to identify and characterize practices, values, strategies as well as often-conflicting interests without prejudging the role of the state or the harm caused by codification.

The studies quoted here are based on extensive reviews of historical material, and the methodology adopted has produced sophisticated and valuable analyses. However, when they compare historical observation with present-day practice, Tucker, Sonbol and Sanadjian base their conclusions on political abstractions; they do not advance empirical material, case studies, observations or statistics to prove that today's practice differs from that in the Ottoman period. Furthermore, they demonstrate a tendency to draw a dichotomy between the application of Islamic law in the pre-modern and post-colonial/modern nation-state periods. This logic causes them to resort to further dichotomies, such as codified versus uncodified; fluidity versus fixity; flexibility versus standardization; modern versus pre-modern; and, in the case of Tucker, judges' subjectivity versus objectivity of binding law. These dichotomies lead them to formulate the pre-emptive conclusion typified by Tucker: 'The legal system that permitted such flexibility is nowhere to be seen today, nor it is really conceivable in the context of contemporary society' (Tucker 1998: 186).

Tucker, Sonbol and Sanadjian portray contemporary Muslim societies and individuals in the Muslim nation-state as if they were mere objects of state law. This portrayal does not take into account the capabilities and knowledge of people (Long 2001) and tends to depict them as passive victims of state law. Nor does it acknowledge processes of interplay between individual agency and societal structure(s) that can subvert the coercive power of state law.

Sociology of law affirms that there is a social space between individuals and legislation. For example, Griffiths (1992: 155) points out that it is naïve to assume that the social space between legislator and individual is a *'normative vacuum empty of norms and structures other than those of the state itself'* (italics in the original). Moore (1978) notes that even in industrial societies, the law does not operate in a vacuum; there is always a degree of informality, which may diverge from the code of law. Gulliver (1997: 21), too, in his study of the relations between adjudication and negotiation in the application of law, points out that 'some societies are characterized by the absence of adjudication, but probably no society is without some forms of negotiation as a means of dealing with disputes.' The depiction of codified law as inflexible and lacking fluidity is derived from what Masud (2001: 5) calls a 'positivist' vision of law.

In contrast to this approach, which defines law in relation to the coercive power of the state, a more adequate approach can be found in Griffiths' propositions (1992: 155). He points out that in order to understand the *relation* between people and law, people should be conceived of as social characters; every 'inter(activity) takes place within and is in the first instance regulated by a complex web of reciprocal relationships and social fields.' Law does not pass from the state to its citizens through cables; it is mediated through social bodies such as the police and courts. The state is only one among 'many arenas in society where regulatory activities take place.' Griffiths (1992: 156) concludes that one should pay attention not to the intention of the law but to the social working of law; therefore, the adequate theory of law 'depends on an adequate theory of social organization; it must be a sociological theory.'

The judges' task is more complex than is apparent at first glance; they have to deal with actors from different social backgrounds and possessing different power resources. Their strategy is to understand the power balance between litigants and the weight each party has in society. To achieve this goal, judges interrogate litigants about their background, ask to which family they belong, in which Palestinian institution they work, where they live and so forth. Judges also use ushers (and court clerks) as agents to help them understand what is going on outside the courtroom. When they are confronted with a difficult case (that is, involving people with overwhelming power, or when the case is exceptionally serious), they consult with the qadi al-qudah and other judges to reach a collective decision. Another strategy is simply to postpone the case until the following week, unless they feel that a quick judgment is required. Judges also maintain communication with community leaders; I have often heard them asking litigants to send their makhatir for consultation. The strategies of judges range from in-court mediation to the application of customary law, out-of-court negotiation, threats and negotiation. Their methods of reasoning are akin to those of their predecessors, for they exercise ra'y (personal reasoning), consult each other (in order to reach consensus, ijma') and also use istihsan and istislah (seeking the most equitable and best solution to serve the interests of the community).

It is not only in the Shari'a court that the subjectivities of judges come to bear. In the contemporary 'West', the subjectivity of court officials plays a significant role in deciding how cases proceed. This is illustrated by Bridges and Steen (1998), who studied the differential attitudes of court officials in dealing with youth problems in the United States. In their study, which focuses on the relationship between punishment and 'race', they observe that official, subjective perception is quite decisive in assessing the character of the offender, which in turn plays a critical role in the decision made by the court. It is interesting to note that the application of the law and officials' subjectivity end up serving the interests of the white male in US courts, while in the Gaza Shari'a courts, judges often take the side of women despite prevalent gender inequalities that allot males many privileges. In one case, the courts are deepening racial inequalities in the society; in the other, they are trying to protect the weaker parties to the extent possible.

In the Gaza Shari'a courts, the fact that the application of family law is not monolithic enables women to seek out points of leverage. However, a valid counter-argument might be raised here: flexibility may also work against women's interests. Flexibility and the incorporation of customary practice may mean adopting and validating so-called honour crimes or justifying female genital mutilation, or the acceptance of other, less violent actions such as preventing women from receiving their share of inheritance under the rubric of 'custom'. In this context, let us recall Moore's contention that law is implemented in a certain context by certain people who have access to unequal power resources and defend particular values and principles. To reveal the degree, intensity and content of the law's flexibility, we need an appropriate methodology. Moore points out that informal mechanisms remain influential because of 'thick layers of formalism and ideological self- representation to be penetrated, [which make it difficult] to find out *what is really going on*' (Moore 1978: 30, italics added).

Levine (2003) contends that the courtroom should be observed through cultural and legal lenses. For instance, criminal law in the United States should not be perceived as reflecting absolute truth, for it is based on values that are culture-specific. Analysing several criminal cases, she shows that some US minorities were criminalized by the American legal system because of their 'different' cultural practices. In her conclusion, she quotes Fox (1985: xii) as criticizing the Western portrayal of Others' legal systems as too culturally bound, which leads to the comforting conclusion that those Others are primitive.

Culture and cultural practices are not fixed or timeless; they are subject to negotiation by people as groups and individuals. Essentializing culture as if it were a package of practices transmitted from generation to generation has proved to be an ideological and political weapon used by both Western Orientalists and indigenous fundamentalists. People's interaction (with each other and their environment) often leads them to change, drop or adopt certain practices in order to realize their well-being. Therefore, there is no exclusive category such as 'Palestinians' customary practices' applied by all Palestinians across time and space. Palestinians have multiple realities and diverse practices, influenced by elements related to their interaction with their environment.

Obviously, there cannot be an abstract notion of *women* or *culture* because that could lead to the trap of false objectivism and universalism. Nor is this study advocating cultural relativism, which in its extreme form defends certain political objectives often constructed by the powerful groups in society at the expense of people's full realization of their rights. Cultural relativism, which is meant to acknowledge people's beliefs and customs within their specific context and culture, has been used and abused by its more adamant advocates who, under the rubric of cultural specificity, actually harm the less-powerful groups in society, be they women, children, ethnic minorities or others. This study is also not claiming that flexibility, as presented above, is objectively 'positive'. It simply stresses that observation in the courts shows that flexibility is acknowledged by the judicial system of the Shari'a court and is thus adopted by various actors, each of whom uses it to ensure certain values and interests.[1]

There is no single recipe, such as advocating fixity or supporting flexibility, to expand women's choices. The richness of women's realities can be captured in different ways. Gender power presents diverse patterns and configurations, which need to be envisaged from different standpoints simultaneously. For example, in 1996 the women's movement campaigned for the right of women to obtain passports for themselves and their children without the permission of their husbands. The campaign succeeded, and this right was 'granted' through a specific decree. Another campaign succeeded in eliminating what appeared to be a 'fixed' regulation, forbidding women from learning to drive a car unless accompanied by a male relative.

Although codified law is meant to restrict judges' subjectivity, in fact it provides them with significant leverage in particular cases. For example, family law does not specify how much nafaqa should be deducted from the husband's income and so leaves it up to the qadi to estimate. Nafaqa should reflect the economic situation of the husband and the standard of living of the wife, and, being familiar with the community and those who apply for nafaqa (poor families, women and men), the qadi can set a reasonable amount in accordance with the economic circumstances of the litigants. However, the amount of nafaqa, as even the judges admit, is not necessarily enough to cover minimal living costs. In estimating nafaqa, judges assume that the wife is living in her parents' house and is being taken care of (in terms of shelter, food, clothing and so on) by her natal family. This assumption works against the interests of the vast majority of applicants, who find themselves faced with a difficult choice: either to endure the hardships of being in their natal family house or to struggle for a better deal with their husbands. The outcome is contingent upon when and how a wife chooses to go to court, the support she gets from her natal and extended family and the role of the court (in ruling in her favour). The exercise of subjectivity by the judges is thus situated within the broader gender discourse in society with minor or greater departure to provide 'justice' as they view it.

On another level, the priority of judges is not so much to follow the text as to contribute to social stability, help to preserve social cohesion and, at the same time, protect the weak members of their community. Social welfare is 'served when local practice serves as the limit for comprehending the relations individuals have chosen to form with each other' (Rosen 1989: 49). Social welfare may mean that individuals should sacrifice their personal interests to serve the wider community. For example, judges prefer that people find a mutually acceptable solution rather than resort to the law. When spouses come to court seeking divorce and the wife does not want to lose her financial rights (in terms of alimony, value of her furniture, deferred dower and so on), the qadi tells her family, 'I will put pressure on the husband to get as much as possible from him, but you too have to be flexible.' If, for example, the total financial entitlement of the wife is around JD 4,000, the qadi might propose that the wife should halve that amount because a judgment giving the wife a larger amount may not be complied with. In one case, when the wife's lawyer estimated her alimony above what her husband could pay, the qadi advised him: 'Do not exaggerate your demands. I will not agree to them. Request what is acceptable, to enable me to respond to you.'

Sometimes, the qadi even forces the wife's family to give up her minimal right to the nafaqat al-idda, that is, the maintenance rights of women during the idda period. This happens particularly when the qadi gets the impression that further conflict could lead to undesirable consequences for the two families and the wider community. The qadi is aware that the parties are not just the wife and husband, but that both are involved in 'multiplex relationships' in which forces such as their families, perhaps even hamayil (clans), may intervene and expand the conflict to serve other interests if it is not resolved.

It is not only when the case involves nafaqa that the qadi acts with regard to the possible consequences of his decision; the same tendency is exemplified in the case of a 21-year-old divorced woman, which was heard in December 2003. The issue was over who should be the woman's wali (guardian in marriage or custody issues). According to Decree No. 1 of 29 August 1994, which was issued by the first qadi al-qudah of Palestine,[2] courts should use the Shari'a to 'facilitate people's affairs when they approach the judges of Shari'a courts, especially in matters related to marriage procedures'. The decree goes on to explain the procedure:

> Suppose that the fiancée's wali is on a trip, then the next of kin should act as her wali. The qadi should grant her permission to marry, provided there are two witnesses who can identify him. If the mature and sensible fiancée has no wali (close or remote), the qadi should act as her wali because guardianship of a mature woman is not obligatory. The marriage should be concluded in the presence of the present wali in order not to deprive the bride of a groom of equivalent status (kafu').[3]

The qadi al-qudah repeated the same concern eight months later. On 2 February 1995, he stated his view in more precise phrasing. The decree reads:

> Wilaya [guardianship] in marriage is preferable (wilayat istihbab) [as opposed to ijbar: obligatory]. Therefore, when the first wali is absent due to death or travel, then the next eligible person [in her family] should act as a wali. If none of them is present, the qadi should act as a wali because the woman should not give up the equivalent (kafu') groom and thus endure damage. These are articles 37 and 40 of the *Personal Status Law* and they should be applied in order to facilitate the marriage procedure.

I observed a case in which a divorced woman, Sana', was accompanied by her uncle and two brothers when she went to the court to conclude her second marriage. The qadi ordered her uncle to bring her father to court, but the uncle replied that the father was working in Israel and did not come to Gaza frequently. The qadi asked, 'When do you expect him to be in Gaza?' The uncle replied, 'Next week.' The qadi then enquired, 'Why are you in a hurry? Wait until her father comes back and then you can conclude the marriage even without my permission.'

I asked the qadi later why he had not granted Sana' the required permission to conclude the second marriage. His response was,

> There is a bad smell in this marriage. If the uncle is sincere, he can wait until her father is back. I suspect that they want to conclude the marriage in the absence of the father. This suggests that a conflict may arise when the father

comes back. The father may quarrel with his brother, sons, daughter and the new son-in-law. Why should the court contribute to a foreseeable conflict instead of promoting harmony?

I suggested that what he had done was against the law, which allowed Sana' to conclude her marriage even in the absence of her father. He answered: 'The law is blind, we are not.' The next day, concerned that I might not understand his reasoning well, he elucidated his motivation further:

> Suppose that a woman decides to marry somebody whom her father does not accept. And suppose that she concludes her marriage in the court according to the teaching of God and His Messenger. What do you think the father's response would be? Some fathers have limited minds. They may kill their daughters or at least force them to divorce. Our society is full of such fathers and we cannot – as a court – turn a blind eye to the consequences of our decisions. Is it wise to conclude such marriages and thus risk the daughters' lives? What is more important, giving licence to a couple to marry or saving the girl's life and future? Moreover, girls in our society have no knowledge of what marriage means. They can be influenced by the love stories they watch on the numerous TV channels that can be accessed all over and thus think that life is rosy. Real life is hard. My refusal is meant to save the girl and her family.

Thus, social harmony took precedence over individual interest. As the qadi expressed it, 'We work according to the principle which emphasizes that avoiding harm has a higher priority than providing benefits.'

The qadi's reasoning echoed arguments put forward by some members of the Model Parliament in 1998, which will be discussed in Chapter 8. Similar logic was also used in 2002 by some young women linked to women's organizations operating in Gaza, who had participated in discussion groups about issues related to family law and reform, during the fieldwork for this study. Some were volunteers in gender awareness-raising projects; others were beneficiaries of training courses provided by women's organizations; yet others had been included in the interviews because of their economic problems or social vulnerability. Many of the participants maintained that they would not get married without the approval of their families. For example, Nisrin, a young Birzeit University graduate, said, 'How can a girl marry without being honoured by her father's blessings? How can a husband respect such a wife?' Family approval is crucial for young girls to establish a new life. The issue of the wali is probably linked to values related to the interdependence of family members. An Al-Azhar University student said,

> Even if I wanted to conclude my marriage without the approval of my father, tell me, where is the man who would dare to conclude such a marriage? Who would accept me without my family? Would his family accept his act and would they respect me?

Salwa al-Qasim, director of the women's unit in the Centre for Human Rights, explained the factors underlying this attitude:

> The issue of guardianship should be read as a social value more than as a legal text. A girl who gets married without her family's approval is disdained by her husband and his family. At least, she would be considered without izwa [in this context, without value]. The next question is related to whether any man is trustworthy enough for a girl to sacrifice her family for him. Another question is related to the economic interdependence of family members, especially in this period of economic crisis. It is common for young men to be incapable of establishing a new life without the support of the family, whether by supplying them with the dower or hosting them and their wives until their wings are covered with feathers [that is, they are self-sufficient]. In our system, the protection network is important for both sexes. More importantly, most marriages take place between relatives, or connected hamayel [clans]. In such relations, no one operates individually or independently. We are part of a larger system that controls us. Even if there are some men who are economically strong, their social attitudes are likely to be more conservative than those of others and thus they are unlikely to marry 'free women'. Therefore, the issue of a wali is embedded more economically and socially than legally.
>
> (Interview, August 2002)

Establishing a new family is not an individual option; it involves the prospective wife and husband, their families and the community as a whole. Even though young men and women understand that their marriage implies a personal bond, they also know that it is unattainable without being rooted, accepted and appreciated by their families and the larger community. For example, take the case of Samah, daughter of a prominent family in Gaza. She obtained a Master's degree from a European university, where she became involved with a Gazan man who had a refugee background. When she returned to Gaza, the man's family visited her father and asked for her hand, but her father refused because the social background of the prospective groom did not satisfy him. The daughter tried to convince her father through some family mediators, but her attempts failed. Samah is 33 years old now, occupying a prestigious position in an agency, living in her father's house, still unmarried. She has no hope of marrying at that age.

The judges' use of discretion is particularly evident in cases related to women's right to maintenance. When a woman sues her husband for nafaqa, the normal procedure is for the court to estimate the amount and to convince the husband to accept it. If one party does not accept the sum offered, the qadi calls on each side to provide a representative who, together with a court representative, will estimate how much alimony should be paid. The representatives of the two parties are relatives who are familiar with their financial situation and therefore can estimate the amount of nafaqa to be paid or received. If the husband rejects their estimate, the qadi tells him that there is only one alternative: a three-member committee, all of them to be nominated by the court, would go to the husband's house and his place of employment to check his income and set the nafaqa accordingly. That would entail transport costs, which would have to be paid by the husband in addition to the nafaqa. In addition, the court committee might set a higher amount than the one suggested initially. The qadi explains these extra expenses and unforeseen consequences to the man and suggests that it would be more economical for him to accept the court's decision. Faced with that threat, the husband may either accept the amount suggested by the court or try to reconcile with his wife (with the qadi's full encouragement), thus minimizing his financial losses. In these processes of negotiation or threats, the qadi may arrive at a solution that enables him to feel that he is preserving the message of the Shari'a, complying with people's customs, not violating the law and protecting the institution of the family as best he can.

Sometimes, the man may accept the qadi's estimate but then fail to pay regularly or at all. In such cases, the wife petitions the court, which then summons the man to explain the reasons for his delay. If the husband is unable to justify his conduct, the *Code of Islamic Jurisdictions* authorizes the qadi to jail him for 20 days. The procedure is for the qadi to instruct the relevant authority in writing to imprison the man. The qadi can do this three times, after which he has no further means to force the husband to pay.

An interview with Nahla Radi, a human rights lawyer who visits prisons to evaluate the extent to which the human rights of prisoners are respected, brought to light interesting details about the way men who do not pay nafaqa are treated in prison:

> The men who have not paid nafaqa [are] housed separately from the other prisoners. The prison director told me, 'I do not consider these men to be criminals. They just lack the money to pay nafaqa to their wives.' The men themselves do not allow me to address them as 'real' prisoners. They tell me, 'We are here because of nafaqa cases, we are not prisoners.' One of them told me that because his wife had sent him to prison, he would not pay even if he were imprisoned a hundred times. He told me, 'How can I view her as my wife? Family means accepting the good and the bad, not imprisoning the husband at the first sign of trouble.'

However, as Chapter 5 will show, in many suits the judges do succeed in helping women who file nafaqa cases, through the use of their discretion.

Although some women use nafaqa effectively to obtain financial support, others use it to achieve results that go far beyond the initial intention of the law. For example, take the case of Su'ad, a woman in her late forties, who has four married sons and two married daughters. One day, her husband, Hatim, found JD 10,000 missing and accused his wife of having stolen it. He beat her, forced her to leave the house and filed a theft accusation against her at the police station, which is a rare action in Gaza. The police could not find any evidence to support his accusation. After waiting vainly for one year for her husband to reconsider, Su'ad sued him for nafaqa. She felt that her husband had robbed her of her honour. 'The accusation of theft has stained my honour forever. For one year, I have not been able to interact with people. What would they say about me if I did? I am a hajja [a woman who has performed the pilgrimage to Mecca],' she told me. For a year, Su'ad had lived with her sons and daughters, spending one week in each of their homes, while waiting for Hatim to reconsider. The sons tried to bridge the gap between their parents, but the father was so angry that he would not allow them to intervene. Su'ad told me:

> I could not continue my life without regaining my honour. My lawyer advised me to use the court to reveal the facts about the theft accusation. I want to save my face vis-à-vis my in-laws. How could my daughters and sons face their in-laws otherwise? They would constantly recall their mother's crisis. The theft spoiled my family's life. I am also tired of living in their houses like a refugee. I want to get back to my place where I was living like a queen.

I then talked to Hala Anwar, Su'ad's lawyer, who explained to me that her client was not really interested in obtaining nafaqa:

> The case is not about nafaqa. Su'ad did not need money. Nafaqa was only an excuse to meet Hatim in the Shari'a court where the qadi could help to restore Su'ad's honour. After we filed the case, Hatim was called to appear before the qadi. I used the opportunity to explain to him the reasons for the case. I told him: 'You know that we are not here to get nafaqa; we are here to sort out the problem once and for all. We need you either to prove your claim that she is the thief or to accept our proposal that she swear on the Quran that she did not steal the money. She is well-known as a person who observes Allah's commands. You yourself took her on the hajj and you are sure that she fears God.' With the help of the qadi, we convinced Hatim to follow this route. He did not have any proof that she had stolen the money, but it seems he was too proud to withdraw his original accusation. He accepted the proposal and added another condition, that her father and brothers also swear on the Quran that she had not stolen the money. We accepted that.

Thus, the litigation was transformed from a nafaqa suit into an opportunity to prove Su'ad's innocence. The Shari'a court has no jurisdiction in civil affairs related to money and theft, nor is it the qadi's official duty to intervene in such family affairs. However, the qadi was motivated by his sense of being a religious and community leader and wanted to use his moral authority to help Su'ad regain her self-respect. On the day Su'ad was to swear her innocence on the Quran, the whole court was very tense. Whenever there is an extraordinary case, the qadi informs the court members about it and discusses it with them. That turns the court into something like a theatre, with court members assembled to watch the proceedings.

As the case involved an oath taken on the Quran, the assembly performed ablutions (wudu') before entering the courtroom. I then discovered that the qadi always performs ablutions before ruling on cases because, he explained, 'we have to touch the Quran, read passages of it or ask witnesses to swear [and] this requires us to be clean'. The wife appeared before the qadi at 11.30 a.m., accompanied by her sons. The husband appeared a little later. When both were present, the proceedings began. They were unusual since there was no need for papers, sijillat or katib; only a copy of the Quran was required.

The qadi called witnesses from the community and the court. Su'ad's lawyer was also present. The qadi asked Su'ad if she was clean (not menstruating) and if she had performed her wudu'. She was prepared for the oath-taking, clean and had finished her ablutions. She looked frightened, and the qadi calmed her down. Then he told her to put her right hand on the Quran and told her to repeat after him: 'I swear in the name of the Great God and His Book that I have not stolen the JD 10,000 from my husband.' Su'ad did so, and then, overcome with emotion, repeated it several times while looking at her husband and crying loudly. The husband turned his face to the wall, apparently to hide tears. It was a moving scene and those present started calling out, 'Allahu akbar!' (God is the Greatest!). Hala Anwar, the lawyer, hugged her client to calm her.

The qadi closed the session and told them that he was going to Su'ad's house to repeat the swearing ceremony with her father and brothers. He took the same copy of the Quran and went off with two witnesses, one a well-known community leader (the mukhtar of the neighbourhood) and the other a court clerk. The qadi used his personal car. Once the father and brothers had sworn on the Quran that Su'ad was innocent, he returned to the court and told Hatim: 'As you know, swearing on the Quran is not a trivial issue. We do that when serious matters are involved. Your wife's honour and that of her family were at stake. Now your request has been fulfilled and the family have proved that your wife was innocent. It is up to you now to declare this publicly.' Hatim nodded his head in agreement.

The qadi continued: 'I order you to send a large group of the best-known and most respectable people in your circle to bring your wife back to her house. I also order you to send her gifts in the form of new clothes; she retains her honour and she deserves to enter your house as a new bride.' The wife had already left the court with her sons. Her lawyer told me later that the husband had followed the qadi's instructions and brought his wife back to his house surrounded by a big crowd of their family members.

In this case, the qadi used his moral authority to apply values that are customarily and religiously observed to reach the desirable end of reconciliation. The courtroom was used as a medium through which the qadi exercised his 'reasonable' autonomy. Nafaqa was used as an avenue to reconcile the couple and preserve Su'ad's honour. The most striking feature of this case is that it did not appear in the court record. The intervention of the qadi was subjective and transmitted orally. This frequent reliance on oral interventions excludes the accumulation of precedents. No trace is left, and thus no legacy or recorded jurisprudence is to be found.

4.3 Conclusion

This chapter has shown that judges' decisions are informed by their understanding of the Shari'a as a set of ethical principles that aim at, on the one hand, protecting the weaker members of the community and, on the other, preserving the social order. In the process, it has examined some dominant ideas in the literature and tested them against the findings of the author's fieldwork in the Gaza Shari'a courts. It has established that judges do exercise a degree of discretion, informed by their self-perception as members of their community rather than as mere implementers of the law. It has also proved that the dichotomy between a technical voice and an ethical voice in Islam, with the legal system being dominated by the technical voice, is false.

The flexibility of the judges' conduct was analysed with reference to the theoretical framework provided in Chapter 1. In particular, the flexible implementation of family law offers leeway to judges to overcome problems resulting from the contradictions between the law and its objectives. When such discrepancies emerge, the qadi invokes 'legal concepts' which, unlike the codified law, are unwritten, flexible, unspecified and, most importantly, ambiguous. Thus, the flexible application of family law in Gaza reflects the flexibility of the wider conceptual framework with reference to which the qadi operates. Furthermore, the multiple identity of the qadi plays a vital role in shaping his rulings. The qadi's familiarity with community norms and customs, his educational background (in Shari'a and fiqh) and his view of himself as a member of his community direct him to find solutions that do not depart from the prevailing morality of the community. Therefore, the way in which 'legal concepts' are applied cannot be viewed in isolation from the qadi's multifaceted identity. This further implies that flexibility might be stretched or tightened in accordance with judges' embeddedness in, and responsiveness to, the norms of their community.

The standards of 'rightness' or 'wrongness' depend on the context within which the dispute takes place. The qadi assesses the wrongdoing of a litigant against what is defined by society as ordinary behaviour. The qadi often does not refer to the legal implication of the man's action; rather, he invokes concepts related to what the society, religion and general morality consider to be acceptable behaviour. This appears to be the yardstick used by the qadi. Interestingly, the same trend – that is, placing the transgression in the framework of socially accepted behaviour – is also observed among litigants. When they communicate with the qadi, they often refer to his moral and religious authority instead of his legal position. Women frequently address the qadi as the father of Muslims, the protector of God's worshippers and so forth. Men do the same thing. Even when protesting against the qadi's interventions, they frame their objections in religious and moral terms.

Is flexibility found only in Palestine? This question can only be answered by conducting a comparative study of Shari'a courts in different Islamic countries. The specificity of the Gaza courts may influence the application of family law. Palestine is still, to all intents and purposes, under occupation, and no state can impose its rules over the Shari'a courts. Thus, the Shari'a courts may have some sense of independence in applying a different system of justice. However, this specificity bears out rather than weakens the analysis in the chapter by revealing the diversity of Shari'a courts' modes of operation, both over time and in different contexts.

The most important question to ask now is: did the developments that occurred after the codification of Islamic family law create a break with the traditional flexibility and fluidity of Islamic jurisprudence? More specifically, has codification really had a drastic impact on the exercise of women's rights, as suggested by Sonbol, Tucker and Sanadjian? If women's rights suffered in the twentieth century, was that a consequence of codification? Should we try to find an explanation for the weakening of women's rights in the legal sphere or should we look in other areas? Answering this question is not within the remit of this study, but observation in the Gaza Shari'a courts suggests that the codification of Islamic law does not in itself provide a satisfactory explanation for such 'regression' in the contemporary era. This study agrees with Tucker's argument that knowledge of the history of Islamic law is needed to answer current questions, and adds that it is also necessary to adopt a suitable and direct observation methodology in order to see how judges and lawyers struggle to maintain the Shari'a on the one hand, while preserving social harmony on the other.

The judges in the Gaza courts have not only studied their own heritage, but they also incorporate the exigencies of contemporary life into their judgments and treatment of litigants. Contrary to Tucker's assumption, according to whom today's judges have lost their subjectivity, Gaza judges are still loyal to the heritage of Islamic jurisprudence, which asserts the concepts of fairness, consideration of the context and protection of the weak. However, they are equally loyal to the tradition of Islamic law that condones a sharp division in gender roles and rights.

With the broad principles on which the judges base their judgments having been established, the next chapter will examine how they deal with the issue that is brought before them most frequently: nafaqa.

Notes

1 In an interesting observation, Moore (2005: 347) points out that 'culture has lost its political innocence'. In her view, 'today, when cultural difference is offered as a legitimation for and explanation of legal difference, cultural context often comes up as an aspect of a consciously mobilized collective identity in the midst of a political struggle, and it arises in relation to constitutions, collective inequalities, insiders and outsiders, and other aspects of national and ethnic politics.'
2 When the Palestinian Authority was established, President Yasir Arafat instituted the post of qadi al-qudah, which was initially occupied by the outstanding qadi Abu Sardana, previously a judge of the Court of Appeal in Amman (Jordan). The role of the wali was one of his first concerns. When he went to Gaza in 1994, he attempted to update the Shari'a court administratively and judicially in accordance with the latest reforms implemented in the Jordanian courts. Abu Sardana's main decrees will be discussed further in Chapter 9.
3 Decree of 28 August 1994 (no number), cited in M. Faris (2002).

Bibliography

Ahmed, L. (1992) *Women and Gender in Islam: Historical Roots of a Modern Debate.* New Haven, CT: Yale University Press.

Antoun, R. (1989) *Muslim Preacher in the Modern World: A Jordanian Case Study in Comparative Perspective.* Princeton: Princeton University Press.

Bridges, G. and S. Steen (1998) 'Racial Disparities in Official Assessments of Juvenile Offenders: Attributional Stereotypes as Meditating Mechanisms', *American Sociological Review* 63(4): 554–70.

Faris, M. (2002) *Ta'amim qadi al-qudah khilal saba' sanawat (Decrees of qadi al-qudah over seven years).* Gaza: No publisher.

Fox, R. (1985) *Lions in the Punjab.* Berkeley and Los Angeles: University of California Press.

Gluckman, M. (1955) *The Judicial Process Among the Barotse of Northern Rhodesia.* Manchester: Manchester University Press.

Griffiths, J. (1992) 'Legal Pluralism and the Social Working of Law', in B. Brouwer, T. Hol, A. Soeteman and A. de Wild (eds) *Coherence and Conflict in Law: Proceedings of the 3rd Benelux-Scandinavian Symposium in Legal Theory*, pp. 151–76. Amsterdam and Deventer: Kluwer Law and Taxation Publisher.

Gulliver, P. H. (1997) 'Case Studies of Law in Non-Western Societies: Introduction', in L. Nader (ed.) *Law in Culture and Society*, pp. 11–23. Berkeley, CA: University of California Press.

Levine, K. (2003) 'Negotiating the Boundaries of Crime and Culture: A Socio-Legal Perspective on Cultural Defense Strategies', *Law and Social Inquiry Journal* 28(1): 39–86.

Long, N. (2001) *Development Sociology: Actor Perspective.* London and New York: Routledge.

Masud, M. K. (2001) *Muslim Jurists' Quest for the Normative Basis of Shari'a.* Leiden: ISIM Publication.

Moore, S. F. (1978) *Law as Process: An Anthropological Approach.* London: Routledge & Kegan Paul.

Moore, S. F. (2005) 'Certainties Undone: Fifty Turbulent Years of Legal Anthropology, 1949–1999', in S. F. Moore (ed.) *Law and Anthropology: A Reader*, pp. 347–67. Malden, Oxford and Victoria: Blackwell.

Rosen, L. (1989) *The Anthropology of Justice: Law as Culture in Islamic Society.* Cambridge: Cambridge University Press.

Sanadjian, M. (1996) 'A Public Flogging in South-Western Iran: Juridical Rule, Abolition of Legality and Local Resistance', in O. Harris (ed.) *Inside and Outside the Law: Anthropological Studies of Authority and Ambiguity*, pp. 157–84. London: Routledge.

Sonbol, A. (1996) 'Adults and Minors in Ottoman Shari'a Courts and Modern Law', in A. Sonbol (ed.) *Women, the Family and Divorce Laws in Islamic History*, pp. 236–59. Syracuse, NY: Syracuse University Press.

Tucker, J. (1998) *In the House of Law: Gender and Islamic Law in Ottoman Syria and Palestine.* Berkeley, CA: University of California Press.

Yngvesson, B. (1993) *Virtuous Citizens, Disruptive Subjects: Order and Complaint in a New England Court.* New York: Routledge.

5 The sociology of Nafaqa (maintenance)

This chapter analyses the various strategies adopted by women in the Shari'a court when claiming maintenance. While placing the discussion within its legal framework, the chapter does not make the juridical aspect of nafaqa its main focus; rather, it examines how nafaqa is implemented and transformed in the course of its application. The argument is that nafaqa, which defines gender relations between spouses according to the principle of 'maintenance versus obedience', has been transformed over time by the action of women as social agents. Women use this provision to serve objectives that differ from those initially intended by the law, which may signify women's ability to transform what is meant to be an instrument for their oppression into a tool for their empowerment.[1]

5.1 Social context

After the establishment of the Palestinian Authority (PA) in 1994, the number of nafaqa and other cases submitted to the Shari'a courts increased rapidly (see Table 5.1). According to qadi al-Karmi, 'the legal system genuinely attempted to regain its power [and] women benefited most from this reinstatement.' If we take 1993 as the base year, the number of cases at least doubled, from 122 in 1993 to 273 in 1994. Most of the cases were nafaqa suits, which rose from 62 in 1993 to 133 in 1994. The total number of cases continued to increase in subsequent years, reaching a peak of 935 in 1997, with nafaqa cases continuing to dominate significantly.

The big increase in the number of cases in 1995, from the previous year's 273 to 414, might be partly attributable to an administrative change. Before the establishment of the PA, women used to combine several petitions to the court in one application; then, in August 1994, the newly appointed qadi al-qudah, Abu Sardana, issued a decree (ta'mim) requiring each demand to be filed separately. Thus, suits concerning nafaqa, tawabi' (value of wife's furniture), children's nafaqa, nursing fees ('ujrat hadana), breast-feeding fees ('ujrat rida'a) and so on could no longer be grouped together. Abu Sardana's official explanation was that each case has its own rationale, but some lawyers saw the decree as an attempt to collect higher fees from litigants. The decree also emphasized the importance of filing suits for children's nafaqa separately from that of their mother's because

74 The sociology of Nafaqa

Table 5.1 Nafaqa suits as percentage of total cases at Gaza Shari'a courts, 1993–2001

Year	Total number of cases	Number of nafaqa suits	Nafaqa suits as % of total
1993	122	62	51
1994	273	133	49
1995	414	238	58
1996	712	337	47
1997	935	316	39
1998	605	276	46
1999	604	277	46
2000	624	260	42
2001	548	298	54

Source: Data from Gaza Shari'a court records.

'the wife's nafaqa may take a longer time to establish, depending on the nature of the dispute, in which case the children could be harmed while waiting for their mother's case to be settled' (Decree of 29 August 1994, in Faris 2002). However, the Shari'a courts only followed the 1994 decree in 1996 and part of 1997; after Abu Sardana returned to Jordan in 1997, they reverted to their traditional procedure of grouping several claims in one case. This is apparent from the decline in the number of suits from 935 in 1997 to 605 in 1998. The separation of court cases was subsequently brought up by qadi al-qudah Al-timimi, who reiterated the reasoning of his predecessor in Decree No. 69 on 14 July 2003.

The establishment of the PA and Abu Sardana's decree by themselves do not provide sufficient reason for the big increase in cases. We also need to examine the elements of this political change and their impact on the dynamics of social relations. When the Palestine Liberation Organization (PLO) returned from the Diaspora in 1994 to establish the Palestinian Authority, thousands of its members and employees were given temporary permits to live in the West Bank and Gaza Strip by the Israeli authorities. Some authors estimate the number of post-Oslo returnees to range from 40,000 to 100,000. The returnees hoped that after some time they would receive permanent residence and invite their family members to join them.

However, a combination of factors turned their dreams into nightmares. The permit processing bureaucracy compelled applicants to submit their papers to several authorities, but, given the time pressure under which the Palestinian security services had been set up in the West Bank and Gaza Strip, they were unconnected and competed against each other. It was not clear which department in the PA was responsible for processing the many thousands of permit applications. Nepotism (wasta) and favouritism appeared and flourished, and that led to a process of manipulation and modification of the application lists. Some requests were favoured and others left at the bottom of the pile. Israel was a full participant in this game, being the actual decision-maker in acceptance or rejection of the applications. It was very reluctant to facilitate the return of Palestinians and normalization of their lives, for that would lead to the entry of thousands more as part of family reunification.

Thus, Israel adopted a policy of procrastination, refusal and vetoes, which then became the legacy of the Oslo process. The application lists became chips not only in the bargaining between the PA and Israel, but also in the power struggle between the different Palestinian security services. Interestingly, Israel was involved in this internal power struggle, too. On certain occasions, a number of returnees were granted papers by Israel to 'reward' a particular security department or even a particular leader for his 'co-operation'. Thus, the development and proliferation of nepotism was influenced and advanced by the very political process of Oslo.

In the meantime, thousands of returnees waited in vain. Some became frustrated and decided to go back to the countries from which they had returned. Others preferred to believe that their odd situation would not last long. Their decision to wait made them more vulnerable because their temporary permits (tasrih ziyara) expired after some time, and they were unable even to leave the Territories. They are now illegal residents in Gaza and the West Bank, where they effectively remain imprisoned.[2] Tamari (1996b: 34) depicts their situation ironically: 'Palestinian expatriates returning to their homeland have fewer rights than foreign emigrants making applications for citizenship in a new country of choice.' A number of Palestinians accepted their situation and carried on with their lives. For some, this meant divorcing wives who were still abroad and marrying Gazan women. Divorce petitions rose from 317 in 1993 to 387 in 1994, and continued to increase in subsequent years to reach 570 in 2001.

There is yet another returnee-linked reason for the rise in nafaqa and divorce cases. Some of the returnees had left Gaza 10 or 20 years previously to join the PLO abroad, leaving wives and children behind them without sorting out their marital status. Some wives had initiated divorce proceedings shortly after their husbands' departure; others had preferred to remain married, perhaps waiting for their husbands to return before doing so. When those men returned, their wives/ former wives initiated nafaqa or divorce cases.

Wives who claimed nafaqa benefited from the new system in the Shari'a court, introduced after the establishment of the PA, which allows the executing department (da'rat al-tanfith) to deduct nafaqa directly from the salary of PA employees. This empowered wives because it minimized the husbands' bargaining power. If the wife won her case, the man could not postpone (yumatil) paying because the implementation department would ask his governmental agency to deduct the nafaqa from his salary.

Another factor that contributed to the increasing number of suits is the clash of value systems between the returnees' families and the men's original families in Gaza. Returnees from Tunis, Iraq, Syria, Lebanon, Yemen, Egypt, Jordan and other countries were accustomed to less conservative rules of conduct than those of Gaza. Besides, the vast majority of returnees were members of the PLO, which had adopted moderate social values with regard to gender roles and performance. The dominant slogan in the resistance movement during its struggle in Lebanon in the 1970s and 1980s was: 'We want to liberate the land and people (tahrir al-ard wa al-insan)', which signifies not only political liberation but also social emancipation. Most returnees were part of that movement in one way or another. In contrast, Gazan society, under prolonged Israeli occupation, was becoming more and more conservative, both politically and socially. That led to the birth and expansion of the Hamas movement in the late 1980s and its bitter conflict with the leftist and liberal factions of the PLO. Hamas's success in restricting women's participation in the first intifada and its imposition of the hijab (headscarf) are but two symbols of its social and political hegemony.[3]

Differences between the two communities – that is, the 'original' Gazans, whether refugees or indigenous, and the returnees – were evident in everyday family interaction. Most returnees lived in the same village or camp they had left 20 years earlier and, out of necessity, they had to stay with their mothers, fathers or brothers until they could rent an apartment or build a floor above their family's house. That process took months or longer. The returnees had to comply with limitations on women's mode of dress, their social behaviour and their conduct within the family. Some returnees' wives were unable to conform to the rules and restrictions imposed by their in-laws, and some families were unable to deal with the continuous 'invasions' of the husband's extended family and clan in their private life.

The returnees also had difficulty dealing with the unforeseen reciprocities that are part of Gazan culture: the daily visits, the unexpected arrival of relatives for dinner and lunch, the constant questioning about the spouse's well-being (or otherwise), rumours and gossip between sisters-in-law, interventions regarding children's behaviour and marks achieved in school, and the rather burdensome system of gift exchange, with relatives having a child every nine months and at least one child in the household getting good grades in school at the end of every year. Because most Gazan households comprise between 7 and 15 members, the returnees found it difficult to protect their privacy.

After some months, a number of them, out of necessity, built small apartments above those of their brothers. This setting, in which the husband's family (his parents and married brothers) occupy the same building, means that the door of everyone's apartment is expected to be open all day. That had not been the norm abroad, where family privacy had been maintained. The mere fact of being in a host country that was sometimes hostile towards Palestinians had been a factor impelling families to preserve their privacy. In Gaza, female returnees found themselves unable to find space for what had until then been their own family and was suddenly part of an extended family. There was growing friction between the two 'communities'. Gazans decided that the returnees had been corrupted culturally. As one Gazan mother told me:

> Their wives do not cover their hair. They are arrogant. My son does not go to the mosque. He no longer uses our dialect; he speaks softly, like Shami (the Syrian and Lebanese dialect). His wife does not pray. She smokes. Our son is a toy in her hands. He does not even have a say concerning his children.

A Gazan teacher voiced bitterness towards the PA and its returnees:

> They grabbed the biggest part of the Oslo pie. All employment opportunities and economic and security facilities are given to them; we were given only the crumbs.[4] Without our intifada, they would not have dreamt of seeing Palestine. They should go back to where they came from. Previously, we had one military governor, now we do not know how many governors we have. Every returnee claims to be an important person.

Returnees, for their part, labelled Gazans as backward (mutakhlifin) or narrow-minded (mahdudin). Some were angry over what they perceived to be ingratitude. One returnee told me, 'Fi-l-ghurba [when we were in the Diaspora], we experienced hell in order to liberate them; we built nothing, while they were building their houses and businesses. After losing our youth in al-ghurba [the Diaspora], we have to start again from scratch.'

Others sympathized with the Gazans' tragedy of 'inhumane' imprisonment and isolation. A returnee commented, They are born, live and die in one neighbourhood. They do not know what is going on outside their small world. They are like ahl al-kahf [prehistoric society]; they need major social surgery to come to terms with our globalized world.

The heterogeneity and diversity of Palestinians as individuals and groups have come to the surface whenever they have been forced to encounter each other and struggle over already scarce, rapidly confiscated resources. Under such circumstances, differences and variations are invoked, exaggerated and fashioned into sweeping generalizations and stereotypes. For example, the friction between refugees and residents after the 1948 tragedy was depicted in popular culture as a war between the 'eternal green grass', that is the land and resources of Gazans and West Bankers, and the 'attacking grasshoppers', that is, the refugees (Muhammad 1997: 111).

The war of words was exacerbated by a number of minor issues. For example, Israel issued green identity cards to returnees, the numbers of which begin with a 4, as opposed to red residents' cards with numbers beginning with a 9. This official marker became a powerful manifestation of segregation between the two groups. By their very association with the PA, the 'green group' were more powerful; it was sufficient to present the ID card without saying a word to convey the status of the cardholder. Moreover, the returnees were granted privileges such as tax exemption on cars and differently coloured and numbered license plates. Residents could judge a person just by looking at the car. The clash between the two groups over employment opportunities, security facilities and travel permits was bitterly translated into criticism relating to morality and behaviour.

On the micro level, this new reality is reflected in the 'power balance' between returnees' spouses. Some men who were originally from Gaza or the West Bank had lived for a long time in the Diaspora, where they had married Palestinian (or non-Palestinian) women whose families had established themselves in the countries of exile. Marital relations between the spouses had thus been set in a context in which the wife's family constituted *the* family for both. 'He was like an orphan, we adopted him,' a mother in the Diaspora would say about her son-in-law. The adopted man was appreciative of the adoptive family; 'I could not live normally without them,' a Gazan in Lebanon told me.[5]

However, once the Palestinian husband returned to Gaza with his wife, the situation changed. A returnee's wife told me:

> When we were in Lebanon, my husband treated me well. I had my family around me and they took care of me. Yet, at the same time, they treated him as a son. I was supported by my parents and brothers. He could not cross certain limits with me. Now, everything has changed. I am living with his family. They support him. They do not like me. They call me a 'ghariba' [outsider, stranger] and they continuously interfere in every detail of my life. I no longer feel that I know him; he is not the same person.

Women always capitalize on their connections, whether political or non-political. When they lose them, no power can balance that of their husbands', especially when the man operates within his family system. This new setting made the lives of some returnees more difficult, and disputes were unavoidable. Some husbands preferred to accommodate to the new restrictions at the expense of their wives' freedom, advising – sometimes compelling – them to wear the hijab, to keep on good terms with the family, to stay at home; in short, to preserve the husbands' image.

Some wives promptly went back to their families abroad. Some men could not compromise; they divorced, sent the wives back to their country of origin and married a relative (or non-relative) from Gaza. These dynamics perhaps contributed to the growing number of cases in the Shari'a court.

Another political factor affecting marriage and divorce was the Israeli economic blockade. In 1996, the Oslo process reached a dead end when the right-wing Benjamin Netanyahu was elected as the new Israeli prime minister. After the eruption of the first intifada, sparked off by the Israeli government's confiscation of a hill in Jerusalem, Israel prohibited unmarried Palestinians from accessing its labour market. The rationale was that married men would be more concerned about the well-being of their families and therefore be less open to nationalist slogans and less 'dangerous' to Israel. This mirrored a similar policy in the late 1980s. The limited and distorted labour market in Gaza could not employ the jobless, and hundreds of thousands of Palestinians were reduced to penury during the nine-month blockade. Palestinian families responded by marrying off their sons, even at a very early age, so that they could obtain a permit to cross into Israel and look for work there.

In 1996 and 1997, the situation became even more complicated. No Palestinian was given access to the Israeli labour market, and all were categorized as 'dangerous'. Palestinian workers then devised a new strategy: long-term residence in Israel. For that, they needed a permanent residence permit or an Israeli identity card. Israeli women (including Palestinian women with Israeli citizenship) can obtain these documents for their husbands, but Israel prohibits polygyny. Thus, married Palestinians would not be able to use that path. However, the voice of the stomach is loud at times of starvation,[6] and families had to survive. Therefore, workers' wives had to make a sacrifice by accepting temporary divorce (talaq raj'i) so that bread-winners could marry a Palestinian Israeli citizen, work in that country and feed the family.

The Israeli authorities soon discovered the stratagem and made marriage to a Palestinian Israeli citizen conditional upon the man being single or having undergone a definitive divorce (ba'in). Even in the face of this rule, workers did not give up. Islamic family law enables men who have repudiated their wives through a final divorce (ba'in) to remarry them under certain conditions, with a new contract and mahr. This enabled the workers to continue obtaining Israeli residence permits. As we have seen, the reason for this strategy was to help their families survive; however, some men took advantage of the situation to abandon their families in Gaza. Their former wives then filed nafaqa suits against them. Such cases probably contributed to the rise in nafaqa cases.

Marriage was also used as a coping strategy by Palestinian refugees after the nakba. In the early 1950s, the United Nations Relief and Works Agency (UNRWA), which had been established to feed and provide services to Palestinian refugees, was desperately looking for professionals to work in its various departments, especially in the educational sector. Initially, it recruited Palestinians who had the minimum ability to read and write as teachers. Many only had primary school education or had studied in katatib in their villages and towns before the 1948 tragedy.[7] Instead of paying such employees in cash, the UNRWA gave them additional food rations. In the late 1950s, after the first generation of trainees graduated, the UNRWA started recruiting its own Palestinian graduates, paying them comparatively high salaries.[8] Because those graduates were then capable of feeding their families, the UNRWA cut off the food rations for their families.

While the UNRWA's notion of a family was the nuclear one, the Palestinian conception is that of an extended family, comprising father, mother, sisters and brothers, whether married or not, as well as grandparents, aunts and uncles, cousins and other relatives. In some settings, the term 'relatives' may reach out to encompass people from the same village or neighbourhood. To continue getting rations without the bread-winners having to give up their jobs, families had to fall back on each other's sense of solidarity and interdependence. They arranged mock marriages between relatives from the same hamula; for female UNRWA employees, the groom would be either a cousin or an old man who understood the nature of the game and received his share of the proceeds (in cash or kind). A UNRWA employee who concluded a mock marriage would show the UNRWA a marriage contract proving that she/he had established her/his own nuclear family (in accordance with UNRWA criteria) and was no longer the bread-winner of the natal family. Thus, the food rations of close kin were not cut off.

Strategies of using marriage and divorce to survive economically reappeared in the 1980s and early 1990s as a result of Israel's economic blockade of Gaza, but the dynamics were different. In 2001 and 2002, qadi Muhammad al-Ansari saw yet another coping strategy emerge. To obtain help in the face of ever-growing

80 *The sociology of Nafaqa*

Table 5.2 Marriages and divorces at Gaza Shari'a courts, 1993–2001

Year	No. of marriages	No. of divorces	Divorces as % of marriages
1993	2810	317	11.2
1994	3052	387	12.6
1995	3316	457	13.8
1996	2843	483	16.9
1997	2919	488	17.7
1998	3104	489	15.7
1999	3306	524	15.8
2000	3430	525	15.3
2001	3558	570	16.0

Source: Data from Gaza Shari'a court records.

economic difficulties, husbands and wives went to court to divorce, and the divorce certificates were then used by wives to claim support from charities, which had sprung up like mushrooms since the eruption of the second intifada. Once the divorce certificate had served its purpose, the couple would return to court to marry again during the 'idda period. Divorced women were also helped by the Ministry of Social Affairs,[9] zakat committees,[10] NGOs and the like.

As Table 5.2 shows, there was a gradual escalation in the percentage of divorces from 1993 to 1997.

The analysis so far has laid the ground for the next section, which discusses the judicial procedures and practice of the judges, lawyers and women litigants in nafaqa cases.

5.2 Legal framework

The *Law of Family Rights* (*LFR*), issued by the Egyptian Governor-General in 1954, is applied in the Gaza Strip. In the West Bank, however, the *Jordanian Law of Personal Status*, gazetted in 1976, still obtains. Both derive from the *Ottoman Law of Family Rights* (*OLFR*) and Islamic Shari'a. Women's right to nafaqa is stipulated in three articles of the fifth chapter of the *LFR*, which is entitled 'Rules of Marriage' (ahkam al-nikah). Marriage as a legal contract is established in accordance with a fundamental balance of gender rights and duties, which is reflected in all the *LFR* articles. The husband is responsible for the maintenance of his wife, and she, in turn, owes obedience to him. In addition, article 39 reads: 'The husband is obliged to prepare a legitimate house (maskan shar'i) for his wife, supplied with all necessary equipment, in the place of his choosing.'[11] Article 38 makes the wife 'entitled to dower and nafaqa as soon as the contract is signed. Rights of inheritance are [immediately] established between them.'

The husband should treat his wife well and allow her to visit her family members (haqq al-ziyara). He can permit or forbid her to engage in wage labour. She has to move to his dwelling and fulfil her marital duties, that is, respond when he calls her to bed. Article 40 states: 'The wife is obliged, after she receives her prompt dower, to stay in her husband's house and travel with him wherever he goes unless there is a legitimate prohibition.' Major Sunni schools structure gender relations within the family on these bases, with some variations that will be addressed in Chapter 7.

5.3 Judicial procedures

When women apply for nafaqa, they go through the following judicial procedures. First, the judge reviews the marriage contract to ensure its validity. The wife who claims nafaqa has to attach her marriage contract to the standard application form, which has spaces for the name, locality and place of origin of both the petitioner and her husband (whether the petitioner is originally from Gaza or from pre-1948 Palestine).

If the woman files a nafaqa suit on behalf of her children, the judge makes sure that the children are the husband's (by checking the children's identity cards or birth certificates). In addition, he makes sure that the mother is dedicated to her children's welfare by asking the wife's witnesses to give evidence on this point. Generally, the judges accept the witnesses' testimony at face value unless the husband raises objections.

When a nafaqa case is brought before the judge, he does not question her right to nafaqa, for it is her inviolable right. It is the main pillar of marriage. To quote qadi al-Karmi, 'Whether the man works or not, whether he is absent or present, the wife's right to nafaqa obtains. The wife does not need to be poor. Whether poor or rich, nafaqa is her right' (conversation with qadi al-Karmi, January 2002). However, the pertaining mechanisms, tools, amounts and time limits are all subject to negotiation. The wife's right is greater than that of children: if the children are not destitute, if they have an inheritance, then the law frees their father of any obligation to pay for their maintenance.

The amount of nafaqa is decided either through acceptance of the judge's estimate by the two parties involved or by a committee of experts (mukhbirin) nominated by the qadi. The committee consists of a male from the wife's family, a male from the husband's family and a male nominated by the court. The court representative in the committee might be a court clerk. Sometimes, a lawyer who happens to be in the courtroom during the hearing is proposed by the qadi, provided he does not represent either party. The family law states that nafaqa is estimated according to the husband's income (article 57 of the *LFR*), but that does not always appear to be the case.

In court, spouses often accuse each other of not telling the truth. Both wives and husbands claim to be poor. The wife alleges that her husband is richer than he admits. The husband, in response, says that he earns much less than she claims. Judges are accustomed to these dynamics. If they feel that no agreement can be reached within a reasonable time period, they threaten both spouses with the nomination of a committee to estimate the nafaqa. Wives seem less frightened by this threat, while husbands are generally reluctant to accept the formation of a committee. If the couple do not accept the amount of nafaqa proposed by the judge, he calls for their representatives to appear in court.

82 The sociology of Nafaqa

The committee members consult for 15 to 30 minutes. The representatives try to have the nafaqa established to their side's advantage, while the court representative proposes a median sum in accordance with Gazan standards of living. After agreeing on a sum, the committee members return to the courtroom to convey their decision to the qadi.

Female lawyers are not appointed to the committee. The rationale behind this exclusion is, to quote lawyer Imad Hamid, 'The shahada [testimony] of women is not on a par with that of men; the equivalent of one man's testimony is that of two women.' However, qadi Muhammad al-Ansara provided a different rationale:

> It is not about shahada per se, it is about saving the female lawyer from the trouble of such work. These committees are involved in a familial dispute. It is out of respect for our female colleagues that we do not expose them to such problems.

These explanations might not be sufficient to understand why female lawyers are not appointed as committee members.

Women used to appear in courts only as litigants, and it was only after 1995 that they became shar'i lawyers. A lot of water has flowed under the bridge since 2004–05. In 2017, Shari'a courts became accustomed to women practising not only as lawyers but also as prosecutors, members (and sometimes chairs) of the institution known as 'Family Counselling'. In the West Bank, women are employed as Shari'a court judges (see Chapter 9 for a discussion of the major changes).

5.3.1 Strategies of judges and lawyers

As noted in Chapter 4, judges find nafaqa a suitable strategy for pressurizing husbands to initiate a reconciliation process. Sometimes the qadi sets the nafaqa at a level where the husband finds it more economical to resolve the dispute than to pay the nafaqa. As stated earlier, the amount paid to wives is rather low, given the cost of living in Gaza. Still, men caught between joblessness on the one hand, and their wives' financial demands on the other, find it difficult to pay even such a small sum of money. Furthermore, the husband sees that as long as the dispute goes on, he not only has to keep paying nafaqa but also leaves himself open to other financial claims by his wife, such as her right to receive the cash value of her assigned furniture, delivery expenses, baby clothing (if she is pregnant), nursing fees and breast-feeding fees. This strategy of using nafaqa, adopted by qadi and wife alike, works as a catalyst to bring the husband back to the negotiation table.

Turning to the court can thus be a strategy to obtain recognition, to renegotiate or to send a harsh message, a threat, without actually taking the case to a conclusion. In certain cases, women use nafaqa suits to get a divorce. One strategy used by lawyers to help their clients involves mutual understanding between the lawyer and the qadi.

During my daily visits to the court, I found that in some cases judges and lawyers seemed to have the same objective. I got the impression that there was a tacit agreement between them concerning the amount of nafaqa to be paid. Lawyer Khalid al-Tayyib confirmed this to me:

> Yes, in nafaqa suits we (the qadi, the katib and I) play our favourite game. The objective underlying the game is to get as much monthly nafaqa as possible from the husband. The game is as follows: the qadi starts by telling the man, 'You have to pay JD 100 as nafaqa to your wife. What is your response?' The man would usually say, 'I cannot pay that much, I can commit myself to paying JD 20,' for example. Husbands always complain of their economic hardship and tell the qadi they cannot pay their wives the specified nafaqa. In this scenario, I would play my role as a lawyer to dismiss the husband's claim that he could not pay the JD 100. The qadi would start negotiating with me (as agreed before the session), telling me, 'The man cannot pay what we propose to him. Can you make a concession?'
>
> The husband would take advantage of the qadi's stance and start bargaining with me. I (as a lawyer) would appear to be angry and tell the man, 'We are not in a market, selling and buying tomatoes. This is the right of the wife as set out in the Islamic Shari'a. Do you want me to work against God's will? Against the Shari'a?' The katib, for his part, would ask the man to come closer to him. He would whisper in his ear that it would be wise to accept the qadi's estimation for, if not, the lawyer would make him pay more. After arguing for a while, I would give the impression of making a great concession. The qadi would settle the amount at between JD 40 and JD 60, which is the scope of nafaqa cases anyway.

The game would not end there. To avoid the problems of a Court of Appeal hearing, the qadi would then tell the husband, 'Now you have committed yourself to paying the agreed amount.' This sentence, when it is written into the case record, designates the husband as the one who committed himself to paying the amount; thus, the amount does not appear to have been set by the qadi. The consequence is that the man cannot appeal the qadi's decision, because he was the one who committed himself to paying that amount of money and signed the record stating that.

5.3.2 Strategies of female litigants

Nafaqa petitions have always constituted the highest proportion of Shari'a court cases. My archival research indicates that in the 19 years between 1920 and 1992 selected for analysis, on the average, nafaqa suits constituted 47% of all cases submitted to the court.[12] While the statistics on nafaqa cases serve to provide a general picture of shifts in women's legal actions in relation to major political and social events, they do not explain the *why* and *how* underlying the cases. Why are nafaqa suits so numerous? Why are they filed more in certain years than in others? How do women approach the court? And how do they present their cases? Interviewing the litigants yields some answers to such questions. Women do file cases for nafaqa to get economic support, but the need for maintenance constitutes

84 *The sociology of Nafaqa*

only one motivation. Women's claims reflect a dual motivation, manifest and hidden. The manifest meaning is formal, juridical and tailored to match the legal rules. However, there is a deeper, hidden motivation determined by individual circumstances (Mir-Hosseini 1993: 78). In order to reveal the hidden meaning and link it to the manifest, this chapter draws simultaneously on statistics from the Shari'a court archives and on women's narratives. It focuses on the period following the signing of the Oslo agreements and the shifting political conditions generated by the establishment of the PA.

Various strategies are adopted by different actors to make sure that some justice is provided to women. However, female litigants are not passive agents in court. They do get sympathy from judges and lawyers, but they also apply their own strategies. Women do not turn to the court until they have exploited all other available avenues. Those who experience marital problems and cannot find a remedy in customary conflict resolution (implicating their natal families in the dispute, inviting family members to mediate, appealing to community figures, inviting powerful persons to mediate, and the like) often turn to the nafaqa provision to achieve their objectives. It is not only women that really need maintenance who use this provision, but also those that want to attain other objectives but cannot do so due to the limited scope for manœuvre provided by the law.

When a marriage is dissolved, the man is obliged to pay nafaqa for the children's maintenance, but some men do not pay and continue to threaten the mother that they will take the children away from her. In such cases, some mothers file a case for the children's nafaqa, only to drop it after the husband formally promises not to (or threaten to) take the children away from her.

Strategic use of tawabi'

Another strategy that goes without much notice in the literature is the use of tawabi' to put pressure on the husband and compel him to renegotiate the terms of marriage. Tawabi', as explained in Chapter 4, is the cash value of furniture (or household goods) estimated as part of the prompt dower when contracting the marriage. However, this definition of tawabi' is recent; when it appeared in marriage contracts in the 1930s, it had a different function, conveyed a different meaning and had a different legal significance. According to Shaykh Judah,[13] tawabi' emerged with the appearance of beds and chairs as part of the household furniture, replacing the usual mattresses and mag'ad (a small mattress placed on the floor) for sitting:

> This trend appeared first in the big cities such as Jaffa and Haifa and slowly spread to other towns and villages. Tawabi' is not part of the Islamic marriage contract, but was incorporated in accordance with modern modes of furnishing. This may signify a degree of flexibility in Islamic law and its ability to integrate even some mundane issues such as new ways of life.

The first contract specifying tawabi' in Gaza appeared in 1938 in the records of marriage contracts (sijillat 'uqud al-zawaj) of notary Shaykh al-Khuzindar. What he wrote in the contract is significant. He specified the prompt and deferred dower as follows: EGP 40 as dower in total, divided into EGP 30 as prompt and EGP 10 as deferred.[14] In the margin, he added: 'In addition to the mahr, a cupboard with two mirrors.' Another contract from the same year specifies EGP 50 as total dower, divided into EGP 40 prompt and EGP 10 deferred. Again, the notary has a note in the margin: 'In addition to the mahr, cupboard with two mirrors, two mattresses, two bed sheets, four pillows, an iron bed and six bamboo chairs.'

This phrasing has legal consequences. It signifies that tawabi' was not part of the prompt dower; rather, it was ziyada, meaning additional. In legal terms, when it first appeared, tawabi' was like a gift to the wife, something she could not claim later or use as part of her legal strategy. Here lay the difference between nafaqa and tawabi': while the former is a guaranteed financial right, claimed when necessary, tawabi' was not so at that time. Women used nafaqa as a legal resort as early as 1920, while claiming of tawabi' has another history, to which we shall return a little later. Tawabi' continued to appear in the margins of marriage contracts in subsequent decades.

Table 5.3 shows the frequency of tawabi' in random samples of 100 marriage contracts in Gaza for selected years between 1920 and 2000. Initially, the chosen years were at five-year intervals, beginning with 1920 (1920, 1925, 1930

Table 5.3 Tawabi' in marriage contracts at Gaza Shari'a courts, selected years between 1920 and 2000

Year	Incidence of tawabi'	Tawabi' as household goods	Tawabi' in cash
1920	–	–	–
1925	–	–	–
1930	–	–	–
1935	–	–	–
1938	2	2	–
1940	2	2	–
1945	14	12	2
1946	14	13	1
1947	25	23	2
1948	11	10	1
1949	27	24	3
1950	25	21	4
1955	21	8	13
1960	45	1	44
1965	53	1	52
1970	62	–	62
1975	92	–	92
1980	91	–	91
1985	98	–	98
1990	95	–	95
1995	99	–	99
2000	100	–	100

Source: Data from Gaza Shari'a court records.

and 1935). The next years were 1938, 1940 and 1945. After 1945, there was a worsening of the situation in the 'historical Palestine', and I wanted to check if unrest, war and refugee status had affected the number of tawabi' cases registered at the Gaza Shari'a courts. Therefore, I researched the marriage contracts for all the years between 1945 and 1950. Subsequently, I resumed the five-year intervals until 2000.

There was no mention of tawabi' until 1938, when it appeared in 2% of the contracts; the incidence increased to 11% in 1948. In 1949 and 1950, the percentages of contracts including tawabi' were 27% and 25%, respectively. However, people still thought of it as household items; they continued to describe it as cupboards, beds and the like. In 1955, tawabi' was still on the increase, with 25% of contracts incorporating it. This rapid increase of tawabi' in the marriage contract was paralleled by another phenomenon: the gradual replacement of a list of household furniture with the cash equivalent of their value. In 1955, we see that 13% of contracts specified cash instead of household goods as tawabi'. This trend continued in the following decade until 1970, when there was no specification of household items in the contracts at all; instead, tawabi' was specified as cash.

That was not the only change. Instead of tawabi' being specified as gifts noted in the margins of the marriage contract, it was defined as part of the dower. The prompt dower now includes the cash value of household furniture to be provided by the groom. The change of tawabi' from household goods to cash was gradual. At first, the dower was divided into two parts and tawabi' was specified as a list of household furniture; for example, 'JD 60 for cupboard and chairs'. After some years, this inventory of household goods to be purchased as tawabi' was no longer specified. All contracts that included tawabi' used the cash value without specification.

This gradual transformation of tawabi', from a response to the modern way of life to part of the prompt dower payable in cash, had enormous effects on the legal strategies of women and lawyers in court. As observed earlier, once a woman receives her prompt dower, she is obliged to live in her husband's house, to obey him and not to leave the house without his permission. The division of prompt dower into two portions has done much to provide women with further room for negotiation *during* their marital life, in that the wife can leave her marital house and go to her parents' house in a state of anger. She can then go to court and demand that the man provide her with her full dower because she has received only part of it. In such a case, the man might argue, 'But I gave her the dower and furnished the house with the specified sum of tawabi'.' The qadi would respond, 'You have written that her tawabi' is in cash, but she has not yet received *this money*. Whether you furnished the house or not is not our problem. The wife should receive her tawabi' exactly as specified in the contract. The tawabi' was written down as cash and thus she has to receive it in cash.' The man would usually respond: 'If she wants the furniture, let her take it.' The qadi would not accept this, insisting: 'You have specified a sum of money in your contract as tawabi'; she should receive exactly that sum so that we can declare that she has received her full dower.'

This interaction between a qadi and a husband, which is typical of the proceedings involving tawabi' in the Gaza Shari'a courts, indicates how tawabi' has become an important tool for negotiation. Unlike deferred dower, which only becomes an issue when the marriage is decaying, tawabi' is an integral part of the negotiation process *during* marital life, not after. Women use it as a bargaining chip to correct aspects of their marital relationship. The legal significance of tawabi' as a powerful instrument in the hands of lawyers and women is evident in Table 5.4.

In 1998, 1999, 2000 and 2001, around half of the lawsuits filed for nafaqa were accompanied by claims for tawabi'. This reflected considerable growth since the 1960s, when only 5% of nafaqa suits included tawabi' claims. By 1977, tawabi' was included in 12% of nafaqa claims. The real increase began in 1986, when 37% of nafaqa cases included tawabi'. In 1988, the percentage was 50%, and it has continued to hover around that level. Lawyer Hala Anwar reflected on this change:

> In the sixties and seventies, women used to take their furniture from their husbands' houses once the marriage was over. For the man, this is not a bad deal because the furniture is likely to be worn-out and no longer serviceable to him. The man will marry another woman, who will oblige him to buy new furniture anyway. Now, with the specification of tawabi' in cash, women no longer take their furniture when they are divorced; they receive their tawabi' in cash, as originally specified in the contract.

Another lawyer said:

> The man becomes vulnerable once his wife files a case of nafaqa plus tawabi' because that is quite a lot of money. The man's financial calculation will be along this line: 'I paid her a dower of JD 2,000 and furnished the house with another JD 2,000. Now she wants me to pay her JD 2,000 (as tawabi') in addition to the nafaqa. That is quite a lot. It is better to make a compromise.'

Table 5.4 Linkage of tawabi' and nafaqa in cases at Gaza Shari'a courts, 1998–2001

Year	Total no. of nafaqa suits	Cases with nafaqa alone No.	%	Cases with tawabi'+nafaqa No.	%
1998	276	161	59	115	41
1999	277	132	48	145	52
2000	260	119	46	141	54
2001	298	136	46	162	54

Source: Data from Gaza Shari'a court records.

In lawyer Khalid al-Tayyib's view, this legal/financial compulsion is likely to guide the man towards reconciliation.

Suing for nafaqa to claim sexual rights

Nafaqa can also be used to claim sexual rights. Women's utilization of the law, and especially of the provision of nafaqa, for attaining sexual rights are rare; or perhaps such cases are rarely noticed because, on one hand, the wife does not overtly manifest her wants and needs in the court, and on the other, the social taboo surrounding sexual issues does not allow women to make such demands overtly.

A woman may claim her sexual rights under the banner of reproductive rights, that is, the husband does not have the capability to father children or does not want to go to a doctor to cure a reproductive problem. Or she may claim her sexual rights in a polygynous marriage because the husband is not treating the wives equally in sexual terms. This was the situation facing a woman whom I met at the Gaza Shari'a courts. She told me that she and her husband had led a tranquil and tender life until he married a second wife. Then, 'he became more accustomed to staying with my co-wife (durra), eating with her and sleeping in her room, leaving me miserable.'

She went to her parents' house and stayed there for several months, but the husband did not reconsider his position. She filed a case for nafaqa, but apparently not because she wanted the money. On appearing before the qadi, she asked him to conduct the session *in camera*. The qadi granted her request, but I was allowed to remain by both the qadi and the litigant. Her husband was also present. She told the qadi,

> I lived with him for nine years without any problem. He is a good man. He even promised to take me on the hajj [pilgrimage]. So why, in God's justice, does he not come to my room? Allah says that we should be equal. I do not need money, I do not need nafaqa, I want him.

The qadi listened to her, nodding his head. After she had finished, he turned to the husband and asked him to respond. The man did not say anything. Then the qadi started a long lecture about the rights and duties of men and women in Islam. It was like a Friday sermon because the qadi was speaking in formal Arabic (fus-ha), citing verses from the Quran, bringing up arguments and counter-arguments. It was clear that he was enjoying the role. Unlike cases in which the qadi might give the impression of being annoyed, bored or bothered by a litigant's arguments, here he was sympathetic and energetic. The qadi's 'sermon' made it obvious that the religious discourse is more than ready to provide lengthy speeches about how people should meet religious criteria in matters related to sexuality.

Suing for nafaqa to regain freedom

Not all women sue for nafaqa in order to achieve reconciliation with a spouse; some do so because they want to be rid of a spouse, either because they do not love him or because they have aspirations other than marriage. In such cases, a wife may deny the husband her body. She can generate conflicts with him, provoke him into injuring her or make up any excuse to leave and go to her family's place, weeping and complaining of mistreatment. This trend is especially found among young wives. In some cases, women use the violence of their husbands to provide a space where their natal family can intervene.

For example, a young wife of 19 years came to court, accompanied by her father, to file a nafaqa suit. She told me that she had never wanted the marriage. She had been involved with a fellow university student, 'but I did not want to marry him either. I want to live my life.' She was in her first year at al-Azhar University when her husband asked for her hand. She did not allow him to approach her the first night and on subsequent nights for a week. Then he became angry, beat her up and took her by force. The next morning, she quarrelled with her mother-in-law, who, with the help of the husband, beat her and locked her in her room until the afternoon, when some of her relatives came to congratulate her on her marriage. Her door was unlocked and the relatives took her to hospital. They phoned her father, who immediately complained to the police. The father brought her to court to claim nafaqa with the aim of obtaining a divorce. She said, 'I will never go back to him, I want to continue my studies and I will use my gold to pay the university fees. I am still young and want to enjoy my life.'

The interesting part of her story is the difference between the way she addressed the court and how she related her story to me. The scribe, in accordance with her request, wrote in her application form: 'I am Maya Salim al-Ma'ruf from Gaza/Zaytun. My ID number is. . ., I am filing a case against my husband Radi Darwish al-kas and his mother Nazira Mustafa al-kas with regard to their attempt to kill me and steal my gold.'

Then she went on to describe in detail what had happened to her, when and where and how she had been taken to hospital. At the end, she specified the exact amount of gold that she alleged had been 'stolen' from her. She requested the qadi to order her gold returned, punish the husband and his mother, and compel the husband to pay her nafaqa. The last sentences were,

> I am a weak and helpless woman. I have nobody but God and you to help me get my rights. I trust your merciful heart to look after me. God the Greatest chose you to bring justice to His worshippers. He looks after His worshippers through you. May God support you in your mission to bring justice to the weak and tyrannized.

The introduction to this chapter referred to the manifest and hidden meanings of women's action in the court. The manifest is formal, legal and tailored to conform to the legal rules. The real meaning is hidden; it is decided by circumstances (Mir-Hosseini 1993: 78). In this case, the wife hid her real agenda not only from the court but also from her father. She successfully worked her husband's violence into a tool to serve her agenda.

Friedl (2003), analysing the shifting meaning of 'marriage' and 'freedom' in contemporary Iran, identifies a gender gap in how young men and women envisage the marriage institution. While men aspire to be liberated from their natal families, young women tend to be more radical; they want to enjoy life, to determine their future and to have more say concerning their marriage. The previous case exemplifies this aspiration on the part of young women. However, it is a difficult aspiration to fulfil in Gaza. The incompatibility between fathers' limited economic means and their use of their daughters' marriage as a coping strategy on the one hand, and the young women's aspiration to 'live their lives' on the other, is likely to remain as long as the political, economic and social circumstances in Gaza continue to deteriorate.

Nafaqa as a tool for revenge

Nafaqa can also be used by wives to take revenge on husbands who have not lived up to their promises. At the age of 18 years, a female high school graduate (who is now a lawyer) married a man who had high school education. She is a refugee of peasant background, whereas he is a refugee of Bedouin background. Intermarriages between Bedouin and peasants are not the norm. Only Bedouin and peasants who fled Palestine in 1948 and became refugees have developed some sort of flexibility in this regard. It seems that the experience of refuge and shared locality have lowered the barriers between these groups.

It is said that Bedouin men have no problem in 'taking' (marrying) peasant women. Bedouin women, however, are not accessible to communities other than their own. The stereotypical view about Bedouins is that they stress the notion of 'ird (honour): 'It is shameful to give one's own 'ird to other people.'[15] Still, peasants feel that they are 'better' than Bedouin; they earn their livelihood through their sweat (yaklu min 'arak jabinhum), meaning that they cultivate their land and draw their subsistence from it, whereas Bedouin have nothing to do with land and land cultivation, which in the eyes of peasants are the only forms of work, and are therefore perceived as being lazy.

These stereotypes and differences have become less of an issue over the decades of refuge and interaction with original Gazans, the UNRWA and Israel, which enforce the collective identity of these two groups more as refugees than as members of a particular socio-cultural group. For the UNRWA, for example, the term 'refugees', be they peasants or Bedouin, designates a group of people who constitute a burden, needing services and making ever-growing financial demands. For original Gazans, the term 'refugee' connotes poverty, social negligence, backwardness, dirt and the like. Israel perceives refugees and their camps as a major threat to its security.

As the girl was of peasant background, it seems that the proposed marriage did not expose the man to social or psychological conflict. In view of the perceived 'Bedouin culture of laziness' and disregard for education, the girl's father set one condition for approving the marriage: his daughter would finish her higher education. The man agreed. The father added that his daughter should be allowed to work in her field of specialization after finishing her studies. Again, the man agreed. After the marriage, he kept his promise and the wife became a lawyer, a career that is still male dominated. During the following five years, the man kept working on his land, a fact that challenges the stereotypical view of the Bedouin. However, after the wife finished her studies and started her practical training, the 'intellectual gap' between the couple grew, and the man gradually developed a sense of envy and discomfort. To complicate their life, the wife was unable to become pregnant. She told me: 'I went to several doctors, but they found nothing wrong with me. They said that my husband should have a test done, which he does not agree to.'

Conflict mounted between them. He married another woman, apparently to prove that he had the ability to procreate. The first wife viewed that as 'just an excuse; he knows very well that the failure is his. I was and still am able to get pregnant. His real intention is to humiliate me and to feel that he still has an advantage (daraja) over me, regardless of my degree in law.' She told him several times that they should not break up because of her education, 'but he continued to feel insecure.' When he married the other woman, he took all the furniture from the first wife's house. He was unable to take her gold, however. 'Thanks to my mother's wisdom, she never agreed to leave it with me. She knew how these Bedouins behave,' she told me. The man was thus again labelled a Bedouin. She sued him for nafaqa because 'I do not need money, I want to take revenge on him. This will be the first case in my career.'

Nafaqa as leverage for remarriage

The following case illustrates the use of nafaqa as a strategy to achieve yet another underlying agenda. When I met Afaf, she had divorced from Muhsin two years previously and had two children, a two-year-old boy and a four-year-old girl. She and her mother blamed the divorce on the continual interference of the mother-in-law in the spouses' life. According to Afaf, the mother-in-law wanted her son to marry one of his maternal cousins. After divorcing Afaf, Muhsin did so. The ex-wife and her mother decided to go to court for an increase in the children's nafaqa. They hoped that, once in court, he could be persuaded to remarry his ex-wife.

According to Afaf, Muhsin only visited their home on Fridays. 'His wife could not protest because he would come to our home directly from the mosque. He had performed ablutions (mutawadi') and his heart was full of God's words (kalam Allah).' Afaf's plan was to convince Muhsin to take her back. 'Even if he has another wife, what does that mean? Co-wives do not *eat* each other (al-darayir ma byaklu ba'ad).' The mother seemed to have convinced Afaf that getting back together with Muhsin was her best option under the circumstances.

They filed a case for an increase in the nafaqa because Muhsin had stopped interacting with the children after quarrelling with his wife. Afaf did not need the money. 'Filing the case for higher nafaqa is only an excuse. I want him to see us again and perhaps get me back to his 'isma,' she told me.

Nafaqa to bring about behavioural change

Some women use nafaqa claims as a way of applying pressure to get a husband to change his behaviour towards them. This is illustrated by the case of a Palestinian woman who returned to Gaza at the age of 27 years after having lived in Cairo for a number of years, during which she married, had two children and then divorced. She brought her children with her to Gaza and they lived with her brothers, who were very strict. She was not allowed to visit friends or go out of the house except to work (she is a secretary in a ministry). As a divorcee with children, even though she is young and beautiful, her prospects of marriage were slim. When a married man with six children proposed marriage to her, she saw it as an escape and accepted even though he was 15 years older than her. 'I agreed to marry him on one condition, that I would continue working in order to pay the expenses of my children who live with my mother. He accepted that,' she told me.

After marriage, he started bargaining with her over her monetary contribution to the household; he wanted her to pay the rent of the apartment and take care of the household expenses. She refused because she wanted to continue paying her children's expenses. She told him, 'You spend one night with me and another one with your first wife, so you have to pay me expenses for 15 days, and I can take care of myself for the rest of the month. I will even pay half the rent.' However, he refused, so she left his house and sued him for nafaqa. In response, he petitioned the court for a house of obedience ruling.

She told me:

> My lawyer says that he cannot take me to the house of obedience unless he pays me the tawabi' and nafaqa. I do not want to leave him because I do not want to go back to live under the restrictions of my brothers. But, by taking this step, I want to set new rules for our relationship.

The struggle in the legal arena has various dynamics and takes different shapes. When the wife takes legal action, the husband is not expected to stand still; he negotiates, bargains, threatens and sometimes resorts to divorce. Women enter the process of dispute settlement without full realization of how the process will proceed. Sometimes, the process itself dictates the final power balance between the two (Moore 1978). I could not follow these two cases as they started just before the planned end of my fieldwork. However, the aim of presenting them here is to demonstrate the various strategies used by women and the diverse motives underlying women's application for nafaqa. In this analytical context, therefore, the outcome of a case is less relevant than the action itself.

Suing for nafaqa to get a separate house

Nafaqa suits can be initiated by women to demand a separate house. As explained in Section 5.2, the norm is that women have to move to the residence of their husband provided it meets the standards set out in article 39 of the *LFR*. According to article 41, the husband's natal family and relatives cannot lodge in that residence without the wife's permission. This is not a big problem in the West Bank, where the process of urbanization proceeded comparatively smoothly and was accompanied by structural changes in the family. Therefore, younger generations have a relatively greater say in decisions about when and whom they marry (see Moors 1995), which reduces the possibility of domestic strife and the need to use the nafaqa rights for living in a separate house.

Gaza, in contrast, exemplifies a paradox: it combines artificial and forced urbanization,[16] economic dependency of younger generations and almost compulsory residence with the extended family. This is a result of scarce economic resources and limited space. The couple may build a room above the parents' house or even expand it into a 'real apartment', but all household activities continue to take place in the parents' house. Furthermore, the mother-in-law aspires to exercise power and authority. She controls her sons' income; she is the one who governs the house budget and decides when, how and what should be done daily, despite her frequent claims that sharing of activities is part and parcel of family intimacy. Thus, the house fails to meet the criterion in article 41, and the wife is entitled to stay with her parents and receive nafaqa from her husband until he provides a separate house. Wives resort to this entitlement only when a conflict arises; when that happens, they use the grey area between social norms, economic circumstances and legal entitlement to materialize their interests – in this case, getting a house that is free of aggravating in-laws.

5.4 Conclusion

This chapter has presented an important aspect of Palestinian family reality: the sociology of nafaqa in the Shari'a court. The gender structuration of family law is based on a strict distribution of rights and duties: women have the right to be looked after; in return, they have to be obedient. The cases presented in this chapter show a bit more complex difference between the richness of social reality and the dryness of legal texts, which in turn generates continuous tensions and unresolved conflicts. Women, indeed people in general, are less responsive to 'fixed' texts than to their concrete needs – no matter how they perceive or articulate them – if, when and how they decide to take them to court. Moreover, the 'fixed' law itself contains areas of indeterminacy, ambiguity and uncertainty. Nafaqa is 'fixed' as an inviolable right. Regardless of their social or economic background, women exploit this fixity and use it for various reasons and motives.

94 *The sociology of Nafaqa*

Yet, the nafaqa provision, despite its alleged procedural clarity, does not clearly establish how, when and why women can decide to use it. And this indeterminacy is successfully utilized by women. It seems then that both fixity and ambiguity are beneficial to the female applicants for nafaqa.

Women claim nafaqa when they intend to divorce, when they want to live in a separate house, when they claim their sexual rights or when they want to take revenge on an unfaithful husband. Even after divorce, they may use nafaqa as a strategy to return to the marital house. Many strategies are devised by women from this supposedly 'fixed' gender relation that allots nafaqa in exchange for obedience. Astonishingly, judges and lawyers, whose function is assumed to be to safeguard the law, supply women with the means to manipulate the law and thus assist them in strengthening their bargaining position vis-à-vis their husbands. This observation is important in relation to the mechanism of the application of the law. The same text is applied in different contexts differently, because people as actors, whether they be judges, lawyers or litigants, are 'not only responsible for obstructing, deflecting and transforming' the law (Griffiths 1992: 162), but they are also the key agents of its implementation. This means that various social processes 'dictate the mode of compliance and non-compliance to state-made legal rule' (Moore 1973: 721).

More importantly, the action of filing a suit, regardless of its outcome, is an empowering step that influences women's position in the family. The cases presented in this chapter show that the majority of women use the mere action of approaching the court as an integral part of their strategy and not just a procedural action. Some cases provide insight into how women even generate the circumstances that allow them to take action. And because the intervention of 'formal' institutions, such as the court, in the private sphere carries a social negative connotation, the sheer threat of taking the husband to court may suffice to adjust the relations between spouses in some cases.

The concept of 'agency' is a powerful analytical tool for understanding/theorizing on how women subvert/resist their domination and whether and how women contribute to the reproduction of their subordination. If agency means choices to be made to realize one's own well-being, does that imply that the direction of women's action should be 'fixed a priori' (Mahmood 2001: 212)? In other words, when a woman decides, for example, to make a certain arrangement to convince her husband to take her back to his matrimonial authority ('isma), does such an action imply that she is contributing – in one way or another – to reproducing her subordination? Acknowledging women's agency means that one should take into account the specific historical and social context that creates the conditions within which women operate and make their choices. In some cases, we observe women appealing to the qadi to get their husband's attention; in others, women approach the court to reinstate a collapsed marriage; in yet others, women appear to be less docile and more defiant. Even choosing to live with a second wife is an act informed by a woman's own knowledge and is constrained by the specific context of her choice. These diverse situations, and thus choices, direct our attention to specificities of women's lives and to multiple manifestations of agency. Women plan, think and employ their skills, knowledge and art in trying to achieve their goals. This practical notion of agency refers to their ability to cultivate their capabilities in order to attain their goals.

Having analysed the issue that forms the bulk of the cases at the Gaza shari'a courts, we shall now go on, in Chapter 6, to examine how the courts deal with the concept that is the twin of nafaqa, namely obedience. How do the judges implement it? How do men use it? And how, in the process, is the house of obedience provision applied in the Gaza Shari'a courts?

Notes

1 During fieldwork in Iran and Morocco, Ziba Mir-Hosseini (2000: 44), too, found differences between the real nature of a marriage dispute and the legal avenue to resolve it; for example, that women's cases may start as maintenance suits but end up as claims for divorce, dower or other objectives.
2 The status of tens of thousands of Palestinian returnees is still the same in 2017. A report by the prestigious Israeli human rights organization B'Tselem, published in 2013 but still valid now, observes that these Palestinians continue to live in limbo since they have no IDs. www.btselem.org/gaza_strip/20130722_stateless_in_gaza, accessed 9 September 2017.
3 For an extensive analysis of this period, see Hammami (1990).
4 Tamari (1996a: 2) compares the unemployment rates among returnees and the rest of population. In 1996, when he wrote his commentary, unemployment among returnees stood at only 2%, in contrast to 35% among 'insiders'. However, Tamari considered the bulk of the returnees to be employees in the PA apparatus, which was not the case. A significant number of the returnees comprised families, which means that perhaps a quarter of them were employed, the rest being their wives and children.
5 I have lived in both communities, spending ten years in Lebanon and Syria and six years in Gaza.
6 This expression is borrowed from the Palestinian historian Salim al-Mubayyidh, whom I interviewed in 2002.
7 Katatib (sg. kuttab) are popular schools where children learn to read and write by memorizing the Quran.
8 The starting monthly salary for a teacher was 24 Egyptian pounds at a time when a family was able to live on only EGP 2.
9 Abu Hazim, director of the department of 'Aid for Critical Cases', told me that poor women often went to the ministry to apply for financial assistance or food rations. Some claimed that they were either divorced or had nobody to look after them. However, they went to the ministry accompanied by their husbands, who waited for them outside the building. Abu Hazim said the ministry turned a blind eye to the illegitimacy of their applications because of the widespread unemployment and extreme poverty in Gaza after the eruption of the second intifada and subsequent Israeli economic blockade. The modesty of the rations those women received from the UNRWA (equivalent to 100–200 New Israeli Shekels per month) may have been another reason for the ministry's compassionate treatment of them.
10 Zakat is the part of the income given by Muslims for charitable purposes. The activities of zakat committees expanded during the intifada to include help to orphans, divorcees, the disabled and other marginalized groups in the community.
11 The maskan shar'i is a separate house that has to be prepared by the husband. It should have all the facilities defined as legal. As we shall see in Chapter 6,

the maskan shar'i can be legally invoked by the wife as a ground for claiming maintenance.
12 Nafaqa suits as a percentage of the total number of cases during the selected years were: 1920–27%; 1927–31%; 1937–31%; 1947–47%; 1948–55%; 1949–52%; 1950–34% (perhaps the decrease was due to the upheaval after 1948 tragedy); In 1968, 1977, 1978, 1986, 1987, 1988, 1989, 1990. 1991, 1992, the percentage of nafaqa suits was 40%, 45%, 49%, 57%, 66%, 68%, 49%, 41%, 63% and 65%, respectively.
13 Shaykh Judah was 86 years old at the time of the interview. Born in Haifa, he had been a Shari'a court judge in pre-nakba Haifa and then in Gaza before retiring.
14 Moors (1995) makes a similar observation about marriage contracts in Nablus. However, as she observes, the replacement of household items (in registering tawabi') with cash appeared much later in Nablus records.
15 This information was given to me by several informants, both Bedouin and peasants.
16 Urbanization is truly artificial due to the creation and expansion of the refugee camps where more than 70% of Gaza's population, mostly of peasant background, live. The UNRWA is still a major provider of food, education, employment and health services for the majority of Gazans (see Roy 1995).

Bibliography

Brown, S. G. (1984) 'Impact on the Social Structure of Palestinian Society', in N. Aruri (ed.) *Occupation: Israel Over Palestine*, pp. 223–55. London: Zed Books.
Faris, M. (2002) *Ta'amim qadi al-qudah khilal saba' sanawat (Decrees of qadi al-qudah Over Seven Years)*. Gaza: No publisher.
Friedl, E. (2003) 'Tribal Enterprises and Marriage Issues in Twentieth-Century Iran', in B. Doumani (ed.) *Family History in the Middle East: Household, Property, and Gender*, pp. 151–73. Albany: University of New York Press.
Griffiths, J. (1992) 'Legal Pluralism and the Social Working of Law', in B. Brouwer, T. Hol, A. Soeteman and A. de Wild (eds) *Coherence and Conflict in Law: Proceedings of the 3rd Benelux-Scandinavian Symposium in Legal Theory*, pp. 151–76. Amsterdam and Deventer: Kluwer Law and Taxation Publisher.
Hammami, R. (1990) 'Women, the Hijab and the Intifada', *Middle East Report* 20(3&4): 24–8.
Mahmood, S. (2001) 'Feminist Theory, Embodiment, and the Docile Agent: Some Reflections on the Egyptian Islamic Revival', *Cultural Anthropology* 16(2): 202–36.
Mir-Hosseini, Z. (1993) 'Women, Marriage and the Law in Post-Revolutionary Iran', in H. Afshar (ed.) *Women in the Middle East: Perceptions, Realities and Struggle for Liberation*, pp. 59–85. London: Palgrave Macmillan.
Mir-Hosseini, Z. (2000) *Marriage on Trial: A Study of Islamic Family Law, Iran and Morocco Compared*. London: I. B. Tauris.
Moore, S. F. (1973) 'Law and Social Change: The Semi-Autonomous Social Field as an Appropriate Subject of Study', *Law and Society Review* (7): 719–46.
Moore, S. F. (1978) *Law as Process: An Anthropological Approach*. London: Routledge & Kegan Paul.
Moors, A. (1995) *Women, Property and Islam: Palestinian Experiences 1920–1990*. Cambridge: Cambridge University Press.
Moors, A. (2003) 'Women's Gold: Shifting Styles of Embodying Family Relations', in B. Doumani (ed.) *Family History in the Middle East: Household, Property, and Gender*, pp. 101–19. Albany: University of New York Press.

Muhammad, Z. (1997) 'Harb al-akhdar wa al-azraq: harb al-'a'id wa al-mukim' (The War of Green and Blue: The War Between the Returnee and the Resident), *Al-siyasa al-filastiniyya* 4(13): 111–16.

Roy, S. (1995) *The Gaza Strip: The Political Economy of De-Development*. Washington, DC and London: I. B. Tauris, for Institute of Palestine Studies.

Tamari, S. (1996a) 'Comment on the IDRC Discussion Paper "Adaptation in the West Bank and Gaza" by Jill Tansley'. <http://prrn.mcgill.ca/prrn/papers/tamari1.html>, accessed 9 September 2017.

Tamari, S. (1996b) *Return, Resettlement, Repatriation: The Future of Palestinian Refugees in the Peace Negotiations*. Final Status Strategic Studies, pp. 1–34. Beirut, Washington, DC and Jerusalem: Institute of Palestine Studies. <http://prrn.mcgill.ca/research/papers/tamari2_01.htm>, accessed 9 September 2017.

6 Obedience, rebelliousness and agency

There is disparity between the letter of the law and its actual practice in the Shari'a court with regard to the institution known as the 'house of obedience' (bayt al-ta'a).[1] House of obedience cases, although considered very important by the courts, are not brought very often to the Gaza Shari'a courts. The main argument in this chapter is that the application of the provision depends not only on the text of family law or the heritage of fiqh (Islamic jurisprudence) and tafsir (interpretation), but also on contextual elements such as the litigant's power or the judge's discretion, which are often decisive.

6.1 Roots of concept of obedience

The textual origin of the concept of obedience is in the Quranic sura IV: 34, which establishes the grounds upon which Muslim exegetists founded their views on gender. It reads:

> Men are in charge of [are guardians of/are superior to/have authority over] women (al-rijalu qawwamuna 'ala al-nisa') because God has endowed one with more [because God has preferred some of them over others] (bi-ma faddala Allahu ba'dahum 'ala ba'din) and because they spend of their means (wa-bi-ma 'anfaqu min amwalihim). Therefore the righteous women are obedient, guarding in secret that which God has guarded. As to those from whom you fear rebellion, admonish them and banish them to separate beds, and beat them. Then if they obey you, seek not a way against them. For God is Excellent, Great.
>
> (cited in Stowasser 1998: 33)

Despite their differences over issues relating to the nature of the Quran and the methodology required to read it, the medieval exegetists were in agreement regarding their interpretation of gender roles and relations. For example, Al-Tabari (d. 923), who belonged to the traditionalist school, said:

> This verse is primarily concerned with the domestic relations between husband and wife. It legislates men's authority over their wives, which entails the

male's right to discipline his wife in order to ensure female obedience both toward God and also himself.

(ibid.)

Another Islamic exegetist, Baydawi (d. 1286?), who belonged to the rationalist school, compared men's superiority to that of rulers over their subjects. In his view, that superiority was justified by men's innate abilities and their acquired qualities. Other exegetists, including Ibn Hazm and Ibn Abbas, identified the conditions under which wives could be declared disobedient. Both stipulated that the wife's obedience is related to sexual enjoyment; the man declares his wife's disobedience only when she refuses to have sex with him (Nashwan 1999: 10).

Even in modern times, Muhammad Abdu, the famous Islamic reformist who exercised considerable influence on the articulation of Islamic modernism, did not challenge the gender discourse of sura IV: 34. Abdu sincerely advocated the amendment of family law through a new, modern and 'gender-sensitive' interpretation of the Quran, but one that was in conformity with the mainstream reading of the verse:

> In the God-willed natural order of the family, the man is charged with leadership (qiwama) to protect domestic life and well-being. He is to the wife as the head is to the body. Men merit this 'superiority' because of qualities they alone possess, some innate and some acquired. Among them, some are of a stronger, more perfect, more complete and more beautiful constitution, as is the case with the males in all species. This physical constitution is linked to a stronger mind and sound perceptions, the ability to earn money and administer affairs in a creative way. Women, in turn, should be gratified that their dependency, even though it is a matter of natural constitution, is actually rewarded with 'remuneration' or 'wage' (dower and maintenance).

(ibid.: 35)

Interestingly, recent Islamic scholars seem to be as conservative as their predecessors. For example, Shaban (1983, cited in Haddad 1998: 16–17) believes that women should be obedient to their husbands. Women have to preserve their husbands' honour and wealth and prevent anyone from entering the house without the husband's permission. In return, the man should treat his wife well:

> It is not fitting for a man to allow his wife to do what she pleases and for him always to follow her wishes. If that were the case, he would lose his ability to control the family. The man should supervise the wife and make sure that she fulfils all her religious duties.

Shaban, like other Muslim conservatives, quotes an oft-cited hadith to support his view: 'If a man calls his wife to his bed and she does not come and he sleeps angry towards her, the angels will curse her until the morning.' He further refers to the following hadith: 'If it is possible for one to prostrate oneself before a being other than God, I would order the wife to prostrate herself before her husband' (ibid.).

In this context, I witnessed several cases that demonstrate how the practice of contemporary judges, in keeping with the time, is less conservative, emphasizing that the use of force in an unhappy marriage is counter-productive. Moreover, their conduct not only suggests a difference between text and practice but also directs our attention to the quality of difference: the text is often more conservative than the practice. This confirms the argument by Dwyer (1990), which emphasizes the importance of reading the text through the eyes of people rather than through the ideological presentation of Islamic law.

One case I observed concerned Inshirah, a woman who had failed to consummate her marriage with Hazem after signing a marriage contract and receiving a substantial mahr of JD 6000. During the khutba period, that is, the time span between signing of the contract and actual consummation (dukhul), she had discovered serious incompatibilities between her and Hazem. She told me: 'We have differences in everything. I like poetry, he likes cars; I love music, he loves food; when we sit together, I do not feel any attraction to him, he does not inspire me.... And, above all, I do not need his money even though I am from an average family'. Hazem's reaction to the non-consummation was a petition to the court for a house of obedience order. He expostulated to the qadi:

> I paid her a very high dower; she cost me more than six women. I bought her an apartment in al-Rimal [an upper middle-class neighbourhood]. I equipped my house with Italian furniture, a TV, a video player, a satellite dish. Everything was prepared to welcome her. I even bought her a car. And after I have done all that, she does not want to conclude the marriage. She wants divorce.... I don't know what this woman wants me to do. [... It is my right to bring her to the house of obedience.

The qadi looked at him sympathetically and tried to explain to him: Marriage is mainly a bond between hearts. If it does not click, you should leave each other. Allah says in the Quran: 'You should either live together in peace or leave each other in good shape' (imsakun bi maruf aw tasrihun bi ihsan) (Sura II: 229). It is not acceptable in our norms and traditions to bring a virgin to the house of obedience.

The husband appealed angrily, 'Please understand my situation. She humiliated my rujula (masculinity) and she refused me as if I were an insect. I want her to come to my house for even one day and then I will divorce her immediately if she wishes. I have invested a lot in this marriage and I do not want to look like a fool in my circle.' The qadi convinced him to take more time to persuade Inshirah and adjourned the hearing for a week. The case was again adjourned several times. Finally, Hazem divorced Inshirah in exchange for 'ibra.[2]

The law is not clear about what to do in circumstances such as these. It only sets out regulations concerning divorce before consummation. Article 49 of the *LFR* states that

> if divorce [decided by the husband] takes place before consummation, the wife has the right to keep half of her mahr. But if judicial divorce [iftiraq] has been demanded by the wife's wali [guardian in marriage or custody issues] due to the lack of kafa'a [equivalence], then the mahr lapses.[3]

The law does not clearly specify how the qadi should act when the wife requests divorce on other grounds (not necessarily relating to kafa'a). Perhaps the qadi, seeing that there were insufficient grounds to grant the wife a divorce, protected her by using 'our customs and traditions' as an excuse to stop the husband from forcing her to the house of obedience.

It seems that the mainstream approach in Islamic fiqh also does not favour forcing women to go to the house of obedience before consummation. For example, Samara (1987: 176), in his review of the positions of different fiqh schools, states that if the man delivers the mahr to the wife upon signing the marriage contract, she has to deliver herself to him because he has done what is expected of him. If she refuses without a reason, the man has the right to get his mahr back. Fiqh, it appears, only deals with the relations between the spouses before consummation in terms of financial obligations. To sum up, it seems that the qadi took advantage of the ambiguous legal framework and the lack of clear-cut precedents for how to deal with a petition for a house of obedience order on the basis of non-consummation of marriage (makhtuba).

6.2 Views of Madhahib

As discussed in Chapter 5, the marriage institution is 'textually' established on a fundamental balance of rights and duties: maintenance is the duty of husbands; wives, in return, should be obedient. The rights and duties of each spouse have been further elaborated by Muslim jurists of different schools. Upon signing the marriage contract, the wife should receive the payments due to her (mahr and nafaqa) and, in exchange, she has to be obedient. Regardless of his hadhhab, the man has clear rights vis-à-vis his wife: ta'a (obedience),[4] ta'dib (chastity)[5] and the duty of the wife to stay at home[6] (summarized by Samara 1987). When the equation is disturbed by the wife's disobedience, chastisement is needed through disciplinary action, beginning with advice, then hajr (sexual abandonment), then beating. Beating, it is advised, should not humiliate the wife nor should it leave marks on her body.[7] Samara (1987: 253–4), who compares the views of the different madhahib with the *Jordanian Law of Personal Status* applied in the West Bank, is of the view that Islam did not order Muslims to beat their wives; rather, it only legitimized what was already being practised. Islam legitimizes beating the same way that the modern state sets penalties to punish those who break the law.

Beating is justifiable when other means fail, and it is less harmful than threatening the structure of the family, he adds. However, that beating should not leave signs on the body; if the man exceeds the limits, the wife has the right to petition the qadi for tafriq (judicial divorce).

One interesting observation in the jurists' texts is that all madhahib link the nushuz (rebellious) act instrumentally with its financial consequence; no nafaqa is due to a wife declared nashiz. The adjective 'nushuz' is derived from the noun 'nashz', which means 'high place' or 'high position'. Thus, nushuz means that the wife assumes a higher social position than that of her husband. It is in this regard that she is considered disobedient. The declaration of the wife as nashiz, and thus the suqut (lapse) of her nafaqa, are entailed by the following acts:

- Leaving the house without the husband's permission, even for reasons related to worship. Leaving the house for work is considered nushuz because it is forbidden for reasons considered more important than work. The Shafi'ite school is more strict than other schools on the matter of permission, decreeing that the wife becomes nashiz if she goes on pilgrimage without her husband's permission. In contrast, the Hanafites do not consider a wife's pilgrimage without her husband's permission to be a nushuz act, provided she goes to Mecca with a muhram (Samara 1987: 219).[8]
- Refusal to surrender herself (tusallim nafsaha) to her husband sexually.
- (According to the Shafi'ites), the wife's failure to obey her husband day and night. If she obeys at night but disobeys during the day (or vice versa), then she is considered nashiz.[9] This means that if the wife leaves the house during the daytime for work, even if she fulfils her sexual duties at night, she is still considered nashiz.[10]
- Refusing to travel with the husband.

This review shows that the ideological representation of gender, especially with regard to the concept of women's obedience, is misogynist to say the least. Legal discourse, as exemplified in the family law applied in Gaza and the West Bank, is influenced by this conservative reading of sura IV: 34. Sections 6.5 and 6.6 will provide case material and observations to examine the extent to which daily experience corresponds to the text of family law. However, first the next section will outline the *Law of Family Rights* applied in the Gaza Strip.

6.3 Contemporary legal text and practice

The *LFR* of the Gaza Strip regulates the issue of obedience as follows. Article 39 states that 'the husband is obliged to prepare a fully equipped maskan shar'i [a house that meets the legal requirements] for his wife in a place of his choosing.' Article 40 specifies that 'after receiving her dower, the wife is obliged (mujbara) to live in the husband's shar'i house and to travel with him to any other place (balda) if there is no reason for not doing so.[11] The husband has to treat his wife well and she has to obey him in permissible (mubaha) matters.' Article 41 states that 'the husband should not lodge his natal family and relatives (ahlahu wa aqriba'hu) in his house without the wife's agreement.' However, his wife's agreement is not needed for lodging 'his young [immature] boy (ghayr al-mumayiz)' in his house. For her part, the wife should also not lodge her children [from a previous marriage] or relatives (awladuha wa aqriba'ha) without the husband's consent. Article 66 states that 'if the wife becomes nashiz and leaves her husband's house, she has no right to nafaqa during the period of her disobedience.'

It is noteworthy that, while the *Book of Personal Status Rulings*, which is frequently used by the judges and lawyers, unequivocally lays down the sexual rights of the husband, the 1954 *LFR* applied in Gaza does not do so. Article 212 of the *BPSR* specifies that the wife 'should not leave the house without his [the husband's] permission and should respond to him when he calls her to bed (yad'uha li-l- firash) unless she has a shar'i reason for not doing so.'

After the establishment of the Palestinian Authority, the first qadi al-qudah, Abu Sardana, reminded the judges of the legal limits of the application of ta'a:

> The execution of the judgment of obedience (hukm al-ta'a), when it reaches its final degree (daraja qat'iyya), should not be made compulsory (jabran), because the wife, while ordered, should not be constrained (tu'mar wala tujbar). If the wife refuses to abide by the judgment without a valid reason (bidun haqq), her punishment in this world (dunya) is that she will be deprived of nafaqa due to her disobedience (nushuz) and her punishment on the Day of Judgment (al-akhira) is that God will sanction her disobedience (ma'siya). I repeat what I said earlier: the mere hukm al-ta'a (the judgment of obedience), when it reaches its final degree, does not license cutting off nafaqa unless the wife's disobedience (nushuz) is proved by her refusal to comply with the judgment (hukm) either through a written certificate from the executive office (dai'rat al-tanfith), which should bear the wife's signature declaring her refusal, or by providing legitimate evidence (bayyina shar'iyya) through filing of another case for ceasing to pay nafaqa.

Article 37 of the *Jordanian Law of Personal Status* (gazetted in 1976), applied in the West Bank, reads: 'The wife should *live* [italics added] in her husband's house.' However, article 40 of the *LFR* (1954) stipulates that 'the wife is *obliged* [italics added] (mujbara) to live in her shar'i house'. Welchman (2000: 231–2) notes that when the Jordanians replaced family law No. 92 of 1951 with the law of 1976, they removed the word 'obliged', thus doing away with the legal justification for forcing the wife to go to her husband's house once he wins a ta'a case.

Although the word 'obliged' (tujbar) still exists in the *LFR*, in practice, a wife is not forced to go to the shar'i house when her husband wins a ta'a case. This is because the *Code of Shar'i Jurisdictions* of 1965 clearly sets out the limits of legal execution. Article 219 of the *Code of Shar'i Jurisdictions* states that 'keeping the child with the custodian [. . .] is compulsory (qahran, that is, with the use of force) except in ta'a cases; when the wife refuses to comply, she is considered disobedient (tu'tabar nashiz).' Thus, the legal consequence for the wife when she

104 *Obedience, rebelliousness and agency*

does not comply with the court order to go to the house of obedience is that she will be considered nashiz but will not be forced to go to the house.

Gazans generally avoid the use of force in resolving marriage disputes. Part of the reason for their reluctance is that the institution of marriage is not simply a relationship between individuals but also a bond between families. It involves people who are relatives within the same extended family or clan (hamula). In this context, a house of obedience case would be humiliating for the wife as well as her relatives, who are usually also relatives of the husband. Table 6.1 confirms that petitions for a house of obedience order were not filed frequently at the Gaza Shari'a courts between 1927 and 2001.

While the total number of Shari'a court cases escalated drastically in the year following the nakba (from 148 cases in 1948 to 236 in 1949), the percentage of house of obedience suits initially increased only slightly (by less than 1%) and then declined radically, from 11.8% in 1949 to 2.4% in 1950. The drastic increase in the total number of cases might be explained by increased population. On the eve of the nakba, the population of the Gaza Strip numbered 70,000, but after the influx of refugees it increased by 250,000 (Roy 1995).[12] Most of the newcomers had fled from their towns and villages around Jaffa and Bir al-Saba' in the Negev. In fact, what is now designated as the Gaza Strip covers only 27% of the area of Mandate Gaza (ibid.). The sudden population increase in this reduced territory explains the sharp increase in the total number of cases. The later decline

Table 6.1 House of obedience petitions filed at Gaza Shari'a courts, selected years between 1927 and 2001

Year	Total number of cases filed	Number of house of obedience cases	House of obedience cases as % of total cases
1927	150	30	20
1937	159	17	10.7
1947	135	14	10
1948	148	16	10.8
1949	236	28	11.8
1950	406	10	2.4
1966	361	13	3.6
1967	181	12	6.6
1977	288	16	5.5
1978	250	9	3.6
1986	217	1	0.5
1987	224	–	–
1996	712	4	0.6
1997	935	10	1
1998	605	7	1.1
1999	604	3	0.4
2000	624	7	1.1
2001	548	4	0.7

Source: Data from Gaza Shari'a court records.

in house of obedience cases, however, appears to have been related to the socio-economic and political upheaval that occurred in Gaza after the 1948 war, with refugees still living in tents because no housing was available for them. It is hard to imagine that men who were searching for shelter for their families would petition for a house of obedience order.

Between 1977 and 1987, ta'a cases dropped from 5.5% to 0. Continuous change in socio-economic circumstances could explain this decline: the generation following the nakba received formal education, people's living conditions improved and the number of trained and employed women grew. The UN Relief and Works Agency was a decisive factor as it took responsibility for providing rations, education, jobs and health services to the refugees, who constituted the majority of Gaza inhabitants. In 1986, only one of the 217 cases was for a house of obedience order; the next year, the first intifada flared up and no ta'a suit was registered at the Shari'a court.

Another element to be considered is that the house of obedience provision imposes a constraint not only on the wife but to a certain extent on the husband as well. When a husband chooses to sort out his familial dispute through a bayt al-ta'a petition, he should generally be able to prepare a shar'i house that complies with the criteria set by the Shari'a court. The male litigant who chooses this route must be quite well-off. However, as noted in Chapter 1, Gaza is very densely populated; for example, 84,077 refugees live in al-Shati' Camp, which has an area of only 0.52 square kilometres.[13] Under such circumstances, a house that met all the Shari'a court's requirements would be rather luxurious. This observation is also supported by Welchman (2000: 381),[14] who notes that only five house of obedience cases were registered at the Gaza Shari'a courts in 1989, 1992, 1993 and 1994, compared with 17 in Ramallah and 20 in Nablus in the same years.[15] Thus, people's legal practice with regard to the house of obedience provision underwent significant modification under the influence of socio-economic and political change, without the legal text being reformed.

6.4 Viewpoints of practitioners

The Shari'a courts are very strict about the criteria for shar'i houses. The criteria were explained to me by Abu Khalid, who works at the Gaza Shari'a courts and has been frequently appointed by judges of the first instance to examine such houses:

> Getting the court's approval of the house of obedience is very difficult. . . . The house should be in an area that is not remote. All equipment needed by the wife should be available. The house should be secure in terms of its doors and windows. If the man's economic status is good, then the house should meet his standard of living. . . . When we examine the house, we search for the slightest reason for considering the house to be illegitimate. We can always find such defects. The lack of baking flour, or of secure windows, are our frequent excuses. . . . To declare the house as not being shar'i,

we sometimes hide behind the gloominess of the house, which is a subjective criterion.

This makes it difficult for a man to get his wife back against her will. As noted in section 6.3, even if the man succeeds in preparing a house that is declared to be shar'i, a wife who refuses to live in it cannot be forced to do so. Of course, her status of being married but neither living as a married woman nor receiving nafaqa may make her life difficult if she does not submit. She is not allowed to remarry, and the husband can keep her nashiz all her life.

Although judges tend not to undermine the gender-based division of roles, they know that when a dispute reaches the stage of a house of obedience case, the relationship has become bitter and the man is likely to be seeking revenge. Therefore, the court does not favour compelling a woman to go to her husband's house. 'Such an act ... may expand the distance between the couple and further embitter relations between their families,' qadi al-Karmi told me. It for this reason that the court makes it difficult for the man to prove that the house he has prepared is shar'i. To quote qadi al-Karmi:

> The court's clerks examine the house and write a report about it. Then the qadi has to be convinced that the house complies with the shar'i criteria. The man should provide a house that matches his financial situation. The house should contain all the modern equipment (al-ajhiza al-haditha) that women need.

Before the husband's petition for a house of obedience ruling is heard, he has to pay his wife's full dower, including tawabi'. For a house to be shar'i, it must be located in the same area where the couple used to live and where neighbours can provide help when the wife needs it. Among other conditions, the house doors and windows should be in good condition. No member of the husband's natal family can be in the house without her permission, but she may invite members of her family of origin to visit her, provided they are her maharim.

I witnessed a case which demonstrated how, to quote qadi al-Karmi, 'our experienced clerks search for any defect to make it difficult for the husband to humiliate his wife'. A wealthy man who petitioned for a house of obedience order had prepared a house containing new and valuable furnishings, but the qadi had been informed that the husband constantly beat his wife and that she had therefore left the house and returned to her family in a state of anger. Instead of filing a nafaqa suit, she wanted to find a solution through her family by asking for a divorce in exchange for waiving her financial rights. The man did not accept the solution proposed by her family, nor did he accept the qadi's advice that the couple live with each other decently and peacefully. Instead, he insisted on 'putting [his wife's] nose down' and said so clearly before the qadi, who noted down the reasons motivating the petition.

The court clerks who had examined the house, while declaring it to be otherwise well-equipped, had reported that it lacked equipment for baking bread. The husband told the court that there was no need for an oven and flour because he bought ready-made bread, but the qadi was not satisfied with that explanation and told him, 'We are in a time of intifada. Suppose there is a curfew, how will your wife bake bread?' He dismissed the petition on that ground.

It is qadi al-Karmi's view that both wives and husbands can be declared nashiz. The husband is considered nashiz if, for example, he does not apply the principles of good treatment (mu'ashara bi-l-ma'ruf) or if he beats his wife cruelly. In such cases, the court rebukes him (yu'azar). Nushuz al-zawj (man's disobedience) also figures in the *Book of Personal Status Rulings*, article 211 of which reads: 'if the woman complains of her husband's disobedience (nushuz zawjiha) . . . and this is established, [the court should] rebuke him.'

Lawyers warn their male clients that a house of obedience order is a constraint on them, too. As explained earlier, the wife must either comply with the court's decision or be declared nashiz and lose her entitlement to nafaqa. On the other hand, the husband has to maintain the house without being able to use it or let his natal family live in it; nor can he sell it or rent it until the dispute is resolved. Should he violate the terms, the wife can immediately apply for nafaqa or tafriq (judicial divorce), and the court will declare the house illegitimate (ghayr shar'i).

6.5 Legal practice in Gaza

Sometimes, men accuse judges of 'sympathy towards women' and deride their knowledge of fiqh. I witnessed this in a case where the husband bluntly refused to pay nafaqa even though a court ruled that he should do so. He told the court that his wife had 'left the house without my permission and she is living now in her family's house. . . . She is nashiz . . . she does not deserve nafaqa. How can I pay her while she is away? I am not getting anything from her [referring to his sexual needs].' The Qadi explained to him that only the court could declare her nashiz, but before it could hear a petition to do so the husband had to give her all the financial rights due to her (kul huquqha al-maliyya): 'You have to give her nafaqa and tawabi'.'[16] Pointing out that the man would have to pay at least JD 50 because his salary was JD 260, the qadi suggested that the better alternative would be to resolve his dispute with his wife through mediators.

However, the man was stubborn and accused the qadi of not knowing Islamic law: 'I am a Muslim, I know the Shari'a, fiqh and the law. What you are saying is wrong. You are rewarding her for her rebellious action. This is not Islamic,' he declared. The qadi then responded dryly, 'All right, we are not as knowledgeable as you are, but we will see who concludes this case.' Then he adjourned the case until the following week. A lawyer who happened to be in the courtroom tried to calm the qadi down, telling him, 'People speak stupidly due to their ignorance; please forgive them'. Another court clerk said jokingly, 'You are upset because you cannot leave the courtroom to watch the football game.'[17] The qadi merely smiled at them.

Abu 'Ali, the usher, ran out and warned the man that he was going to lose his case because of his disrespectful comments. The man returned and apologized to the qadi: 'Tell me, what can I do with this woman?' he asked. 'She has made a hell of my life. . . . She sucked my blood with her endless demands and every now and then she brings her brothers to scold me. I want to discipline her ('arabbiha) and teach her brothers a lesson.' Instead of responding to the question, the qadi told him to return to the court the following week. Later, he told me, 'I will teach him a lesson. You will see that nafaqa of less than JD 80 will not satisfy me. He did not accept the JD 50? Well, he will learn who knows fiqh and who does not.'

In another case, too, the qadi used similar tactics to persuade a man to change his mind about having his wife ordered to the house of obedience. Su'ad, a woman in her late twenties, wanted to be divorced from Salim because his father, who was living with them, frequently insulted and beat her. She left with her daughter for her family's house and then filed for nafaqa for herself and the daughter. On the day of the hearing, Salim told the qadi: 'I will not pay her anything until she comes back to my house.' The qadi replied: 'You have to give her all her rights before you get her back.'

However, Salim had another proposal: 'Sir, I have another wife who is willing to accept my father in her house. So, I will put this one in my new house and have the other one live with my father and me.' The qadi was not willing to let the husband shirk his responsibilities and cautioned him,

> If you complicate the case, your wife will continue staying away and you will pay her nafaqa all your life. Your wife is not a slave; you cannot expect me to order her to go to your house. My advice to you is either to return to each other with good will or leave each other in good shape.

The qadi postponed the case until the following week to give the man time to consider his choices. The next week, the man returned and said: 'I agree. I will divorce her in exchange for renunciation of her financial rights, but I want to specify here that she should not claim any nafaqa for herself or for the daughter. This is my condition.' As Su'ad was willing to give up her financial rights, she accepted that condition.

This legal arrangement through which women relinquish their financial rights in exchange for divorce is called mukhala'a. It is not to be found in the *Law of Family Rights*, but the *Book of Personal Status Rulings* devotes a long chapter to it. The 24 articles of Chapter 39 of the *BPSR* constitute the main reference for judges in such cases. In practice, couples who choose this route agree that the wife will give up all or part of her financial rights in exchange for a final divorce (talaq ba'in baynuna sughra). This leaves only one way for the couple to get back together later; they have to sign a new marriage contract with new mahr.

This type of divorce requires the agreement of both spouses, unlike a unilateral divorce decided by the husband in which (1) the procedure depends solely on the husband's will, and (2) the status of the divorce is different. While mukhala'a requires mutual consent and is final (ba'in), unilateral divorce is revocable (talaq raj'i), with the husband having the right to call his wife back to his 'isma during her 'idda period. Welchman (2000: 272–80), who reviewed the positions of the different madhahib regarding this arrangement, notes that the Hanafites hold that 'if the mukhala'a is undertaken for something other than the dower, then all other rights (primarily the dower and the maintenance) are also automatically renounced.' This position differs from that of the Shafi'ites and Hanbalites, who maintain that 'the other rights were only lost if certain explicit formulas were used' (Welchman 2000: 275).

In Gaza, mukhala'a follows the Hanafi doctrine: the wife renounces all her financial rights in exchange for divorce. It is agreed in court in the presence of the qadi. I attended a number of such sessions and found that the judges follow the same routine with all litigants. For example, they do not ask the wife what financial agreement was concluded between her and her husband. Instead, they warn her that divorce in exchange for ibra' means that she will lose her deferred dower and nafaqa. They ask her whether she understands the consequences of her decision. The qadi may say: 'This divorce will cost you all the rights assigned to you by the Shari'a. Be aware of that and do not be hasty. Think about it.' When children are involved, mukhala'a also means that the wife relinquishes her right to compensation for care ('ujrat hadana) and breast-feeding ('ujrat rida'a). Moreover, mukhala'a may require the mother, instead of the father, to cover the child's nafaqa (article 286 of the *BPSR*).

The law approves any agreement between the spouses concerning the amount of compensation ('awad), thus legitimating the husband's demands in return for his acceptance of mukhala'a.[18] Welchman (2000: 275) contends that it is acceptable (although disapproved of) for the wife not only to renounce her rights but also to pay an additional sum. Thus, all Sunni schools validate compensating the husband for granting his wife a divorce.

Lawyer Hala Anwar once drew my attention to a case that involved a novel use of the house of obedience provision. Essentially, the case amounted to a plot between husband, wife and lawyer to use the provision to deal with a troublesome brother.

Adiba, 25 years old, lived happily with her husband Faris, but their marriage was periodically disturbed by a long-standing conflict between Faris and her brother, who were joint owners of a shop. The brother used Adiba as a pawn whenever he wanted to hurt Faris. She told me:

> Whenever there was a conflict between them, my brother would come to my house and force me to leave with him. It was always painful to leave my [five] children suffering from my absence.... When I was in my brother's house, his wife used to discredit me and speak ill of my husband.... One day, lawyer Hala Anwar was giving a lecture in our neighbourhood, which I attended. I asked her (in private) what I should do. Hala Anwar understood the case. She said that if my husband called me to the house of obedience (talabani li bayt al-ta'a), my brother would not be able to take me away again. I phoned my husband and told him to go to Hala Anwar's office and arrange everything with her. Hala Anwar helped him to file the case.

110 *Obedience, rebelliousness and agency*

Hala Anwar recounted what happened then:

> I sat with Faris and worked out the 'plot' with him. We agreed that he would apply for a house of obedience ruling and send a copy of his application to the brother through a family figure. This would make the brother understand that Faris was serious about his legal action. Of course, Faris did not intend to go through the entire procedure involved. It was a tactic.

The plot seemed to work successfully. The go-between depicted Faris's suit as a serious legal action, and the combination of threat and mediation convinced the brother to send his sister back to her husband's house. It is worth noting that not everyone is aware of the implications of legal action, particularly with regard to the house of obedience. As is evident from this case, the provision could have neither led to any sanction against nor affected the economic well-being of the brother or his sister. The brother's decision was probably more informed by viewing the case as a 'social scandal' than by any legal understanding.

Another aspect of this case was the wife's action. Her 'plot' with the lawyer does not tell as much about the house of obedience as about women's strategies. Women operate within a complex matrix of relationships, where loyalty and attachment are subject to continuous reconfiguration. When Adiba realized that her brother was guarding his own interests at the expense of hers, her loyalty to him became more a burden than a power resource. Therefore, she chose to privilege her nuclear family. This case is also exceptional because the ta'a provision, often a tool of women's oppression and humiliation, was used by Adiba for negotiation, accommodation and power redistribution.

6.6 Synthesis

This chapter has examined some legal and social issues regarding the roots and application of bayt al-ta'a, with special attention to its practice in the Shari'a courts of Gaza. It began with a review of the Quranic root of the concept of ta'a and its interpretation by various schools of fiqh. The aim was to clarify the current Islamic family law with reference to its historical source and to study the relation between the conceptualization of obedience in the gender discourse of various schools of thought in Islamic history and its transposition into a 'fixed' legal text organizing gender relation between husband and wife. The chapter also drew attention to the *Law of Family Rights* articles that specify when, how and under which conditions a man may call his wife to the house of obedience. A brief examination of the difference between the law applied in the West Bank and that in the Gaza Strip was also provided. A number of court cases relating to ta'a were examined to show that the text is only one dimension in the administration of bayt al-ta'a. Indeed, aspects relating to the wider context and to the specificities of the cases being heard appeared crucial.

There is persistent discrepancy between the text and the practice of family law. The cases presented in this chapter show that there is little correspondence between the two. Practice has undergone significant change without the letter of the law being reformed. This paradox of text versus practice is likely to remain a permanent feature of the application of family law as long as the text and legislators only pay lip-service to structural changes in society. The practice of law in the court has always been characterized by pluralism, flexibility and a degree of ambiguity, whereas the text remains characterized by rigidity, restriction, stability and, in some aspects, superficial clarity. As law is ideologically conceptualized (Moore 1978), it does not necessarily correspond to a social system full of inconsistencies, oppositions, contradictions and tensions. In the Shari'a courts, as we have seen in this chapter, there are rich individual and situational disparities. These indicate that social change is continuous, notwithstanding great variations in pace and degree (ibid.).

Historically, the massive influx of Palestinian refugees into the Gaza Strip after 1948 negatively and irreversibly impacted on people's social and economic life as well as their legal actions. Their economic integration and absorption was almost impossible. Gaza is small, isolated and circumscribed. It possesses only meagre resources. As Roy (1995: 81) points out, 'with no raw materials, no mineral deposits, no access to markets except across 200 miles of the Sinai Desert, and a limited amount of land and water, the Gaza Strip offered little economic potential.' In 1948 and subsequent years, the Gaza Strip did not even have enough stone to construct houses for the hundreds of thousands of refugees (ibid.). It was only six years after the 1948 tragedy that tents were gradually replaced by poorly built camps provided by the UNRWA. The tragedy of dislocation impacted not only on the refugees but also on the already impoverished indigenous population of Gaza. Their living conditions declined further after 1948, and they became 'economic refugees' (Roy 1995: 79). After 1948, Gazans, whether indigenous or refugees, relied on the UNRWA to provide food, kerosene, education and health care.

These profound changes in modes of livelihood in Gaza may explain why, after 1948, the practice of calling a wife to the house of obedience declined sharply. When a man can provide no shelter whatsoever, it is unlikely that he will ask a court to confine a 'disobedient' wife to a maskan shar'i. These structural elements played a great role not only in reducing the number of ta'a cases but also in shaping the identity, purposes and motivations of applicants. After the exodus, it was probably only the well-off who thought of bringing their wives to a house of obedience.

'Obedience' is meant to maintain a social order based on gender hierarchy. For various madhahib, cutting nafaqa and declaring the woman nashiz sufficed to achieve this goal. These penalties sufficed to control rebellious women. When the Shari'a was codified, the legislators had to find a legal avenue for complying with the gender discourse of the madhahib on the one hand, and for underpinning gender hierarchy in clear, compulsory terms on the other. Cutting maintenance did not prove sufficient to maintain the social order. Therefore, the law-makers not only conceived the house of obedience provision but also established mechanisms of enforcement. According to Jordanian law No. 92 of 1951, applied in the

West Bank, the police could force women to comply with the court's judgment. Later, this mode of enforcement was replaced by the qadi's intervention to get couples to the negotiation table, either by restoring their marriage or dissolving it. Compulsion is legally forbidden in Gaza, but other enforcement mechanisms are intact.

The question thus arises as to why these attempts were made. Why do women have either to be forced to return to married status or to divorce their husbands? The answer lies in the ambiguous status of rebellious women (nashiz). The nashiz woman is neither married nor divorced. She remains a wife because the marriage contract is still valid, but in reality she does not practise her marital life. This ambivalent condition is the last that any law should advocate. One of the fundamental objectives of law, family or otherwise, is to protect the social order. To achieve this, the law defines and fixes a clear-cut personal status. In the case of family law in Palestine, men's and women's social status should be unequivocal: either married or not. The vagueness of nushuz destabilizes the social order and thus prevents the law from accomplishing its fundamental purpose. Therefore, the law had to devise methods to avoid such vagueness. At one point, force was the method chosen, whereas at another, the task was devolved to the qadi. Both methods in fact aimed at preventing the emergence of ambiguity. However, in both situations, the law is founded on gender asymmetry, itself symbolized by the 'maintenance versus obedience' equation. It thus generates ambiguity and will continue to create such aberrations as the status of 'rebellious woman'. The mechanisms for preserving gender hierarchy might be modified, but the basic feature of asymmetrical power distribution will remain unaffected as long as the law's informing gender discourse obtains.

This analysis leads us to the next point related to the actions of judges. They do not tolerate 'grey zones' such as nushuz. Therefore, we see them sometimes discouraging men from resorting to the house of obedience provision; at other times, they accept divorce as a better alternative to the undesirable situation of nushuz. The grey zone, where the woman is neither divorced nor married, is indeed the last situation they advocate. Chapters 1 to 4 referred to the judges' protective attitude towards female litigants in the context of their dual concern to protect the weak while preserving the social order. This is nowhere clearer than in ta'a cases. Judges appear to protect women by discouraging men from claiming their right to ta'a; they put forward enormous restrictions and obstacles to help keep people married, or they facilitate divorce, but their motive is two-fold: to protect women from the shame attached to nushuz and to preserve the social order by not generating the ambiguity that nashiz status entails.

When women do not submit to the ta'a judgment, the only thing that can happen to them is that they forego financial claims on the husband. Sociologically, one may ask two interrelated questions. First, why is this the only requirement that is not enforceable? Second, why do people resort to it infrequently? An answer is suggested by a practising lawyer: 'The wider social implication of such a forcible act is more dangerous than not executing a judgment.' In other words, the shame attached to alien intervention, whatever its nature, by police or otherwise, has wider social ramifications than failure to preserve the force of law. Furthermore, the action of judges in dissuading a husband from filing a house of obedience petition is meant to prevent the situation from developing to a point where they are forced to declare a woman nashiz. Thus, the shame attached to the nashiz woman is indeed more destabilizing to the social order than maintaining the rule of law. The shame, moreover, is likely to stain the reputation of the husband as much as it tarnishes that of his wife.

Gaza is small. It is metaphorically depicted by its inhabitants as a house with thin walls: 'If I cough in the north, those in the south will hear me,' is a common expression in Gaza, describing the forced proximity of their relations emerging from their distorted historical trajectory. This leads to a vague notion of privacy, where everyone appears to know everything about everybody else (and is eager to do so). It is thus not only the hamula system and its imposition of sanctions on its members that impels people to comply with socially acceptable codes of conduct. The whole Gaza Strip appears to be a large hamula in which inhabitants are accountable to each other, especially with regard to their moral reputation (sum'a wa sharaf). Gazans, in times of both rest and strain, often say, 'We lost everything and were left with nothing but our reputation (sum'a).' Sum'a and sharaf are nowhere more critical than in the field of personal conduct. If a man's wife becomes nashiz, she will be socially stained as a 'distorted woman' (mara mush mniha), but he will be accused of being a weak man or not a man at all (mush zalama). In a context in which reputation plays a great role in determining one's weight in society, the shame attached to nushuz must be avoided. Nushuz is a manifestation of shame, and this makes people very reluctant to resort to the house of obedience provision.

Like all members of society, judges are influenced by the dominant gender discourse, which legitimizes the unequal division of rights and duties within the family. Judges thus promote justice as long as their 'just' solution neither disturbs the community's norms nor questions the gender asymmetry inherent in law and social practice.

Another issue pinpointed in this chapter is the qualitative and quantitative difference in the exercise of ta'a at different times and in different places. In Egypt, as one litigant said, the conditions and quality of bayt al-ta'a are entirely different. Even within Palestine, the number of ta'a cases filed in Gaza and the West Bank are different. If bayt al-ta'a is bound to disappear due to elements related to modern modes of conduct, then how would one interpret the discrepancy between the number of bayt al-ta'a cases in Gaza and the West Bank (Ramallah and Nablus), especially considering the higher population of Gaza in comparison with that of the West Bank towns examined? The West Bank is perceived as being more socially sophisticated or (modern). Gaza, however, is treated as backward. Yet bayt al-ta'a is practised more often in the West Bank. These contradictions and analytically challenging observations may call for total abandonment of the notions of 'backwardness' versus 'sophistication', 'modern' versus 'traditional', because they fail to account for the complex symptoms observed. Local specificities cannot be captured by adhering to an overarching framework of analysis, especially when this framework is based on dichotomies. Interrelated and contextual elements characterize the application of bayt al-ta'a across time and space.

6.7 Conclusion

This chapter has examined some legal and social issues regarding the roots and application of bayt al-ta'a in Gaza. It discussed the mutually constitutive relation between the Shari'a court and the community. It then reviewed the textual roots of the concept of obedience and its interpretation by various schools of fiqh and showed how the discourses of various Islamic schools 'fixed' the gender code in the legal text of contemporary family laws. The ethnographic examination showed a persistent discrepancy between how law is formulated from above and how it is redone from below. In Gaza, the applied law is characterized by pluralism, flexibility and a degree of ambiguity, whereas the text remains characterized by rigidity, restriction, stability, and, in some respects, superficial clarity. As law is ideologically conceptualized (Moore 1978), it does not necessarily correspond to a social system full of inconsistencies, oppositions, contradictions and tensions. What we see is a combination of complex elements that needs to be carefully unpacked in order to understand the dynamics of bayt al-ta'a. There are norms to be recognized, the individual agency of the judges and, finally, historical contingency related to the 1948 tragedy. All of these elements intertwine to produce such a reality.

We shall now go on, in Chapter 7, to examine how the courts rule on another important issue: custody rights over children when a marriage has broken down and the spouses cannot be reconciled.

Notes

1 Bayt al-ta'a is the house to which a wife can be legally ordered to move after a Shari'a court accepts her husband's petition to declare her as being disobedient to him. It has to conform to certain strict requirements that will be spelled out later in this chapter.
2 Renunciation of financial rights granted by marriage.
3 I witnessed another case in which a couple appeared in court to conclude a divorce before consummation (talaq qabl al-dukhuul). The woman brought the dower and all the gifts and gave them to the qadi to verify and return to the man. The qadi checked them and then asked the man to re-check them. He specifically asked the man to look in the bag containing the gifts to ensure that nothing was missing. After the qadi declared them divorced, the man approached the qadi and asked him: 'Can I file a house of obedience case against my second wife? She left the house and I want to bring her back.' The qadi looked at him with disdain and responded, 'You have to put her nafaqa and tawabi' on my desk before you file a case. As you have received your rights from my desk, you have to give others their rights on the same grounds . . . leave now and fear God.'
4 'The righteous women are obedient' (sura IV: 34).
5 'As to those from whom you fear rebellion, admonish them and banish them to separate beds, and beat them' (sura IV: 34).
6 'The righteous women . . . guard in secret that which God has guarded' (sura IV: 34).

7 In the modern era, most Islamic thinkers still consider moderate use of force a way of chastising the wife. For example, Shaban (1983) advises the husband to use gentleness and to avoid striking the face. However, there are those who believe that beating is the proper way to deal with a wife's disobedience, for 'psychology books inform us that women do not enjoy sex until they are beaten up. Although this phenomenon may be rare, it has deep roots in the essence of womanhood' (Ali Shalaq 1982, cited in Haddad 1998: 17).
8 A muhram is a person whose degree of consanguinity with the ward prevents him or her from marrying the ward.
9 Ibid.
10 Both Shafi'ites and Hanafites hold this view. Article 169 of the *BPSR* (derived from Hanifite teaching) states that the professional woman who remains outside her home during the day in spite of having been forbidden to do so by her husband ('asathuu), and with her husband at night, receives no nafaqa as long as she continues to go out. Also, Welchman (2000: 224) cites article 156 of the Hanifite *Kitab al-nafaqat* of Qadri Pasha, which also states, 'If the wife has delivered herself (that is, to the ihtibas of her husband) by night and refuses by day, or delivers herself by day and refuses by night, then she is nashiz.' For example, if the wife is a professional woman who works by day in her own interest and comes back to the husband by night, she is not entitled to maintenance.
11 This implies that there is a possibility for a wife not to travel with her husband without being declared nashiz.
12 In 1948, there was only one Shari'a court in the Gaza Strip. In 1949, a new court was established in Khan Younis to serve the population in south Gaza (interview with Shaykh Muhammad Juda, 2002).
13 Statistic from UNRWA. www.unrwa.org/where-we-work/gaza-strip/beach-camp, accessed 21 August 2017.
14 The fieldwork for this Welchman study was carried out in 1999.
15 I will return to the difference between Gaza and the two cities in the West Bank in section 6.7 of this chapter.
16 Later, on 3 March 1997, a decree was issued by the qadi al-qudah, which stated that a man's failure to pay nafaqa did not justify refusing his petition for ta'a. If the nafaqa was not paid, and if the court was unable to get it from him, then the wife could ask for tafriq (judicial divorce). When the husband wanted to file for ta'a, he should owe neither the prompt dower nor the tawabi'; he should have a maskan shar'i (a house that meets the legal requirements); and there should be no evidence of violent behaviour. This has stopped qudah from forbidding husbands to file for ta'a as long as they owe nafaqa (Faris 2002: 49).
17 The case was heard in July 2002, when the World Cup matches were being played.
18 Article 276 of the *BPSR* states that 'it is permissible that the man yukhali' (divorces on a mutually agreeable basis) his wife in return for compensation greater than that which he has paid her (akthar mimma saqa ilayha).'

Bibliography

Ahmed, L. (1992) *Women and Gender in Islam: Historical Roots of a Modern Debate.* New Haven, CT: Yale University Press.
Botiveau, B. (1997) *Al-shari'a al-islamiyya wa al-qanuun fi al-mujtama'at al-'arabiyya (The Islamic Shari'a and Law in Arab Societies).* Cairo: Sienna.
Dwyer, D. H. (1990) 'Law and Islam in the Middle East: An Introduction', in D. H. Dwyer (ed.) *Law and Islam in the Middle East*, pp. 1–15. New York: Bergin & Garvey.

Faris, M. (2002) *Ta'amim qadi al-qudah khilal saba' sanawat (Decrees of qadi al-qudah Over Seven Years)*. Gaza: No publisher.

Griffiths, J. (1992) 'Legal Pluralism and the Social Working of Law', in B. Brouwer, T. Hol, A. Soeteman and A. de Wild (eds) *Coherence and Conflict in Law: Proceedings of the 3rd Benelux-Scandinavian Symposium in Legal Theory*, pp. 151–76. Amsterdam and Deventer: Kluwer Law and Taxation Publisher.

Haddad, Y. (1998) 'Islam and Gender: Dilemmas in the Changing Arab World', in Y. Haddad and J. Esposito (eds) *Islam, Gender and Social Change*, pp. 3–30. New York: Oxford University Press.

Moore, S. F. (1978) *Law as Process: An Anthropological Approach*. London: Routledge & Kegan Paul.

Nashwan, K. (1999) 'Responsibilities in the Family', internal discussion paper presented at a women's movement meeting during the campaign for elimination of the 'house of obedience' provision in the family law.

Roy, S. (1995) *The Gaza Strip: The Political Economy of De-development*. Washington, DC and London: I. B. Tauris, for Institute of Palestine Studies.

Samara, M. (1987) *Ahkam wa athar al-zawjiyya: sharh muqaran li-qanuun al-ahwal al-shakhsiyya (Rules and Consequences of Marriage: Comparative Commentary on the Law of Personal Status)*. Jerusalem: No publisher.

Shaban, M. A. (1983). *Family System Between Christianity and Islam: Comparative Study (Nizam al-Usrah bayn al-Masihiyah wa al-Islam: Dirasa Muqaranah)*. Cairo: House of Sciences (Dar al-Ulum).

Shalaq, Ali (1982). *Women and Their Roles in Arab Unity (al-mara wa dowruha fi al- wihda al-arabiyya)*. Beirut. Centre for Arab Unity (Markaz Dirasat al-wahda al-arabiyya).

Stowasser, B. (1998) 'Gender Issues and Contemporary Quran Interpretation', in Y. Haddad and J. Esposito (eds) *Islam, Gender and Social Change*, pp. 30–45. New York: Oxford University Press.

Welchman, L. (2000) *Beyond the Code: Muslim Family Law and the Shar'i Judiciary in the Palestinian West Bank*. The Hague: Kluwer Law International.

7 The articulation of gendered parenthood
Care vs guardianship

This chapter has three objectives. First, it identifies the areas of gender asymmetry in the legal text with regard to custody, which divides gender roles into two distinct categories, female-oriented physical care (hadana) and male-oriented guardianship (wilaya). Second, it identifies the various strategies adopted by men and women in claiming (or refraining from claiming) their custody rights. In the course of fulfilling these objectives, the chapter investigates how judges rule on various aspects of custody.

7.1 Legal text

As mentioned in previous chapters, the Shari'a courts in the Gaza Strip rely on two legal references for the application of family law: *Law of Family Rights* (*LFR*) of 1954 and *Book of Personal Status Rulings* (*BPSR*), which follows the School of Abu Hanifa and was compiled by Qadri Pasha in 1875. The *LFR* provides less-detailed instructions than the *BPSR* on how judges should treat custody cases. This makes judges more reliant on the *BPSR* for their rulings. Welchman (2000) also observed this among judges in the West Bank. In organizing custody rights, the *BPSR* reflects a certain world view regarding gender, age, lineage, religion and morality, with gender being the fundamental issue. The *BPSR* divides custody rights into wilaya (guardianship, authority, decision-making and maintenance), which is exclusively the domain of the father or male relatives, and hadana (care, feeding, clothing and bodily hygiene), which is assigned to mothers or female relatives (see Welchman 1999; Layish 1975; Samara 1987; Zahra and Malek 1998). This hierarchical division of custody into different domains is consistent with the gendered philosophy of law, which identifies fathers as final decision-makers while mothers may or may not be seen as care providers.

The concepts of wilaya and hadana cannot be conveyed totally by the term 'custody'. The most salient feature of hadana is that it does not entail major decision-making regarding the child. Its Arabic root means to hold in one's arms, to embrace and to place on the lap. The *Lisan al-'Arab* gives a broader definition of hadana: 'to nurse, to bring up or to raise a child' (quoted in Zahra and Malek 1998: 156). According to Samara (1987: 368), hadana means 'taking physical care of the child who is still unable to do so by itself. The one who has the right to do this is the hadin (the carer).' Wilaya, on the other hand, refers to notions of authority and decision-making. It is divided into two aspects: guardianship of a person and guardianship of property (wilaya 'ala al-nafs wa wilaya 'ala al-mal). The guardian in the context of this chapter is the wali, who has the right to exercise authority over both a person and the property of that person. Zahra and Malek (1998: 157) define wilaya over a person as 'the power to conduct and oversee the ward's personal affairs such as marriage, education, discipline, medical care, career prospects and the like'. Wilaya over property is the 'power to conduct, administer and conclude contracts and other legal acts relating to the property of the ward' (ibid.).

The division of custody into hadana and wilaya is distinctly gendered. While mothers cannot transgress this gender border, men may cross the limits established by the law, as we shall see later in this section. The *BPSR* devotes one full chapter, comprising 14 articles, to custody issues while the *LFR* has only a single article. Article 118 of the *LFR* specifies one important thing: permission is given to the judge to allow mothers to extend the period of their hadana over boys until they reach the age of nine and over girls until they reach the age of 11, if 'the judge believes that [the child's] interests will be served by that'. In this way, the *LFR* stretches the time limit of mothers' hadana by two years beyond that previously stipulated by article 391 of the *BPSR*.

The *BPSR* does not specify the criteria that make a mother eligible to care for her children while she is still married (article 380), but the situation is very different if the mother is divorced or widowed. The mother has to fulfil certain conditions (shurut ahliyyat al-hadana) to qualify as carer of her children. These requirements are given in article 382 of the *BPSR*: 'The hadina [carer] should be free (hurra) [as opposed to slave], adult (baligha), sane ('aqila), a woman of integrity (amina) and not apostate (ghayr murtadda).' Moreover, if, after her divorce or widowhood, the mother marries a stranger, that is, a non-muhram to the child, her right of hadana lapses. Article 383 also states that her right/duty of hadana lapses even if she concludes a subsequent marriage without consummation. However, she regains her right of hadana if her remarriage with the non-muhram partner is terminated.

This implies that the law categorizes mothers into two groups. Mothers who are still married qualify as carers by virtue of that marital status; the law does not question their qualifications. Married mothers are eligible carers not on their own merit but because their marital status suffices to certify them as carers. The law thus places the burden of examining the virtues of the carer mother on the husband's shoulders. As long as he supervises her, she is a qualified carer. Once the marriage is over, the mother falls into a different group and assessment of her eligibility as carer is transferred to a public institution. In other words, failing to qualify as a married woman automatically leads to questioning of the mother's qualities as a carer.

When a mother fails to qualify as carer, her right to hadana is transferred to other females by article 384. In this transference of hadana, the potential carer's proximity to the child's mother ranks higher than her proximity to the child's father. In particular, article 384 states that

> if the mother dies or if she marries a stranger [non-muhram to the child] or if she is not eligible for hadana, her right of care is transferred to the maternal grandmother of the child. If the latter is not alive or is ineligible, the hadana is conveyed to the paternal grandmother.

In other words, when the degree of proximity to the child is the same, the mother's side ranks higher than that of the father. The article goes on to transfer the child to his or her sisters. It makes a further distinction between sisters:

> The shaqiqa sister [sister from the same father and mother as the child] is more qualified than the sister who is not shaqiqa [sister sharing one parent only]. In such a case [hadana is transferred] to the sisters of the mother, then to the sisters of the father, then to the daughters of the child's sisters.

The article continues to list the other relatives who have the right of hadana over the child in a strict order.

One important observation is that the law does not make the female carer's religion a condition. Article 381 states that 'the non-Muslim carer (hadina dhummiyya) is eligible to care for the child the same way as a Muslim carer until the child understands religion (hatta ya'qal dinan) or until [it appears that] there is a danger of the child is becoming familiar [ya'laf] with a religion other than Islam.' This arrangement comes from the general principle of Islam that the Muslim man has the right to marry a non-Muslim woman, while Muslim women are not allowed to marry non-Muslim men.

Another aspect of hadana rights is the issue of travel. Articles 292 and 293 organize the rights of a divorced couple with regard to travel with their wards. The father should not travel with his child if the child is still under the mother's hadana (article 292). If the divorced mother marries a stranger (non-muhram to the child), the father is allowed to take his ward when travelling until the mother regains her hadana or until the next-in-line female carer is available. Article 293 states that the divorced mother needs permission from the father before travelling with her ward. However, if she wants to travel to her country (village or town), where her marriage contract was signed, she has the right to take the child with her without the consent of the father, even if her country (village or town) is far from the father's place of residence.

Thus, there are six criteria on the basis of which hadana is assigned:

1 The carer should be female.
2 When both carers' degree of proximity to the child is equal, the mother's side wins over the father's.

3   The carer who is more closely related to the child through both parents (that is, in both the maternal and paternal lines) ranks higher than one whose proximity stems from one parent.
4   All female carers should be muhramat (sg. muhram). In other words, the carer should not be eligible to marry the child in the future.
5   She does not need to be a Muslim to qualify as a carer.
6   She should not be married to a person who is not muhram in relation to the child.

The woman's hadana right is transferred to the child's agnates only when there are no females of the same degree of proximity, or if there are, they do not meet the established criteria. When hadana passes to the agnatic side, there is an interesting rank ordering. Whereas females are classified according to their degree of proximity to the child, with a clear preference for the mother's relatives, in the case of males the ranking is arranged according to the order of inheritance. Article 385 states that 'when no eligible female exists, or if they exist, do not fulfil the criteria, then the hadana is transferred to the male agnates ('asabat) according to the prescribed inheritance order. Hadana is transferred to the father, then to the grandfather, then the shaqiq [full] brother, then to the uncle on the father's side, then to the sons of the brother.' The article goes on to set out another principle: 'If there is more than one eligible [male], hadana is transferred to the person who is most righteous (aslahahum), [which, in this context, means the one who best serves the interest of the child], then to the most religious, then to the eldest.' Another principle is shared religion: 'It is conditional in the agnates' identification that they should be of the same religion. If the child has two brothers, of whom one is Muslim and the other is non-Muslim (dhummi), then the child is transferred to the Muslim.'

Thus, when hadana is transferred to the male agnates, the criteria are:

1   Order of inheritance
2   Degree of righteousness, religiosity or precedence by age
3   Quality of Muslim as opposed to non-Muslim
4   Status of muhram

It is remarkable that the male members from the mother's side (silat al-rahim) are denied the right of hadana unless there are no eligible agnates, whereas in the case of females the law alternates between females on the mother's side and females on the father's side with a specific preference for the mother's side. Only when there are no agnates ('asabat) or only ineligible agnates, such as dissolute (fasiq) or unreliable (ghayr ma'mun) persons, is hadana transferred to the silat al-rahim. And here, the line of transmission does not follow the same order of inheritance. The main criterion once again becomes the carer's proximity to the child's mother in the following order: 'the grandfather of the child, then the child's uncle, the son of the uncle, then the uncle of the mother' (article 386).

The case of Um Kamil, a maternal grandmother of two girls, who was entrusted with their hadana after their mother was divorced and married a non-muhram to the children, illustrates this aspect of the law. The children's father did not pay maintenance for them for seven years after the hadana was transferred to the grandmother. Lawyer Hala Anwar, who worked on the transference of the hadana, said the transfer was carried out without problems:

> When the divorced mother intended to marry again, I requested the court to transfer hadana to their grandmother before the mother's remarriage took place. This is my usual strategy to make sure that the children will remain accessible to their mother. By so doing, I block the legal route for the fathers, who tend to make trouble for their ex-wives once they know that they intend to remarry. They often send threats to their ex-wives, saying that access to their children will be endangered if they remarry. In legal terms, I file a case to transfer hadana to the grandmother with solid excuses such as the mother's absence, which appear convincing to the qadi. Usually, I get away with this, because, when informed, fathers do not oppose my request as long as I do not demand that they pay children's maintenance. They get upset only when they find out that their ex-wife has remarried. At that point, they cannot withdraw their previous agreement to let the maternal grandmother care for their children.

This strategy sheds light on the lawyers' awareness of the common practice of fathers; they invoke their rights regarding their children only when they are confronted with their financial duties. Some fathers use such action as a threat to prevent the carer from seeking the children's nafaqa through the Shari'a court. For others, filing a case for custodianship is the only way to deal with their growing financial difficulties. In other words, when mothers or carers claim the children's maintenance, fathers are faced with a difficult alternative: either to pay nafaqa in cash or to take their children back. The latter choice is viewed as more economically viable.

While the girls, Asil and Riham, were in their grandmother's care, their mother was able to support them financially because she had remarried a well-paid Palestinian. After the outbreak of the second intifada, the stepfather lost his job and the grandmother needed financial help. Therefore, she found herself forced to confront the father with his financial responsibilities. Um Kamil asked the mukhtar (clan leader) to mediate between her and the father, but he was unsuccessful because the father was also unemployed. This dilemma forced her to sue the father for nafaqa. During the hearing, the father denied the grandmother's right to continue her hadana and sued to bring the children back into his custodianship. The grandmother said that was not what she wanted; she demanded a little financial support to meet the growing expenses of the children. However, the father insisted that the children should be returned to him because 'it is a shame that the daughters of the al-Gazali family should be brought up by an alien family'. The grandmother replied in surprise, 'I do not understand why you forgot your children for several years and it is only now, when I have asked you to help me, that you have remembered they are from dar al-Gazali [the al-Gazali family].'

Asil, at the age of 11, was old enough to be placed in men's custody, while eight-year-old Riham was still under her grandmother's hadana. However, the judge tried to convince the grandmother to give them both up:

> Eventually, they will be taken from you, so why should you cause yourself more pain? . . . We don't want to separate the sisters from each other, it is better for them to live together under their father's protection. You should feel happy because the burden will be taken off your shoulders and put on their father's.

Then he told the father: 'For several years, you did not even thank Um Kamil for caring for your children. Now, you have to compensate her for her good care.' Towards the end, the judge turned to the mukhtar: 'Are you a real mukhtar or playing this role as a hobby? The mukhtar should be able to act as a man; you should have obtained financial compensation for this old woman. Otherwise, what is the benefit of your being mukhtar?' This statement by the judge implies certain assumptions about the role of a mukhtar. The judge reproached him for not acting according to what would be expected from a reasonable mukhtar.

Finally, the judge ruled that the children should go to their father. He did not say that Riham should continue to be in her grandmother's care, nor did he wait for Um Kamil to give her consent. After the two parties had left, the judge asked the mukhtar to stay in the courtroom. He told him that the court would postpone implementing the judgment until the father had paid something to Um Kamil to pacify her. The mukhtar promised to pressure the father.

In this case, the judge attempted to find a practical solution by not following the exact wording of the law, because that would have resulted in the sisters being separated, which in his view would not have been in their interest. All the parties involved left the court with some gain: the father received both daughters without being forced to pay maintenance, the daughters continued to live together; and the grandmother was granted financial compensation.

The law also regulates the status of maharim (sg. muhram) with regard to guardianship. Article 386 states:

> If the child is a male, the female cousins from the mother's and father's sides have no rights of hadana. Equally, if the child is female, no cousin from either side has rights of hadana. In cases where the female child has nobody but her cousin, the qadi should check whether this cousin is righteous. If he is, the qadi will give her to him. Otherwise, the qadi should find a female [non-relative] who is trustworthy and a woman of integrity to give the child to.

This is in conformity with Islamic law, which allows marriage between cousins. In the framework of patrilineality and in light of the political economy of family relations, this may reflect a preference for marriage among cousins on the father's side. By favouring paternal cousins, the law solidifies ties within the extended patrilineal kin group and thus defines this unit as the significant locus of solidarity.

Two questions were asked in section 7.1: Why are asymmetrical criteria applied to men and women in arranging hadana rights? Why is the order of inheritance applied to men while the order of kinship proximity is applied to women? Samara (1987: 373) suggests that women are preferred over men in matters of hadana because they are compassionate, soft, delicate and patient. He adds that the order of hadana is determined according to the degree of proximity of the carer to the mother because grandmothers from the mother's side appear to be more compassionate than grandmothers from the father's side. Although Samara describes the madhahib's positions regarding the issue of hadana, he makes clear his own preference for male and female agnates over uterine kin:

> the basis and rules of Shari'a have always preferred the agnates in matter related to inheritance and wilaya. . . . Shari'a never favoured the uterine kin. Therefore, those who favour mothers' relatives in granting hadana do that without valid reason.
>
> (Samara 1987: 373)

In particular, he declares his agreement with the opinion of Ibn Taymiyya, who maintained that

> the mother is favoured in hadana over the father not because of her lineage but because she is female. If her lineage is preferred, then all men and women from her side would be favoured over men and women from the father's side. As the males from the mother's side have not been indicated, then neither should the females from her side.
>
> (cited in Samara 1987: 373)

Ibn Taymiyya's analysis and disagreement with other madhahib appears consistent with the logic of law, which clearly prefers patrilineality in matters related to inheritance, lineage (nasab) and guardianship.

In any legal arrangement, rights and duties are distributed according to the logic and philosophy of the lawmaker. In our case, the woman's access to her children is perceived as a duty rather than a right. The law arranges hadana in a way that stresses the duty of the carer vis-à-vis the rights of the child. Here, the best interests (rights) of the child appear to take precedence over those of the carer. In other words, hadana does not involve claims by the carer as to decisions related to the future of the child; that falls in the domain of guardianship. In guardianship, the arrangement is turned into the duty of the child and the right of the guardian; in other words, the child has no right to refuse the guardianship of his agnates.

For example, a nine-year-old female child cannot refuse a marriage arranged for her by her guardian. Male agnates have different relations with their wards than children do with their female carers. Agnates have a hierarchal relation with the children in that they can act as their guardians. Because guardianship is arranged according to inheritance order, when agnates assume the role of carers, they are chosen in the same order.

Furthermore, females do not need to be Muslims to claim their right of hadana, whereas this is a precondition in the case of males. This privileged position enjoyed by non-Muslim mothers (as carers) is not due to their higher status, but rather to the prohibition imposed on them not to exercise guardianship, whereas men who are ordinary custodians need to be Muslims to do so.[1]

One more point needs to be made about the gender difference in matters relating to parenthood: the law does not question the guardianship rights of the father, no matter what qualification he may possess. He can exercise his guardianship in matters related to the child's marriage, future and fortune. It is only when the father squanders the wealth of his child that the judge may assign someone else to preserve those assets – but without changing the guardianship of the child's person (article 425). This stands in contrast with what is demanded by the law from mothers, who have to be qualified as carers. In other words, mothers are initially presumed to be unqualified, whereas fathers are considered to be qualified by definition. This gender-based double standard reveals asymmetries that affect the behaviour of men and women during litigation. As we shall see in the following case, while women struggle to hold men responsible for their legally assigned financial duties, men can misuse the rights assigned to them by virtue of this gendered distribution. Judges, for their part, do not question this particular legal arrangement; rather, they expect both parties to behave decently, that is, to fulfil their duties as the quid pro quo that legitimates their rights. When a father does not do so and instead misuses the law for nefarious purposes, judges use the law relating to the father's eligibility to deny him custody over the children. The case of Adala, a 35-year-old primary school teacher, in which the deputy qadi al-qudah personally intervened with advice that enabled a mother to frustrate the father's attempt to use custody as a bargaining chip in a nafaqa case, is one example of this.

Adala, who had recently been divorced from Ziyad when I met her, was teaching at an UNRWA school, so she was earning a salary higher than that at a government school. Ziyad had left her with 10 children, ranging in age from 3 to 15 years, and had married another school teacher. After the divorce, Adala filed for nafaqa for her children, and the judge ruled that Ziyad should pay JD 25 for each child, which added up to more than 60% of his salary. Because Ziyad was a government employee, the court could deduct the nafaqa directly from his income. After a few months, in order to put pressure on Adala to drop her claim, Ziyad filed for custody over the two eldest girls, aged 14 and 15. Adala was worried that her daughters would become servants in his household and opposed the transfer of their custody to Ziyad.

She hired Khalid al-Tayyib, who is reputed to be one of the best lawyers in Gaza, and he decided to make Ziyad's ineligibility as a custodian the core of his case. He told qadi al-Karmi, 'The father is not eligible to be a custodian because he has beaten his daughter twice in the street. The most disgraceful act was when he took off her headscarf and uncovered his daughter's hair. Samahir [the eldest daughter] is a mature Muslim woman and it is forbidden for her hair to be seen in public ['awra]. That was not the act of a protective father.'

He produced witnesses to back up this statement.

Ziyad's lawyer interpreted the incident differently. He told the court, 'My client's daughter is 15 years old now and she has reached the age at which the custody of men is needed. I agree with my colleague that Ziyad has beaten his daughter in public twice but he did not exceed the limits of disciplining children. The beating did not cause anguish. This is part of his role as a father.' With regard to the headscarf, the lawyer said, 'If her hair became visible during the quarrel, that happened accidentally, of course.'

After hearing testimony over several sessions, the judge denied custody of the two daughters to their father. He based his judgment on article 386 of the *BPSR*.[2]

The father then took his case to the Court of Appeal, which overturned the judgment and referred the case to qadi Muhammad al-Ansari, who ordered Adala to hand over Samahir and Ilham to their father. Citing 'articles 16, 18, 38, 39, 46, 48, 81 and 83 of the *Code of Islamic Jurisprudence* and article 391 of the *Law of Family Rights*', he said, 'the daughters are of age to be placed in men's custody' and outlined the factors in the case on which he had based his judgment:

We took into consideration the following facts:

1   The father's right of custody should not be jeopardized by the fact that he did not file a legal case earlier.
2   The witnesses have testified that the father is an ordinary, reliable and protective Muslim. Therefore, he is eligible to take his daughters under his supervision.
3   The testimony concerning Ziyad's beating of his daughter seems to have been magnified by some witnesses.
4   The most important thing is that his daughters have become mature (baligh) and need the guardianship of men.

Khalid al-Tayyib's next step was a semi-formal one, of bringing the matter to the attention of the deputy qadi al-qudah.[3] The lawyer made an appointment for Adala to meet him, and at the appointed time, she and six of her children went to the deputy qadi al-qudah's office, accompanied by Khalid al-Tayyib. The lawyer explained to the deputy qadi al-qudah that Ziyad was not seeking custody because he wanted to care for his two daughters; rather, his action was intended to pressure the mother to withdraw her demand for nafaqa. The deputy qadi al-qudah then said he would ask qadi al-Karmi to reassess the case 'because, obviously, he is very familiar with it and his judgment was more in line with the Shari'a than the second one'. Then he advised the mother to get all her children to participate in the following strategy:

> When the hearing takes place, let your daughters ask him to take them all. On our part, we will put pressure on him to take all the children. He has remarried and his wife is unlikely to accept your 'army', fearing they would spoil her house and life, especially your youngest 'monsters'. They are not hers. The best thing we can do is to send them to her and give her an unpleasant surprise. She has to get mad. This depends on your children's behaviour. Once they are there, they should be noisy, break plates, play football indoors and switch the TV on and off all the time. In sum, they have to drive the wife crazy. Your children will be returned to you the next day.

Accordingly, on the day of the hearing, the two daughters told qadi al-Karmi that they would like very much to live with their father but did not want to be separated from their brothers and sisters. The judge told Ziyad, 'Now you have an excellent opportunity to take all your children to live with you. Your ex-wife does not object to that and the children want to live with you, so what is your decision?' The father had no option but to accept all the children. Adala sent them to their father's house the same day; once there, they made a nuisance of themselves with their unruly behaviour, and within an hour they were returned to their mother's house.

As a quid pro quo for keeping her children, Adala also accepted the deputy qadi al-qudah's instruction to reduce their nafaqa so that Ziyad would not be left with only 40% of his salary. She decided that it would be enough to receive JD 100 instead of JD 250.

The law assumes that both agnatic and maternal kin are acting in good faith, but in practice the agnates generally try to use their legal precedence to further their personal interests. In this situation, the role of the judge is to mediate between the spirit of the law and the manifestation of self-interest, while simultaneously considering the rights of the weakest party, that is, the child; this, irrespective of gender asymmetry. There is a dialectic relationship between the ethical requirements of Islam and the divinely sanctioned principles of gender asymmetry, which did not appear to be the main premise of Adala's husband.

7.2 Hadana in practice

As in the previous two chapters, the court cases presented here reveal the discrepancy between law and practice. They show the various ways in which negotiations in the Shari'a courts proceed. The main point is that while the law considers that litigants should work in good faith, men do not do so. The judges, who do not question the right of men to wilaya, find it difficult to defend fathers' positions because they violate the 'division of labour' prescribed in the law, which grants fathers wilaya but in return requires that they fulfil certain responsibilities.

Various complex webs of relations determine the outcome of a hadana case. Such cases only end up in the Shari'a court after all other avenues for resolving the conflict have failed, indicating deep disagreement and bitterness between the spouses and their respective networks. Socio-economic factors are also important elements in deciding the fate of the children, since hadana is bifurcated, with physical care being given by the mother's side of the family and the maintenance cost being the responsibility of the father's side of the family. Instead of paying children's nafaqa, some fathers (or agnates) prefer to raise them in their own homes, considering that to be more economical. When the carers are widows, they face additional pressures. If they want to keep their children with them, they have to maintain a positive relationship with their in-laws, for the law by itself does not guarantee them hadana. Some in-laws file suits against mothers just because of their embittered relations. Young mothers with a few children would find it difficult to marry again, or would probably be forced to give up the children eventually for legal or social reasons, so they are told by their own families to give up the children to the in-laws (see also Moors 1995). Furthermore, extra children in the household would increase the expenses of the mother's natal family. Also, social disapproval, based on the allocation of rights and duties among agnates and the mothers' relatives by Islamic law, would make the mother's family reluctant to cover the expenses of a child belonging to another family.

The pressures that widows face when they want to keep their children with them, especially when a substantial amount of money is involved, is illustrated by the case of Salha. The case is also special because the 34-year-old widow, who worked as a cleaner in a hair salon, succeeded in bending customary practice to her advantage. I met Salha on 29 June 2002 in the waiting room of the Gaza Shari'a courts. She was an orphan from a poor family and her husband, a distant relative (qaraba min ba'id), married her with almost no dower. 'I got only a gold ring,' she told me. She and her husband, a taxi driver, succeeded in building a small house in the al-Shati' camp, but the husband died in a traffic accident before repaying the home loan. However, he had taken out life insurance, and the assurance company promised a relatively high payout to his family.

Salha had four children: Rima (14), Sa'ad (12), Sami (10) and Muna (7). Their paternal uncle took the children from her so that he could claim the insurance payout as their guardian. In addition, he wanted to marry Salha's eldest daughter to his son. Taking advantage of Salha's weak position as a poor widow with no family to support her, he threatened that if she claimed the children, she would be barred from seeing them again. As stated earlier, article 391 of the *BPSR* allows divorced or widowed mothers to keep their children until the boys reach the age of seven and the girls the age of nine. The *LFR* applied in Gaza enables the judge to let mothers extend the period of their hadana over boys until they reach the age of nine and girls until they reach the age of 11, if 'the qadi believes that their interest will be served thereby'. If the mother remarries, the law transfers the children to other female relatives in the order given in section 1 of this chapter. Thus, Salha was legally permitted to keep Sami and Muna with her if the judge agreed.

She entered the courtroom during an interval between two cases, introduced herself to the judge and explained her dilemma: 'I know that the law does not serve my case, . . . but I will not give up my children.' She repeated her determination several times. Then, without allowing the judge to respond or to give her permission to continue, she started crying piteously and told him,

> I gave birth to my children through Cæsarean operations. I watered them with my tears and love. For many years, I protected them from the slightest draught. Now, their uncle has taken them from me after their father's death. Isn't it enough for me to lose their father? What justice on earth is this?

The judge listened in silence and then tried to convince her to negotiate with her brother-in-law. However, Salha continued to plead with the judge to intervene:

> You are the father of Muslims, I am your daughter in the eyes of God. What will you tell Allah in the next life when he asks you about my orphans and me? They lost their father, they will lose his insurance compensation and now they have lost me. These orphans will work as servants in their uncle's house. Is that Allah's justice?

Playing on the judge's identity as a man, as a symbol of justice, as a father, and as a protector, she continued her appeal, emphasizing her vulnerability, but gracefully, using words and phrases that would make the judge feel ashamed not to help her. After a while, the judge asked her to return home and send her family's mukhtar to consult with him (in this context, mukhtar means leader of the clan). The next day, the mukhtar went and sat with the judge. They agreed to resolve the dispute between Salha and her brother in-law at the mag'ad (the common house where the hamula meetings take place). The judge used his spare time to intervene. For one week, he kept up communication with the family's powerful figures, including the mukhtar, who in this particular case was also the mukhtar of Salha's husband's family (they were from the same hamula).

Although the judge knew that the case was eligible to be heard in the court, he did not choose that formal route, perhaps because he thought that the delicacy of the issue required informal intervention. Involving a mukhtar and the attempts to resolve the dispute outside of the court were obviously not part of the judge's formal duties. However, as an inhabitant of Salha's camp, he felt obliged (and perhaps was delighted) to play the respected role of rescuer, even informally. His action was in conformity with Islamic law, which, as Rosen (1989) points out, favours the injured party over the one that inflicts injury. Similar behaviour is observed in other contexts. For example, in Morocco, the judge often pushes the responsibility towards 'those highly localized personnel and procedures. . ., [that is,] customary practices on which relationships themselves depend for their coherence' (ibid.: 37).

Holding the uncle responsible through the hamula was a way of exerting pressure on him through the collectivity. The judge might also have wanted to advance his influence in the camp, a trend that has become more visible in post-Oslo Palestine, in which not only conventional political parties enhance their influence, and thus legitimacy, in the public sphere through such interventions, but also the religious establishment as individual figures as well as institutionally. On another level, using the community to exert pressure on the accused party is an ordinary practice of administrative superiors (see Moore 1978). Eventually, through mechanisms of negotiation, persuasion and agreement, a solution was reached that allowed Salha to keep her children and even obliged the brother-in-law to pay their nafaqa to her.

The negotiation within the mag'ad is a collective endeavour involving the active participation of male clan members. Each participant who has been allowed into the mag'ad has the right and duty to play a part and to propose a solution.[4] The mukhtar and the most authoritative figures in the community (who are normally the eldest) have the authority to speak the last words. However, the consent of the mag'ad members is the main legitimation of the decision. The accused person, not wanting to be marginalized and rejected, accepts the sanction ordered by the mag'ad members in order to retain his reputation, honour, property and, above all, membership of the hamula, without which he cannot survive. Thus, the mag'ad functions as an instrument for stabilizing social peace and avoiding a feud when other mechanisms fail. The mukhtar's role and the mechanism of mag'ad decision-making bring solace instead of adversity. If the mukhtar (as representative of the collective) proposes a solution, then the first consideration of the implicated member is how to preserve his own honour and reputation within the community. Implicated members of the clan or family do not lose face by obeying the mukhtar's decisions; on the contrary, their acceptance of the mukhtar's decision is viewed by the hamula members as an indication of loyalty, grace and genuine membership.

Customary law, as an institution, has stronger influence than formal law does. It operates in a context where mechanisms of negotiation, persuasion and agreement are acknowledged more than coercion and force are, especially in the Palestinian situation, where coercion is often linked with the brutal practices of the Israeli occupation. Moreover, people who are involved in mediation based on customary law are members of the same community or hamula. For example, the mukhtar is often identified as the authorized person in matters relating to 'private' life. The hamula members grow up with an awareness of his status and authority; he is the one who leads social events, visits the hamula members during feasts and makes decisions about the hamula's collective concerns.

There are two types of mukhtars: the leader of a hamula, as we have seen, and one who has been officially selected for that rank. The official rank was initially introduced during the last decades of the Ottoman Empire to designate the representative of a particular community, village or neighbourhood. He is responsible for, among other things, providing the authorities with information regarding the personal status of inhabitants. He can also provide the people in his area with certificates needed for formal processes. An official mukhtar also plays a vital role in keeping the peace in his neighbourhood with regard to conflicts between families and clans, especially in communities structured in hamayil. He maintains his position by sharing the celebrations and sorrows of the community, attending weddings or funerals and protecting vulnerable members. It is also said that the title of official mukhtar is passed from father to eldest son, which would indicate monopolization of the post by a specific family or hamula.[5]

The official mukhtar has to be agreed upon by both the community and the state. This does not involve a 'democratic' election; rather, a consensus has to be reached among the inhabitants, otherwise the mukhtar cannot fulfil his duties. The mukhtar receives the PA's approval and is given an official stamp to certify documents. Despite their diminished authority in recent decades, as well as the processes of urbanization and modernization, which imply new modes of governance, the role of official makhatirs remains vital in some areas such as the Shari'a courts. They still constitute the formal authority on which the Shari'a courts rely to certify that no religious prohibition precludes the marriage of a couple and so give them shar'i permission ('adam mumana'a) to marry.

In the Salha case presented earlier, where children became pawns in an uncle's attempt to gain control over wealth, the judge discussed the matter with the mukhtar so that communal pressure could be brought to bear on the uncle. On the other hand, he had to take into consideration that the uncle's intention to arrange a marriage between paternal cousins (the children of two brothers) was in accordance with the representation of agnatic precedence. Therefore, while recognizing agnatic pre-eminence in principle, the judge subordinated the way he dealt with the case to precepts of justice such as the children's manifest interest. When the uncle misused his agnatic rights, the judge sanctioned him by obliging him to pay the child's nafaqa. Thus, the judge emphasized that agnatic rights also entail agnatic duties.

When money is involved, in-laws frequently try to use the law to take it away from women. When possible, judges try to prevent this outcome. The case of Nisrin, who ended up in court after caring for her children for five years following a divorce and the subsequent killing of her ex-husband by Israeli forces, is another example of such a case. Nisrin's husband, who was unemployed, had left her with two young children without paying their maintenance. She and her family had decided there would be no point in filing a case for nafaqa since he would probably not be able to pay it. She lived with her mother and brothers, and found a job in a clothing factory. While at work, Nisrin used to leave her children with her mother. She managed her life well because the factory was close to where she lived, so she could see her children during the one-hour lunch break.

After her ex-husband was shot dead by Israeli soldiers, he was considered a martyr and the Ministry of Social Affairs and other charity organizations made quite a large amount of money available to the family.[6] The martyr's father and brothers then tried to take the children away from Nisrin in order to legitimize their status as a martyr's family and thus receive the money. When Nisrin refused to give the children to them, her in-laws sued for custody. They called witnesses to testify that she worked in a factory from dawn to night and thus could not look after the children. They also claimed that the mother's family did not like the children, that they were kept playing outside the house, which endangered their lives in view of the intifada.

The judge asked the in-laws whether they had paid anything for the children during the past five years. When they replied in the negative, he told them, 'Why did you not think of the interests of the children before your son was killed? And why is it only when there is money involved that you thought of the children's interests?' After listening to the witnesses, whose testimony proved to be weak, the judge dismissed the in-laws' application for custody, saying that their right to custodianship would be legitimate only if the mother remarried.

This hypocritical recourse by the in-laws to agnatic precedence in order to gain material benefit is a recurrent form of behaviour; children are instrumentalized in these disputes. However, the judges seem to be consistent in their ethical stance. Unlike in the case of the grandmother Um Kamil (outlined in section 7.2), where the grandmother had no financial resources, Nisrin's ability to support her offspring convinced the judge of her capacity to serve the interests of her children.

Cases like these came up frequently in the courts after the eruption of the second intifada, during which many young men were martyred. Most were either single or newly married. When money is involved, the children of martyrs often become implicated in the competition between the mother and her in-laws over who is the legitimate representative of the martyr's family. Usually, the martyr's parents immediately take the children from their mother and send the mother back to her parents. Some arrange a marriage between the widow and the martyr's brother. At the Ministry of Social Affairs, social workers complain about these contests. The money is often given to the martyr's father on the assumption that he will share it out fairly, which usually does not happen. The problem is widespread enough so that the Centre for Women's Empowerment in Gaza has published a booklet focusing on the social experiences of women with their in-laws after the martyrdom of their husbands.

We saw earlier how Salha, when facing a custody problem, appealed to the judge not in his capacity as a judge, but as a community leader, a person who could use his informal authority to put Islamic law on the right track and thus maintain a balance between rights and duties. The following case demonstrates what happens when a judge is approached in his capacity as a judge. How, then, does he strike a balance between rights and duties? How does he act to protect the best interests of a child?

In trying to protect women when they feel that their rights have been harmed, judges sometimes find their task made difficult not only by those inflicting the harm but also by those whose interests the court is trying to protect. One such case was that of Um Hashim, who was well known during the first intifada as an activist and is still admired for the capacity she showed for organizing demonstrations and informal schooling at that time. A divorced mother of seven children, she found herself in court, facing a custody battle over two of her daughters.

132 *The articulation of gendered parenthood*

Um Hashim, who was 50 years old at the time of the hearing, had been divorced from her cousin Abu Hashim for two years. She lives in the al-Shati' camp with her children. Her eldest daughter trained as a gynaecologist in the former Soviet Union and now lives in Amman (Jordan) with her husband. The second daughter was 21 years old at the time of the case and had recently graduated from a university in Gaza. She was working as a teacher at a secondary school. Um Hashim had two working sons, one a police officer and the other a waiter in a restaurant. The rest of her children were still in school. Two of them were girls ages 14 and 16. The youngest child was a nine-year-old boy.

The crisis in Um Hashim's marriage started in 1996 when the sewing factory owned by Abu Hashim had to close down because of the Israeli blockade. Abu Hashim went through a serious depression, which resulted in his becoming a drug addict. Um Hashim attempted to save the family from further economic hardship by preparing special meals for the wedding celebrations of middle-class families. She succeeded in paying for the children's education but could not meet the growing expense of Abu Hashim's drug addiction. She took him to Egypt for clinical therapy and spent months (and money) in vain. He became violent and started bringing his friends to the house to smoke drugs and drink alcohol. The financial problem was worsened by his continuous demands for money to buy drugs. Eventually, they divorced in 2000, but their disputes did not cease. The latest incident concerned Rim, the daughter who worked as a teacher. Abu Hashim wanted her to give him her salary, but Um Hashim refused. This coincided with the daughter's betrothal, for which her father, as the wali, had to give his approval. Abu Hashim refused to do so and instead filed a suit for custody over Rim and her two teenage sisters.

When Um Hashim appeared in court, she explained the case to the judge, who was aware of the circumstances as he lives in the same camp. He told her, 'I can act as your daughter's wali if the groom is kafu' and if Abu Hashim refused the marriage without legitimate reason.' He summoned Abu Hashim to appear in the court. The following colloquy took place on 30 April 2002:

JUDGE: (ADDRESSING ABU HASHIM): As you know, Mas'ud has asked for your daughter's hand. Why have you refused?
ABU HASHIM: I don't want to marry her to him. Isn't that my right?
JUDGE: It is not an absolute right. Allah gave you this right to protect and safeguard your daughter's interests, not to damage her future.
ABU HASHIM: Sir, I am 52 years old and this is the first time in my life that I have entered a court building. It is shameful that I must come to court to defend my rights as a father. Does Islamic law permit you to turn my daughter against me? Does Islam order us to allow our daughters to decide whom to marry? If that is what you think, it is not surprising that our society is falling into chaos. Our judges have become as corrupt as others. I would prefer to die rather than be forced to accept such shame.
JUDGE: Instead of sitting here complaining to me, you should go and enquire about the man who wants to marry her. If you find him a good man, kind,

with good manners, from a good family, having a good profession, then you should bless this marriage. But let me warn you, if you do not prove that the man is not kafu', I will act as her wali and marry her to him.[7]

ABU HASHIM: That would be better for me than to be forced to accept someone who was chosen by her and her mother.[8]

JUDGE: Look, this is the time of utmost happiness in her life. It would not be nice for her to marry without your consent. That would be bad for both of you. It would also be bad for your daughter's image in the eyes of her in-laws. If I were you, I would go and felicitate her and say 'mabruk' [congratulations]. Believe me, it would be your victory. Let me tell you one more thing. She is 21 years old; this may be her last chance to marry. No-one looks for a woman to marry of her age. She has become old. All her age group have half a dozen children now. I am sure you don't want to see her become an 'anis [spinster]. One more tip: your positive response will help you in your custody case over the other girls, you can be sure of that.

The shifting strategy of the judge from threat to persuasion did not work. Abu Hashim insisted that he would not accept the marriage because it had not been his choice. Instead, he decided to continue with the custody case. The judge knew that the actual reason for Abu Hashim's inflexibility was that he wanted to get control over his daughter's salary, but he did not confront him, preferring to continue with persuasion. He adjourned the hearing until the following week. Meanwhile, the judge advised Um Hashim to be wise and reach a compromise with her husband. 'Don't jeopardize Rim's future if the issue is about money,' the judge told her. Therefore, Um Hashim started searching for a suitable mediator.

She was unable to obtain support from her hamula. Because she was Abu Hashim's cousin, the hamula members were relatives of both parties. Moreover, she believed that they were hostile to her because, 'they consider me liberal because I sent my eldest daughter to study abroad. They have hated me since the days of the first intifada because I used to work for the DFLP women's group.[9] They say that this group is communist. They were happy that my marriage ended in disaster.'

Therefore, Um Hashim decided to use her social and political network to materialize her interests and sought help from her DFLP group. She was still on good terms with them even though she had left the group a long time ago. A DFLP representative went to Abu Hashim and bargained with him over the 'price' of his acceptance.

Realizing that he would not be able to get his daughter's salary, Abu Hashim demanded her dower instead. However, Um Hashim refused: 'This is my daughter's property; nobody should take it from her, especially a drug-addicted father.' She was in a dilemma. She did not want to lose a good son-in-law, but she also wanted her daughter to have izwa when signing the marriage contract so that her dignity would be maintained in front of her in-laws.[10] That dignity would be undermined if the father did not appear at the daughter's wedding ceremony.

The father's presence is the daughter's symbolic capital before the groom's family. No matter what is going on inside the family, the father's attendance and blessings are important. She told Abu Hashim that she would give him $300 if he agreed to be sensible. The deal was that Abu Hashim would receive the whole dower (JD 3,000) during the marriage ceremony but would take only the amount they had agreed on. However, Abu Hashim did not keep his word. Instead of taking $300, he took $1,000.

At the next court session, Um Hashim appeared before the judge, shouting and yelling: 'Is this the behaviour of a father? Instead of giving her a gift, he stole her dower to buy drugs!' The judge tried to calm her: 'Money comes and goes; the main issue is your daughter's dignity. You saved her face in front of her in-laws. Her marriage contract is signed and everything else should be secondary.' Um Hashim left the court in an angry mood: 'These are just words; they will not buy gold for my daughter. I am the person who will pay the stolen $1,000, nobody else.'

Abu Hashim continued his attempts to blackmail Um Hashim for as much money as he could get from her. He continued his custody suit, insisting on using the court and manipulating the law to achieve his goals. Um Hashim did not have the ability to pay for a lawyer, and her personality was so excitable that lawyers found it difficult to interact with her. Even the female lawyer Hala Anwar, who defended poor women free of charge as part of her work with a Palestinian human rights organization, refused to represent her because of her quick temper. The judge asked Um Hashim to produce witnesses to prove Abu Hashim's ineligibility for custodianship, but she failed to do so because her hamula was standing by Abu Hashim.

Um Hashim requested the judge to listen to her daughters' testimony. He agreed, but she failed to appear in court with them because they had examinations. The judge wanted to help her and told her: 'If you had phoned me, then we could have made it a formal postponement. But absence without justification, in addition to its being manifestation of disrespect for the court, has allowed Abu Hashim to win points over you.' When she appeared at the fourth court session, she was accompanied by her younger daughters. The judge asked her to sit silently because he knew from his previous experience that she became upset very quickly. He then questioned witnesses about Abu Hashim's fitness to have wilaya over the daughters.

JUDGE: Do you view Abu Hashim as being eligible for custody? Before you answer, you have to understand that eligibility means that the father is reliable and capable. I mean a man with good manners, of good morality and good behaviour.

UM HASHIM (INTERRUPTING): Tell the judge in the name of Allah whether Abu Hashim prays or not.

JUDGE (WHO WAS UPSET BY THE INTERRUPTION): We are not interested in knowing how faithful he is to God. (Then he turned to the witness.) Where do you think the interest of the daughters lies, is it in being with their mother or with their father?

WITNESS: It is in being with both, the father and the mother.
JUDGE (IRRITATED): I don't want ideal answers; you know that they are divorced. From your knowledge of Um Hashim and Abu Hashim, who is the one who can best ensure the daughters' well-being?
UM HASHIM (INTERRUPTING AGAIN): Tell the judge whether Abu Hashim is working or not, tell him whether he has a penny in his pocket or not. (Then she turned to the judge.) You know that their father is an addict, so how can you forget this? The girls are your responsibility. If you give them to him, then Allah will punish you. Anyway, nobody can take them from me. You can kill me before you decide to give them to him.

The judge was exasperated by her constant interruptions: 'This case is the longest I have ever experienced! Since February, we have been trying to finish it and every day another aspect appears. It is like mushrooms; one case produces endless cases.' Then he turned to Um Hashim:

> I gave you many opportunities to prove that he is ineligible, but you did not even appear in court for the last three sessions, nor did you bring your own witnesses. I can't help you if you do not know how to help yourself. The only skill you have is in interrupting the normal proceedings of the court. Even lawyers are unable to deal with you because of your bad temper and lack of respect for court proceedings. Your old conflict with Abu Hashim cannot be resolved here, nor are we here to allow you to take revenge. If you speak again, I will order you to leave the courtroom immediately.

People in the courtroom (lawyers who were waiting for the next case, police officers and friends of Um Hashim) started pacifying both the judge and Um Hashim. Some told her quietly that she was losing her case because of her anxiety and loud voice. Others directed their words to the judge, urging him to calm down and accept human weakness: 'She is just a woman, what else can you do with her than be patient? Allah will reward you for that.'

The judge cooled down, perhaps due to her having become calm and the prayerful appeal. However, Abu Hashim continued his criticism of Um Hashim:

> She is not a good mother. Yes, I am still unemployed like half the population of Gaza, but ask her with whom she was working and how she brought us money when we were together. She was working with Abu Mansur (a well-known corrupt leader in the security forces) and that is why I want to protect my daughters. I don't want them to be spoiled.

At that, Um Hashim lost her temper completely. She rushed around the long table separating her from Abu Hashim and started flailing at him with her handbag. She slapped his face and shouted at him: 'Never talk about my honour in this way; I will kill you if you repeat that. You deserve to be thrown into the garbage.' She kept repeating these words while beating him.

The judge, lawyers and even the police officers were taken aback. The judge shouted at her to go and stand near the door. He became very upset: 'This is an illegal act. Nobody can do this in my courtroom, but what can I do with you, you are a woman. If you were a man, I would immediately put you in jail.' He then adjourned the hearing. People around him started soothing him, describing the drama as unprecedented. Lawyer Hala Anwar said that Abu Hashim was not a man since he had let the incident happen: 'How can he accept such an act from a woman?'

Um Hashim left the court without even looking at the judge. During the two following sessions, witnesses continued testifying in favour of Abu Hashim. That was to be expected since they were his cousins. The judge had no option but to order Um Hashim to give her daughters back to Abu Hashim. Later, Um Hashim appealed to the Court of Appeal, which returned the case to the judge, asking him to enquire further into the eligibility of the father. Um Hashim visited the judge in his house, which (as mentioned earlier) is located in the same camp where she lives. He suggested to her that she produce a certificate to prove Abu Hashim's addiction. She travelled to Egypt and obtained the certificate; the trip cost her 2,000 New Israeli Shekels, which she had to borrow because it was beyond her financial capacity. She commented: 'If there were fairness in the court, I would not be paying this much to prove my case.'

The case finally ended with the judge declaring that Abu Hashim did not meet the criteria of a protective father. He then expressed pleasure over Um Hashim's final victory: 'We need to maintain the well-being of the daughters. And that is difficult with an unemployed, addicted and morally corrupt father.' I interviewed the judge a few weeks later and asked him about his perception of Um Hashim. Astonishingly, he showed admiration for her defence of her daughters: 'This woman is extraordinary, she is worth 10 men. She fought for her daughters until the end with grace and dignity. Although she made stupid mistakes, she has done a good job keeping her females protected.'

7.3 Conclusion

This chapter has reviewed how the gender-based double standard of hadana is articulated in the text, which reveals asymmetries that also appear in the behaviour of mothers and fathers during litigation. Gendered parenthood is institutionalized by family law and various ideologically driven people and institutions in society. It is symbolically protected by its long-lasting connection with Islam and by the historical construction of mothers' identity as carers and fathers' identity as guardians. However, approaching hadana in its social working puts people's strategies instead of the text at centre stage (see Griffiths 1992: 157). It requires taking into account the mothers' and fathers' counter- or consensual actions, and it needs to include the ways in which the interplay between the text and people is mediated through judges. Such an approach also needs to investigate how these various actors perceive the law and to what extent gender, class and religious perceptions influence these processes.

Chapter 1 referred to the duality of order and change in the social working of law. Order (law) always exists, but it never takes over. It leaves gaps of indeterminacy, which makes adjustment – that is, change – necessary. The interplay between order and change provides people with sufficient space to adjust the law in their interest. Hadana in this context is subject not only to the order of law but also to the particular social relations within which mothers and fathers operate. Fathers try to manipulate the law, both by keeping the rights assigned to them and by evading the duties attached to those rights.

As we saw, mothers, who are severely disadvantaged by the text, struggle to correct its asymmetry by holding men (fathers or agnates) responsible for their legally and socially prescribed duties. They do this by using the means available to them. In one case, a mother resorts to customary practice, whereas in another a mother depends on wage labour to provide for her children. In the case of Um Hashim, the mother combined various strategies of negotiation, submission and contestation to reach her objectives.

As mentioned in Chapter 1, litigants operate in 'multiplex relationships' (Gluckman 1955: 20–1). Any individual relationship is part of a complex network of multiple bonds. The implications of any dispute between spouses reach far beyond their 'private' life, in the sense that the social relations between their respective families are directly implicated. Judges know that any disruption in one area of these multiplex relationships causes equivalent or greater disruption in a series of other relationships. Therefore, they attempt to reconcile the parties while seeing to it that the harmed party obtains satisfaction by rebuking the wrong-doer (as in the case of Um Kamil).

When judges find that strict adherence to the written code would lead to an unjust outcome, they strive to interpret the law in a way that brings it more in harmony with its objectives. In the case of Salha, the judge not only reinterpreted the law and employed customary code but also overlooked the law. Moreover, in addition to the customary code, the judge employed other 'legal concepts'. In all the cases in this chapter, the salient feature was the judges' attempt to protect the vulnerable member in the relationship, namely the child. They employed 'particular justice', in which the judge balances the rights of the child with those of its mother (or father), and then emphasizes the protection of the child at the expense of the rights assigned by law to his parents. Also striking is the judges' occasional dependence on orality. The out-of-court negotiation (in the case of Salha), threats (in the case of Kawthar) and advice to female litigants (in the case of Um Hashim) are not recorded anywhere; thus, legal theory is deprived of one of its richest resources, the ongoing modification of the system entailed in day-to-day jurisprudence.

Notes

1 In the West Bank, the *Jordanian Law of Family Rights* makes further restrictions on mother's hadana. If the mother works outside of the home, she has to make sure that the child's well-being is not affected by her being away from him or

her. In her study of Jordanian family law as applied in the West Bank, Welchman (2000) found that, in practice, the religious courts do not deprive a mother of custody simply because she works; she can maintain her hadana as long as she leaves the child in the care of a suitable person.
2 Article 386 of the *Book of Personal Status Rulings* states that if there is no legitimate guardian, or if the guardian is insane, dissolute or unsafe, the child should not be transferred to him. The article also stipulates that, in such cases, girls should be transferred to their (*muhram*) male kin, that is, grandfathers, uncles in the mother's line and so on. Qadi al-Karmi's ruling was not fully in accordance with this article, but it settled the case in a way that would serve the interests of the daughters and their mother.
3 The deputy qadi al-qudah is known to be easy to approach despite his ministerial rank in the PA hierarchy.
4 Entry into the magʻad is an honour given to male clan members who are mature in age and conduct.
5 In 2004, a precedent was set in Jordan when the government appointed a woman as mukhtar in the al-Zarqa' district (*Al-Quds Al-ʻArabi* newspaper, 12/13 June 2004). *Aray* newspaper reported that a number of women were appointed as mukhtars in Gaza in August 2015. https://goo.gl/M9gA1N, accessed 3 August 2017.
6 In such cases, the sum can be as high as $10,000, depending on the number of charity organizations the family can contact. In Nisrin's case, no sum was mentioned, but in view of the in-laws' determination to get it, the amount must have been quite large.
7 The Shariʻa justification for this is that the major wali is entitled to replace the minor wali. Thus, a judge can replace the father. The term 'wali' can mean many things depending on the context. It can mean protector, master, guardian and even a slave. In this discussion, it meant religious authority and protector of Muslims simultaneously. According to Gibbs and Kramers (1953: 629), in the Quran the term 'wali' appears in the context of several meanings: a near relative, whose murder demands vengeance (XVII: 33); friend of God (X: 62) or ally of God. It is also applied to God: 'God is the friend of those who believe' (II: 257). The title of wali was given to Prophet Muhammad, and it is one of the names of God in the Muslim rosary.
8 In March 1998, when I was active in the Model Parliament campaign, I had occasion to debate family law reform with the same judge at a public meeting. In his address to the public, he said, 'It is unacceptable for a father to wake up one day discovering that his daughter has married someone he does not accept. This is against the letter of Islam and against our traditions and customs. Most marriage contracts take place between young women and men, who are not in a position to distinguish between good and bad. Those who want to abolish the wali's rights [male guardian's rights] are alien to our society. They attack its fundamental unit, the family. They promote a Western agenda socially while their counterparts promote the same agenda politically. The objective is the same: to destroy our society and religion.' This stark contradiction between the judge's political conceptualization of family law, as expressed in a public arena, and his actual stance in a Shariʻa court is akin to the contradiction between the text and practice. In debating family law, judges adhere to the ideological stance of family law, whereas in practice they seem to be more responsive to the concrete cases brought before them. It draws our attention to the importance of scrutinizing the discrepancies that emerge between the ideological conceptualizations of Islamic family law and its highly differentiated contextual implementation. This leads to the conclusion

that in its implementation, family law proves the reciprocal determinations of jurisprudence, gender asymmetries and personal strategies.
9 The Democratic Front for the Liberation of Palestine (DFLP) is one of the PLO factions.
10 Izwa literally means a crowd of men, but socially it conveys the sense of power and respect linked with having a large number of males in the family.

Bibliography

Gibbs, H. A. R. and J. H. Kramers (1953) *Shorter Encyclopaedia of Islam*. Leiden: Brill.

Gluckman, M. (1955) *The Judicial Process Among the Barotse of Northern Rhodesia*. Manchester: Manchester University Press.

Griffiths, J. (1992) 'Legal Pluralism and the Social Working of Law', in B. Brouwer, T. Hol, A. Soeteman and A. de Wild (eds) *Coherence and Conflict in Law: Proceedings of the 3rd Benelux-Scandinavian Symposium in Legal Theory*, pp. 151–76. Amsterdam and Deventer: Kluwer Law and Taxation Publishers.

Layish, A. (1975) *Women and Islamic Law in a Non-Muslim State*. Jerusalem: Shiloah Center for Middle Eastern Studies, Tel Aviv University.

Moore, S. F. (1978) *Law as Process: An Anthropological Approach*. London: Routledge & Kegan Paul.

Moors, A. (1995) *Women, Property and Islam: Palestinian Experiences 1920–1990*. Cambridge: Cambridge University Press.

Rosen, L. (1989) *The Anthropology of Justice: Law as Culture in Islamic Society*. Cambridge: Cambridge University Press.

Samara, M. (1987) *Ahkam wa athar al-zawjiyya: sharh muqaran li-qanun al-ahwal al-shakhsiyya* (*Rules and Consequences of Marriage: Comparative Commentary on the Law of Personal Status*). Jerusalem: (No publisher).

Welchman, L. (1999) *Islamic Family Law: Text and Practice in Palestine*. Jerusalem: WCLAC.

Welchman, L. (2000) *Beyond the Code: Muslim Family Law and the Shar'i Judiciary in the Palestinian West Bank*. The Hague: Kluwer Law International.

Zahra, M. and N. A. Malek (1998) 'The Concept of Custody in Islamic Law', *Arab Law Quarterly* 13(2): 155–77.

8 Civil society, women's movement and family law reform

Between 1997 and 1999, the Palestinian women's movement took the lead in campaigning for family law reform as part of their vision of the state that was anticipated after the signing of the Oslo Accords between the Palestine Liberation Organization (PLO) and the state of Israel in 1993, which led to the establishment of the Palestinian Authority. The campaign sparked the first major social debate in Palestinian history. As in other Arab and Muslim countries, the discussion on family law featured the following elements: struggle for power and hegemony among the main actors, debate on the place of Islam, the Shari'a and religion in the lives of people, and contending positions on who could claim the right to exercise ijtihad (independent reasoning).[1] There were also divisions over notions of national and cultural authenticity and the ways in which various expressions of traditionalism and modernism were contested.

8.1 Background

Islamic family law regulates gender relations, sexuality and family life. It constitutes the legal framework that regulates the transmission of wealth and lineage (nasab) from one generation to the next. It defines the moral and social aspects of marriage and deals with nearly all the social and financial consequences of divorce, especially questions concerning the custody of children and alimony (see Moors 2003; Fawzi 2001). Family law thus directly and constantly affects the daily life of people. Over time, however, family law has been transformed from a religiously inspired law regulating relations within the institution of the family to a set of complex institutional arrangements generating discourses involving the state, religious institutions, political parties and civil society, including the women's movement.

Until the collapse of the Ottoman Empire, family affairs were the domain of religious scholars, who dealt with them according to the rules of different schools of Islamic jurisprudence (madhahib). At the end of the nineteenth century and the beginning of the twentieth century, with the emergence of post-colonial nation-states, Muslim reformists and state officials worked together on codifying the scattered books and rules of different Islamic schools in a unified national canon known as the personal status code.[2] Religious scholars were allowed authority over the domain of family law and rituals, but it was understood that they would refrain from interfering in constitutional, fiscal and administrative matters (Masud 2001).

The profound changes that Muslim societies underwent during the twentieth century influenced every aspect of life. Processes of modernization, urbanization and education, and fundamental shifts in demographic patterns such as decreasing rates of fertility, polygyny and early marriage, led to a growing conflict between the legal regulation of family law and new socio-economic realities. These processes led to further modification and reforms, albeit slight, of codified family law.

Two paradoxical phenomena emerged at the beginning of the 1970s. Firstly, the structural changes mentioned fostered a growing visibility of women as both economic and political actors. This was expressed in slogans and activities promoting a more gender-balanced representation in the economy and politics. Secondly, the changes paved the way for new players to enter the political arena. While communists and nationalists were no longer able to mobilize the public around attractive slogans, the Islamist movements succeeded in putting states on the defensive. They called for the Islamicization of society through a revision of gender relations from the legal and social standpoints. Both of these phenomena recharged the discussion on the substance, scope and frame of reference of family law.

In the 1990s, the struggle between the proponents of a broader application of the Shari'a and the advocates of women's rights intensified. Political groups were forced to take a position. It is noteworthy that, although the object of family law is the regulation of gender relations and sexuality, the debate went so far as to address 'non-gendered' subjects and to involve institutions that had previously been concerned with different agendas. Family law was no longer strictly a matter of gender, sexuality or religion; rather, it was a metaphor used to express political and economic interests.

In their quest for political power, Islamists used the issue of family law as a lever to expand their sphere of influence and thus to further undermine the legitimacy of the state. Modernists found room to edge into the rather limited political space. Women's organizations, for their part, engaged in the debate, wishing to break through prevailing limitations in the field of gender relations. Members of the religious establishment considered the reform debate and its potential implications a threat that could render them far less relevant and endanger their relatively privileged socio-economic status (Shaham 1999). Family law thus became a powerful political symbol, almost synonymous with Islam (Buskens 2003), and all parties involved in the debate wanted to present themselves as credible players in the political arena.

Unlike in the 1980s, when women's groups concentrated on issues of employment, education and political rights (Moors 2003), the 1990s witnessed the active participation of women in the family law debate, a new field in which they could make their voices heard. In many settings, however, the actual substance of the debate was drowned in dogmatic, rhetorical confrontation (an-Na'im 2001) between 'Islamic' and 'Western' values (Moors 2003). The opposing groups used vague notions of Islamicization and Westernization to delegitimize and discredit each other.

The debate on family law in Palestine presents certain similarities with those underway in other parts of the Arab world, in that personal status is used by many political actors to further their interests and gain power. For instance, when a project for family law reform was tabled in the Legislative Council in 1997, it elicited hostile reactions from the Islamist parties. Their discourse, despite contextual differences, showed many resemblances to the Islamist discourses in other Arab countries. Similarly, the religious establishment, fearing to lose influence over Shari'a courts, launched attacks on the women's movement activists, linking them with the 'West' and the 'conspiracy against Islam'.

8.2 Political context of the debate in Palestine

On paper, Palestinians have an independent government, the Palestinian Authority (PA), created after the signing of the Oslo Accords in 1993. However, the reality is different. There is no country, only two disconnected territories: the Gaza Strip, ruled by Hamas, and the West Bank, ruled by Fatah. The PA does exist as an institution, but it has no independence, sovereignty and control over Palestinian borders and resources. Moreover, the Oslo Accords gave Israel the right to supervise and exercise security in most areas, and it misuses that right by restricting the movement of Palestinians and Palestinian goods. It has also facilitated the creation of settlements on Palestinian land, which house hundreds of thousands of hostile Jewish settlers, whose numbers continue to increase steadily.[3]

The situation is worsened by the PA's lack of previous experience in governance, the undemocratic political structure and the existence of a strong Islamist opposition. These deficits are combined with a severe shortage of natural resources and almost total economic dependence on Israel and the international donor community. The first handshake in 1993 between the leaders of the PLO and Israel was presented as a peace process between 'equal partners', while in fact it was a problematic meeting between two asymmetrical powers and resulted in prosperity for Israel and impossible living conditions for Palestinians. The hostilities since 2000 show that signing a 'peace accord' on paper without establishing justice on the ground easily enables the iron fist of the powerful to prevail. As Hammami and Hilal (2001) observe, Israel now enjoys control over Palestinian public funds and hampers Palestinian workers' access to the Israeli labour market while fragmenting the Gaza Strip and the West Bank into dozens of encircled areas. Thus, it has made the PA's ability to practise self-rule, or even to carry out its assigned job as guarantor of Israeli security, a virtually impossible task.

The debate on family law began during the first years after the Oslo Accords. A central feature of Palestinian politics during that period was that while many Palestinians were enthusiastically debating the laws and challenging their newly established government on the basis of equal citizenship, they were aware of the framework on which their new reality was being constructed, namely an internationally imposed agreement that (a) deprived them of their fundamental right to self-determination and independence; (b) approved and sustained their inequality with Israel; and (c) by virtue of being signed by Palestinian representatives and approved by the international community, was a written surrender and acceptance of continued unequal relations with Israel. The Oslo Accords established a new mode in international relations, based on an acknowledgement of colonial relations by co-opted representatives of the colonized themselves.

The PA's discourse since the signing of the Oslo Accords has increasingly focused on negotiation at the expense of resistance, thus delegitimizing the resistance-based discourse of Islamists. The negotiation discourse has portrayed the Israeli abuses of Palestinians' human rights as mere violations of the peace process. Islamists, on the other hand, view the PA as no more than guardians of Israel's security (Sh'hada 1999). Avoiding the discourse of rights, as Johnson (2004a: 113) points out, weakened the legitimacy of the emerging authority and made both the PA's search for legitimacy and Islamist opposition based on rights credible. This influenced the responses of these two players on the gender issue, particularly in the field of family law.

Anyone living in Palestine in 1995–99 would have been struck by the passion of its people in discussing every bill submitted to the Legislative Council, the huge number of workshops and public meetings devoted solely to debating proposed legislation, and regular media coverage of activities related to debates on law. This process created symbols of what constitutes an ideal citizen and interpreted those symbols, placing them within a specific political and institutional context. Another element that encouraged people to debate the laws was related to Palestinians' historical experience: since the early twentieth century, they had been subjected to a succession of overlapping legal systems of non-Palestinian origin, which had served them very harshly. Various ruling powers had used the law to dispossess and alienate the population as well as to suppress protest against such policies (Welchman 2001). Thus, the celebration in the second half of the 1990s, to a certain degree, expressed strong rejection of those rules.

The Palestinian Legislative Council, elected in 1995, faced a complex intertwining of the different legal systems applied in the Gaza Strip and the West Bank (Ottoman, British and Jordanian laws, and Israeli military orders). In both areas, Shari'a courts continued to have control over the application of family law, the *Jordanian Law for Personal Status 1976* in the West Bank, and the *Law of Family Rights* of 1954 (issued by the Egyptian Governor-General appointed after the 1948 war), with particular reference to the *Book of Personal Status Rulings*, in the Gaza Strip.

The post-Oslo political circumstances created a contradictory environment for the women's movement.[4] On the one hand, there was a conducive atmosphere: nationalists continued to recognize the role of the women's movement as vital, and it was still the most active social movement (Hammami and Johnson 1999: 319). The project of a Palestinian 'state' was still in the making, and there was thus room for negotiating gender; laws were being drafted and social groups could lobby for change. On the other hand, the Palestinian Authority as an administrative body lacked power and resources; thus, the struggle for independence and self-determination remained the top priority. The likelihood of political compromises between the strong conservative Islamist movement and the Palestinian Authority at the expense of the gender issue was a real concern.

These circumstances provided the political opportunity for the women's movement to initiate programmes and activities for legal reform (Abdulhadi 1998; Johnson 2004b: 146–7). It raised issues related to equal citizenship at a time when the nationalist movement was at its 'lowest ebb' (Abdulhadi 1998: 661). The nationalists' failure to address issues relating to social rights, democracy and freedom of speech was striking (Hammami and Johnson 1999: 319). The nationalist movement had faced severe setbacks abroad since the early 1980s due to the Palestine Liberation Organization's military defeat in Lebanon; and in the occupied territories, it was confronted with the rise of alternative political initiatives in the wake of the intifada.[5]

More generally, the nationalist movement was weakened by the collapse of the Soviet Union. The 1991 Gulf war was another breaking point because it altered the international and regional balance of power, putting the PLO in danger of being reduced to nothing more than a disintegrating and destitute bureaucracy located in Tunis. Its only aim was survival, and its only claim to legitimacy was that it represented Palestinians (Bishara, in Usher 1995). After 1993, political disputes over the Oslo Accords made it difficult for the nationalist movement to meet the expectations of its supporters.[6]

The women's movement's public appeal reflected a particular political strategy. Instead of grounding its equality discourse on gender rights, the movement communicated its message through idioms of nationalism, state-building and democracy. Its ability to enter 'monopolized public space' (Bishara 1998) with new claims and demands allowed nationalists to reassert their presence in the political arena.[7] Linking the gender question with the broader national cause had two major consequences: first, reclaiming of the national ground from the Islamists, and second, paving of the way for a new democratic alliance with the nationalists (Hammami and Johnson 1999).

Despite the ideological differences and heterogeneity within the women's movement, a common element emerged, namely a shift towards the public questioning of gender relations. This process was paralleled by gradual institutionalization of the women's movement itself through establishment of women's study centres and grassroots organizations focusing on empowerment and awareness, as well as the setting up of women's departments within ministries. Furthermore, a number of organizations established programmes reflecting the importance of family law reform and the provision to women of adequate advice and counselling on divorce, child custody, sexual abuse and domestic violence. Birzeit University, which started a new women's studies programme at the MA level in 1994, offered additional courses on women and law, notably focusing on Islamic family law. Other organizations encouraged their young activists to study Islamic family law and to engage in careers as lawyers; some women received grants from international donors to study Islamic family law. Several women's organizations started initiatives to review legislation and organized conferences and workshops to propose new legislation on the basis of gender equality.

8.3 Model parliament for women and legislation

The activities and initiatives of the women's movement culminated in the campaign for family law reform known as the Model Parliament for Women and Legislation (MP) between 1997 and 1999. The MP project resulted from a four-year review of gender-based laws by a number of women's organizations and human rights centres. Established in 1997, the MP project aimed to propose Palestinian legislation based on equality and human rights. The campaign for family law reform engaged a wide spectrum of political and social groups. For the first time, political actors of diverse backgrounds and interests used Palestinian television stations, radio, newspapers and posters to communicate a politicized gender discourse.

The suggestions for reform were subject to discussion and negotiation within the preparatory committee and then the wider community. The final text proposed that:

- The age of marriage should be set at 18 years for men and women.
- Spouses should not need to have the permission of a guardian to conclude the marriage contract.
- Assets acquired after marriage should be regarded as joint property, and a court should decide how to divide them in the event of divorce.
- Nafaqa should be paid from the date of separation and not the date on which the application for alimony is submitted to the court.
- The Palestinian Authority should create a fund from which support would be provided to the applicant until the court ruled on the application, after which the payments made would be refunded by the other partner.
- Inheritance rules and regulations should be formulated and enforced to protect women and guarantee their right to receive their legal and legitimate share of inheritance.
- Polygyny should be regulated so that court permission would be needed for its practice.
- A man should only be allowed to marry a second wife for serious reasons such as health problems, and he should then have to inform his first wife, who would have the right to ask a court for divorce on that ground.
- Divorce by either spouse should only be possible through the decision of a court.
- Because of the possibility of intimidation, a mother's renunciation of her custody rights should not be accepted.
- Custody decisions should apply to children up to the age of 18 years.
- If the divorced mother remarries, a court should decide which parent should be granted custody in accordance with the best interests of the children (Nashwan 1998).

The chief campaigners of the MP asserted two principles: first, the need to guarantee the broadest possible participation of groups from various localities and political backgrounds; and second, while maintaining plurality, stronger political groups should be prevented from manipulating the campaign and thus diverting it from its objectives.[8]

Two discourses had emerged during the year before the opening of the MP. The first argued for termination of the existing power structure of marriage and its replacement with a relationship based on equality.[9] The other insisted that any reform should preserve the Islamic quality of Palestinian legislation. Reform should be derived from the Shari'a.[10] They feared that overlooking the cultural, political and social connotations of Palestine's Islamic identity would impact negatively on the women's movement in the eyes of the wider society and give its opponents additional ammunition.

The shape that family law should take relates not only to the ideology of particular actors but also to their view of how family law should be defined, implemented and authorized. In the Palestinian public sphere, the family law debate was both open and controlled. It was characterized by the inclusion of new participants and publics, yet various control mechanisms were imposed by powerful actors to silence certain identities, prohibit given subjects or impose chosen methods of deliberation (Moors 2003). Actors often shifted the debate from one domain to another. For example, at times, religious leaders asserted the right of ahl al-ikhtisas (religious specialists) to exclude specific participants from the process of deliberation. At others, they transferred the debate from the social and political domain to a more morally charged and religiously sensitive sphere. At yet other times, they stirred up the public by stressing the danger of any reform of the family institution. The articulation of arguments and the processes of exclusion or inclusion of subjects and identities were just indicators of how the power structure can compromise the course of deliberation, even in the absence of formal acts of exclusion (see Fraser 1993).

The religious establishment influenced the debate through speeches in mosques, at public meetings, on television programmes and in newspaper articles. Some judges kept their distance from Islamists, perhaps fearing that their attitude would be interpreted as a form of opposition to the newly established PA, while others were explicit in their association with the Islamists.

The differences in viewpoint within the religious establishment show that it is not a monolithic institution. There are those who construct their discourse merely on ideology, motivated by their politico-economic interests, and others who take a practical stance due to their daily contact with the problems and dilemmas of people in matters of personal status. These differences demonstrate the importance of taking into consideration the attitudes of practitioners: when they become involved in the debate, they often express more balanced and concrete views. This stance, as Masud (2001) contends, indicates that the normative basis of law lies not in the debate but elsewhere; it is in the social reality that has been disregarded by both camps. Masud (2001: 5) observes that the current debate in the Muslim world regarding the role of Islamic law indicates the existence and persistence of three levels of contradiction:

1   The political conceptualization of the Shari'a is based on a moral stance while law is likely to be more pragmatic.
2   On the social level, women suffer from the contradictions between the ideals of the Shari'a and the social norms that obtain among Palestinians.
3   On the religious level, a contradiction between legal norms and Islamic ethical values still exists. While practitioners throughout Islamic history have tried to reconcile social norms and Islamic law by invoking principles of necessity, convenience, preventive measures, state of emergency and so forth, contradictions persist because these measures have not been incorporated as 'norms' in legal theory.

As the campaign continued, more actors joined the debate. Academics from Birzeit University wrote articles and produced programmes on Palestinian television in favour of the MP. The majority of Legislative Council members expressed their sympathy with the MP campaign in newspaper interviews and by attending MP sessions. Several lawyers expressed diverse attitudes and arguments. Almost every day, articles on the issue of personal status appeared in the newspapers. Arguments and counter-arguments were put forward from various quarters. Some groups in the Gaza Strip (and the West Bank) used other means of publicity. The walls, which had been freshly painted after the arrival of the PA, were taken over by some groups as a legitimate public space to convey their agreement or disagreement with the MP. Some MP posters were replaced by handwritten statements denouncing what they termed an attack on 'Islam and the Shari'a' and threatening MP members. In this sense, the population was actively engaged in the debate not only through the usual forums, such as active discussion in seminars or workshops, but also by voicing their opinions through all available avenues. The Palestinian public sphere hosted conflicting and competing publics (see Fraser 1993; Eley 1993) as it witnessed one of its most intense debates ever. Family law had sharply divided Palestinians into at least two camps: those who supported pluralism and freedom of expression and those who aimed at monopolizing Shari'a and Islam.

A survey by the women's study programme at Birzeit University showed that the question of reform was affected by highly conflicting interests and values. The analysts demonstrated that, while respondents were committed to equality and justice, these sentiments co-existed with their desire to preserve gender hierarchy within the family (Hammami 2004: 143). In a similar vein, contradictory attitudes existed with regard to legal reform. People believed that they had the right to determine what religious law should be, but, simultaneously, they favoured expanding the role of religious authorities. The study concluded that these contradictions might obtain within each individual. Legal reform should thus take into consideration not only notions of equality but also other controversial values and interests.

8.4 Conclusion

This chapter aimed at answering the first set of questions posed in Chapter 1. It investigated the identity and positions of the participants in the debate, the way they conceptualized family law and the idioms they used to communicate their positions.

The main factor affecting any activity in Palestine is the Israeli occupation. Checkpoints on Palestinian territory prevent the free movement of goods and people. Settlements, in conjunction with these barricades, fragment the population and land. With Israel controlling Palestinian internal revenue and income from Palestinian exports, the PA has limited power and resources at its disposal. Thus, the need for independence and self-determination overshadows everything else.

These conditions explain why Palestinian public discussion on family law differs in one important respect from that conducted in other Arab countries. Whereas debate in the latter reflects tension between the state and civil society, the Palestinian debate developed in the context of the national struggle for liberation and state-building. Thus, in Palestine, not only is the question of who may claim the right to interpret the sources of law central, but so is the clash between appeals for reinforcing equal citizenship rights, as opposed to cultural and religious specificities, in the framework of the national struggle for independence. This aspect has influenced participants' discourse and shaped their argumentations. They often refer to the substance of family law, yet frequently argue with reference to nationalism and state-building.

With this in mind, the chapter analysed the Model Parliament for Women and Legislation, which was the climactic focus of the debate on reforming family law in Palestine. Four main features were observed:

1 The question of who is allowed to speak about family law authoritatively while depicting other voices as irrelevant was posed clearly.
2 Neither the women's movement nor the religious establishment were unified. While the Gaza MP based its discourse on the Shari'a by stretching the principle of takhayyur (selection from different schools of fiqh) to its utmost limits, the West Bank MP referred to the principles of human rights. The religious establishment, too, did not emerge as a monolithic bloc, with some of its members accepting the need to remedy certain gender-based injustices in family law.
3 Analogously to the debate in other Arab countries, the Palestinian discussion appeared both open and controlled – open in that it included new participants and publics, yet controlled in that powerful actors silenced certain identities, prohibited given subjects or imposed chosen methods of deliberation (see Moors 2003).
4 Significant among the controlling mechanisms was the strategy of both opponents and supporters of reform in shifting the domains of debate from one sphere to another. Religious leaders in some instances asserted the right of ahl al-ikhtisas (specialists) to exclude particular actors from the process of

deliberation; in other instances, they transferred the debate from the social domain to the political or entered a more morally charged and religiously sensitive sphere.

Still, they always stressed that reform would pose dangers for the institution of the family. The women's movement (in both Gaza and the West Bank), in contrast, was less successful in shifting course. The main thrust of its discourse was to articulate gender needs and interests in idioms relating to nationalism, state-building and democracy. This strategy was generated from the movement's conscious attempt to locate its arguments around issues less relating to sexuality and sexual rights (see Peteet 1999), which family law regulates.

The discussions and deliberations were a marathon social exercise, not only for the women's movement but also for other social actors. Family law reform was a political project in which diverging assumptions about the role of the Shari'a, Islam and gender were put forward as an expression of the 'social will' (Hammami 2004: 126) that each group claimed to represent. This chapter showed the deep divisions that split Palestinian society over the issue of family law.

A noteworthy aspect of the entire exercise was that there was an implicit assumption among the MP reformers (in the West Bank and Gaza) not only that the law is unjust, but that it is applied straightforwardly and lacks the flexibility I observed during the fieldwork. It is in this regard that the findings of this study, which indicate that women have the ability to manipulate the law (regardless of its extent) and judges have the freedom to, and do, exercise ijtihad so as to ensure 'justice' for female litigants who come before them, are particularly important.

Notes

1 See Moors (1999), which compares the text of family law with social practice in the Arab world, and Moors (2003), which explores various positions, styles and modes of argumentation that appeared in the 1990s. Welchman's contribution to Moors (2003) reviews the debate in Palestine, whereas her previous work (Welchman 2004) assesses the legislative and lobbying initiatives related to Islamic law. Welchman (2000 and 2001) examines the debate over and application of family law in the West Bank from a legal perspective. Buskens (2003) links the debate on family law with the emergence of a public sphere in Morocco and the struggle of various political actors for legitimacy and power. Shaham (1999) examines Islamic marriage contracts in Egypt. Mir-Hosseini (2000) compares the application of family law in Iran and Morocco. Moghadam (2001) studies the emergence of Islamist feminists and their engagement in the reform debate. Wurth (2003) shows which perspectives emerge from the different positionalities of women in Yemen. Hammami and Johnson (1999) and Sh'hada (1999) analyse the Model Parliament for Women and Legislation in Palestine.
2 The process of codification was discussed extensively in Chapter 2.
3 Since 2004, Israel has withdrawn settlers from Gaza and closed down four West Bank settlements, while simultaneously expanding the remaining West Bank settlements. Thus, this rapid and steady enlargement is continuing to multiply the number of settlers in spite of the process being illegal according to international law.
4 Women's involvement in the national struggle has been extensively researched in the last two decades. Researchers have focused on investigating whether the

national struggle provides sufficient room for women's emancipation or presents an obstacle to it. Most feminist scholars have confirmed that national movements are predominantly patriarchal and that women are often co-opted during national struggles. Palestinian nationalism, as Peteet (1999: 71) observes, is characterized by 'contradictory potential'. On the one hand, it acknowledges the multiplicity of women's positionalities; on the other, it has 'denied them the status of either independent agency [and has not] accept[ed] them as a basis from which to launch political organizing'. Since a detailed history of the women's movement in Palestine does not fall within the ambit of this study, it will not be reviewed in this book. However, there is a vast amount of literature that focuses on particular sections of Palestinian women's activism, often linked with the secular national movement. See, for example, Peteet 1991, 1999; Hiltermann 1991; Jad 1995; Abdo 1999; Hammami 1990; Hammami and Kuttab 1999; Sayigh 1993; Ameri 1999; Dajani 1994; Gluck 1997; Sharoni 2001; Abdulhadi 1998; Kuttab 1993. For literature related to the question of women and nationalism in the Third World, see, for example, Kandiyoti 1991, 1997; Joseph 1986, 1991; Badran 1993; Molyneux 1998,2001; Hatem 1993; Jayawardena 1989; Chatterjee 1989; Mohanty et al. 1991. For a more general theorization on women and nationalism, see, for example, Yuval-Davis 1992, 1997; Pettman 1996; Walby 1996.

5 The intifada (meaning 'uprising') was a mass protest against the Israeli occupation of the West Bank and Gaza. It started in December 1987 and continued until the beginning of the so-called peace process initiated by the US after the Iraqi defeat in the Gulf war of 1991. It shifted from mass-based actions to prolonged, institutionalized actions. The main objective of the uprising was to exhaust rather than evict the occupying power through a combination of local and international pressure. The most remarkable features of the intifada were not only the participation of Palestinians from all sectors and classes but also the ease with which mobilization was carried out and support structure built within a few months of its eruption (Hiltermann 1991).
6 For more details on the Oslo Accords, see Usher (1995).
7 Bishara (1998) contends that the post-Oslo period witnessed a growing demobilization of political activities in the West Bank and Gaza due to the multiplication of PA security services.
8 'Stronger political groups' in this study is a reference to Fatah, the leading political party in the PA, and Hamas, its Islamist rival.
9 This view was expressed mostly by members of NGOs that were for the most part funded by Western NGOs, who adopted the mainstream discourse of human rights and democracy.
10 This view was by and large adopted by activists of the General Union of Palestinian Women. Most of them were members of the ruling party, who on the one hand stressed the need for reform, and on the other hand hesitated to antagonize the Islamists.

Bibliography

Abdo, N. (1999) 'Gender and Politics Under the Palestinian Authority', *Journal of Palestinian Studies* XXVIII(2): 38–51.

Abdulhadi, R. (1998) 'The Palestinian Women's Autonomous Movement: Emergence, Dynamics, and Challenges', *Gender and Society* 12(6): 649–73.

Ameri, A. (1999) 'Conflict in Peace: Challenges Confronting the Palestinian Women's Movement', in A. Afsaruddin (ed.) *Hermeneutics and Honor: Negotiating Female 'Public' Space in Islamic/Ate Societies*, pp. 29–54. Cambridge: Harvard University Press.

an-Na'im, A. (2001) 'Rights at Home: An Approach to the Internalization of Human Rights in Family Relations in Islamic Communities', paper presented at the Second Workshop on Islamic Family Law at the Robert Schuman Center for Advanced Studies, European University Institute, in Florence, 21–25 March.

Badran, M. (1993) 'Independent Women', in J. Tucker (ed.) *Arab Women: Old Boundaries, New Frontiers*, pp. 29–49. Bloomington and Indianapolis: Indiana University Press.

Bishara, A. (1998) 'Reflections on the Reality of the Oslo Process', in G. Giacaman and D. J. Lonning (eds) *After Oslo, New Realities, Old Problems*, pp. 212–26. London: Pluto Press.

Buskens, L. (2003) 'Recent Debates on Family Law Reform in Morocco: Islamic Law as Politics in an Emerging Public Sphere', *Islamic Law and Society* 10(1): 70–132.

Chatterjee, P. (1993) 'The Nationalist Resolution of the Women's Question', in K. Sangari and S. Vaid (eds) *Recasting Women*, pp. 204–53. New Delhi: Gayatri Press.

Dajani, S. (1994) 'Between National and Social Liberation: The Palestinian Women's Movement in the West Bank and Gaza Strip', in T. Mayer (ed.) *Women and the Israeli Occupation: The Politics of Change*, pp. 33–61. London: Routledge.

Eley, G. (1993) 'Nations. Publics, and Political Cultures: Placing Habermas in the Nineteenth Century', in C. Calhoun (ed.) *Habermas and the Public Sphere*, pp. 289–339. Cambridge: MIT Press.

Fawzi, E. (2001) 'Family Law in Egypt: Current Situation and Prospects of Further Development', paper presented in at the Second Workshop on Islamic Family Law, held at the Robert Schuman Center for Advanced Studies, European University Institute, in Florence, 21–25 March.

Fraser, N. (1993) 'Rethinking the Public Sphere: A Contribution to the Critique of Actually Existing Democracy', in C. Calhoun (ed.) *Habermas and the Public Sphere*, pp. 109–43. Cambridge, MA and London: MIT Press.

Gluck, S. (1997) 'Palestine: Shifting Sands: The Feminist-Nationalist Connection in the Palestinian Movement', in L. West (ed.) *Feminist Nationalist*, pp. 101–29. London: Routledge.

Hammami, R. (1990) 'Women, the Hijab and the Intifada', *Middle East Report* 20(3&4): 24–8.

Hammami, R. (2004) 'Attitudes Towards Legal Reform of Personal Status Law in Palestine', in L. Welchman (ed.) *Women's Rights & Islamic Family Law: Perspectives on Reform*, pp. 125–44. London and New York: Zed Books.

Hammami, R. and J. Hilal (2001) 'An Uprising at a Crossroad', *Middle East Research and Information Project* 31(219): 2–8.

Hammami, R. and P. Johnson (1999) 'Equality With a Difference: Gender and Citizenship in Transitional Palestine', *Social Politics* 6(3): 314–43.

Hammami, R. and E. Kuttab (1999) 'The Palestinian Feminist Movement: Strategies Towards Freedom and Democracy', *The Alternative Information Center* XV(4). <http://aic. netgate.net/nfw/April99/9904po3-09.html>, accessed 11 March 2000.

Hatem, M. (1993) 'Toward the Development of Post-Islamist and Post-Nationalist Feminist Discourses in the Middle East', in J. Tucker (ed.) *Arab Women: Old Boundaries, New Frontiers*, pp. 29–49. Bloomington and Indianapolis: Indiana University Press.

Hiltermann, J. (1991) *Behind the Intifada*. Princeton: Princeton University Press.

Jad, I. (1995) 'Claiming Feminism, Claiming Nationalism: Women's Activism in the Occupied Territories', in Amrita Basu (ed.) *The Challenge of Local Feminisms:*

Women's Movements in Global Perspective, pp. 226–48. Boulder, CO: Westview Press.

Jayawardena, K. (1989) *Feminism and Nationalism in the Third World*. London: Zed Press.

Johnson, P. (2004a) 'Palestinian Interim Governance: State Legitimation, Legal Reform and the Shari'a', in L.Welchman (ed.) *Women's Rights and Islamic Family Law: Perspectives on Reform*, pp. 112–24. London and New York: Zed Press.

Johnson, P. (2004b) 'Agents for Reform: The Women's Movement, Social Politics and Family Law Reform, in L. Welchman (ed.) *Women's Rights and Islamic Family Law: Perspectives on Reform*, pp. 144–63. London and New York: Zed Press.

Joseph, S. (1986) 'Women and Politics in the Middle East', *Middle East Report* 16(1): 3–8.

Joseph, S. (1991) 'Elite Strategies: Iraq and Lebanon', in D. Kandiyoti (ed.) *Women, Islam and the State*, pp. 176–201. London: Palgrave Macmillan.

Kandiyoti, D. (1991) 'Introduction', in D. Kandiyoti (ed.) *Women, Islam and the State*, pp. 1–22. London: Plagrave Macmillan.

Kandiyoti, D. (1997) 'Identity and Its Discontents: Women and the Nation', *Dossier, Women Living Under Muslim Laws Series, no. 20*, pp. 7–23. Grabels, France: International Solidarity Network of Women Living Under Muslim Laws.

Kuttab, E. (1993) 'Palestinian Women and the Intifada: Fighting on Two Fronts', *Arab Studies Journal* 15: 69–85.

Masud, M. K. (2001) *Muslim Jurists' Quest for the Normative Basis of Shari'a*. Leiden: ISIM Publication.

Mir-Hosseini, Z. (2000) *Marriage on Trial: A Study of Islamic Family Law, Iran and Morocco Compared*. London: I. B. Tauris.

Moghadam, V. (2001) 'Feminism and Islamic Fundamentalism: A Secularist Interpretation', *Journal of Women's History* 13(1): 42–5.

Mohanty, C., A. Rosso and L. Torres (1991) *Third World Women and The Politics of Feminism*. Bloomington: Indiana University Press.

Molyneux, M. (1998) 'Analyzing Women's Movements', *Development and Change* 29(2): 219–47.

Molyneux, M. (2001) *Women's Movement in International Perspective: Latin America and Beyond*. New York: Palgrave Macmillan.

Moors, A. (1999) 'Debating Islamic Family Law: Legal Texts and Social Practices', in M. L. Meiwether and J. Tucker (eds) *A Social History of Women and Gender in the Modern Middle East*, pp. 141–77. Boulder and Oxford: Westview Press.

Moors, A. (2003) 'Introduction: Public Debates on Family Law Reform: Participants, Positions, and Styles of Argumentation in the 1990s', *Islamic Law and Society* 10(1): 1–12.

Nashwan, K. (1998) *Miswaddat muqtadayat li-qanun ahwal al-shakhsiyya filastini muwahhad* (Draft Requirements for a Unified Palestinian Law of Personal Status), Gaza: Discussion Paper from the Palestinian Model Parliament: Women and Legislation.

Peteet, J. (1991) *Gender in Crisis: Women and the Palestinian Resistance Movement*. New York: Columbia University Press.

Peteet, J. (1999) 'Gender and Sexuality: Belonging to the National and Moral Order', in A. Afsaruddin (ed.) *Hermeneutics and Honor: Negotiating Female "Public" Space in Islamic/Ate Societies*, pp. 70–88. Cambridge: Harvard University Press.

Pettman, J. J. (1996) 'Boundary Politics: Women, Nationalism and Danger', in M. Maynard and J. Purvic (eds) *New Frontiers in Women's Studies: Knowledge, Identity and Nationalism*, pp. 187–203. London: Taylor & Francis.

Sayigh, R. (1993) 'Palestinian Women and Politics in Lebanon', in J. Tucker (ed.) *Arab Women: Old Boundaries, New Frontiers*, pp. 175–95. Bloomington and Indianapolis: Indiana University Press.

Shaham, R. (1999) 'State, Feminists and Islamists: The Debate Over Stipulations in Marriage Contracts in Egypt', *Bulletin of the School of Oriental and African Studies* 62(3): 462–83.

Sharoni, S. (2001) *Rendering Conflict and Peace in Israel/Palestine and the North of Ireland*. <www.evergreen.edu/users2/sharonis/millfinal.htm>, accessed 22 July 2001.

Sh'hada, N. (1999) 'Gender and Politics in Palestine, Discourse Analysis of the Palestinian Authority and Islamists', ISS Working Paper No. 307. The Hague: Institute of Social Studies.

Usher, G. (1995) 'Bantustanisation or Bi-Nationalism? An Interview With Azmi Bishara', *Race and Class* 37(2): 43–50.

Walby, S. (1996) 'Women and Nation', in G. Balakriohman (ed.) *Mapping the Nation*, pp. 235–54. London: Verso, in association with New Left Review.

Welchman, L. (2000) *Beyond the Code: Muslim Family Law and the Shar'i Judiciary in the Palestinian West Bank*. The Hague: Kluwer Law International.

Welchman, L. (2001) 'Palestine: Staking Out the Territory: Family Law Debates in Transitional Palestine', paper presented at the Second Workshop on Islamic Family Law, at the Robert Schuman Center for Advanced Studies, European University Institute, in Florence, 21–25 March.

Welchman, L. (ed.) (2004) *Women's Rights and Islamic Family Law: Perspectives on Reform*. London and New York: Zed Press.

Wurth, A. (2003) 'Staled Reform: Family Law in Post-Unification Yemen', *Islamic Law and Society* 10(1): 12–34.

Yuval-Davis, N. (1992) 'Nationalism, Racism and Gender Relations', ISS Working Paper No. 130. The Hague: Institute of Social Studies.

Yuval-Davis, N. (1997) *Gender and Nation*. London: Sage.

9 Change, a step at a time

Chapter 8 introduced the reader to the Model Parliament for Women and Legislation, which was the climactic event in the Palestinian campaign for family law reform. The general argument in the chapter was that the debate on family law is better examined within the framework of struggle for power and legitimacy between the various political actors conceptualizing and contesting each other's views in the public arena. In Palestine, this struggle took place in the context of state-building, in which the family law debate was intertwined with conflicting views regarding the identity and the socio-political structure of the upcoming state. After the Model Parliament was concluded, the women's movement as well as the religious establishment worked on producing legal texts of family law to be presented to the Palestinian Legislative Council. This study would be incomplete without examining those legal proposals; they are presented here by answering the following questions: What was the conclusion of the public debate on family law (1997–98) in Palestine? What sorts of texts were produced? And how did the main actors express their views on gender, Islam and Shari'a in legal terms?[1]

As we have seen in the previous chapter, the campaign for family law reform faced strong opposition from the religious establishment and Islamist parties. This reaction led the women's movement to decide (after the Model Parliament completed its activities) to work on the question of family law reform by following a different strategy. In particular, the West Bank activists opted for 'low-key' lobbying instead of a loud, popular campaign. This meant that the focus was on activities such as meeting with politicians, lobbying decision-makers, influencing Legislative Council members and so forth, in order to muster wide political support for its new family law draft. This strategy was meant to counteract that of Islamists and religious leaders, who have better access to the public thanks to their means of communication and a discourse that invokes people's religious sensibilities.

This chapter briefly reviews the drafts produced by the women's movement[2] and the qadi al-qudah. The analysis was developed against the background of the incipient process of state formation in Palestine following the signing of the Oslo Accords in September 1993. Each actor emphasized the importance of establishing Palestinian law instead of 'inherited legislation' and claimed legitimacy and appropriateness to create the legal framework for the Palestinian family in the upcoming state. Each draft takes the importance of unifying Palestinian personal status law as its point of departure, and each asserts the need for personal status law to be modernized (tahdith) to meet the needs of the contemporary Palestinian family.

The chapter reviews the drafts with an eye to the logic, premises and conceptions for a unified Palestinian family law. It thus examines the legal translation of the actors' visions in which each departs from a particular frame of reference. The main issues to be analysed relate to marriage, guardianship (wilaya), nafaqa, children's hadana (care) and the minimum age of marriage, for these constituted the main points of contention during the debate among Palestinians.

9.1 Law, society and social change

For feminist scholars, law is one of the ostensible fields for examining gender inequality (Weedon 1987; Fraser 1997). Law, as a constitutive part of state institutions, defines wrongs and rights according to certain sets of values and interests (Jamal 2001). And here again, feminist legal theorists have different approaches to the role of law in society: while liberal ones think of law as capable of integrating women's experiences, radical feminists argue that law is inherently masculine; post-modern feminists examine the way in which 'law constitutes and is constituted by gender' (Anleu 2000: 67). Many feminists view law as a tool for ending gender inequality (Singh 1989). Quoting Htun and Weldon (2010), Celis et al. (2013: 4) observe that law has been used to consolidate male domination.

Recent socio-legal commentators have started questioning the meaning of legal change, especially with the growing inequalities in societies (Frohmann and Mertz 1994: 829). The main point is that legislation cannot by itself change society; change is greatly influenced by contextual factors such as family structure, kinship relations, descent, religion and other socio-economic variables (Singh 1989). Social change requires acknowledging the wider political processes in a given society; therefore, some scholars suggest that it is important not only to legislate but also to see how the legislation is implemented (Singh 1989), whereas others suggest that legal change should go hand in hand with wider political democratization (Johnson 2004).

Sociologically, law can be viewed as both facilitating and obstructing the process of social change (Smart 1986: 117). Viewing law as the strategy or resource for social change may easily 'lead to an instrumentalist conception and the inevitable question of whether or not specific instances of legislation . . . have been successful' (Anleu 2000: 234). Moreover, legal reforms can be misused by politicians or redefined by administrators and may in the end generate incentives for opponents to mobilize and oppose them (ibid.). The involvement of various actors and groups in debating the law means that their world views have to be translated into legal terms, which then leads to competition over the right to control the law (Bourdieu 1987).

9.2 Background: integrating the Shari'a with the PA

State-building was an ongoing process in the period between the establishment of the Palestinian Authority (PA) in 1994 and eruption of the second intifada in September 2000. The second intifada (2000–2005), which was a mass protest against Israeli policies, turned into violent confrontation, with Israel reoccupying most of the West Bank and Gaza Strip. As a consequence, thousands of Palestinians died, and the process of state-building could not be continued.

Weber (1968: 56) defines the state not only as a political community 'that claims the monopoly of the legitimate use of physical force within a given territory' but also as a 'legal authority' (ibid.: 215). The period between the signing of the Oslo Accords (1993) and the effective establishment of the PA (1994) was one of preparation. As part of this preparation, Abu Sardana, a leading scholar, member of the Jordanian Court of Appeal and founding member of Fatah, the leading party in the PA, was urgently invited to Tunis to help draw up the legal framework of the proposed state.

Abu Sardana presented his views on the identity of the emerging state at a meeting held on 19 June 1994. He expressed dissatisfaction with the draft Constitution compiled by Anis al-Qasem, a prominent Palestinian legal scholar, who had not incorporated the question of religion in general, and the Shari'a specifically, in the draft, leaving it until the Palestinian state was actually realized (al-Qasem 1992, cited in Johnson 2004).[3] Qasem thought that 'such an issue should be decided upon in an atmosphere of freedom when the time comes for the preparation of a permanent Constitution' (al-Qasem, quoted in Welchman 2003: 51). Abu Sardana raised questions about the three integral parts of the landscape of any Arab state: ifta' (the act of issuing fatwas), Shari'a courts and awqaf (Islamic endowments). In Abu Sardana's view, the Shari'a judiciary is the foundation that keeps society on the right track, maintains the family and organizes relations between its individual members. The institution of ifta shari is as important as the Shari'a court, and because of its special status in any Muslim community, it should be an independent body with a religious scholar (alim) heading it (Abu Sardana n.d.: 51).

Abu Sardana was most concerned about the status of Shari'a courts as the legal institution governing family relations of Muslim Palestinians. He proposed three actions:

1 Unification of family law in the West Bank and Gaza
2 Modernization (tahdith) of family law
3 'Jordanization' of the unified law

As regards the third point, he considered the Jordanian law to be more modern than the one applied in Gaza. Abu Sardana was concerned about modernization and emphasized it all through. For example, during one meeting, he reminded the judges that the rule of law had been undermined by the Israeli occupation during the last quarter century; therefore, they should start working again according to the rule of law.

Within five months of his appointment as qadi al-qudah, Abu Sardana was based in an impressive, newly constructed building housing the Shari'a courts in Gaza. His first action was to replace all personnel of the previous Israeli administration, who were then transferred to other PA departments.[4] He then replaced the stamps and symbols used in the offices of Shari'a courts with those of the Palestinian Authority. Twenty-seven new application forms bearing the PA emblem were printed for daily use in the courts. Within one year of his appointment, the number of judges and clerks in the Gaza Strip had doubled. A new court was established in the South (Abu Sardana n.d.: 162–3) and was followed later by a number of courts in various districts.

Abu Sardana issued a number of decrees that reflected his view of the future state of Palestine, with family law being governed by the Shari'a. Two fundamental elements had to be intact: first, ijtihad as a matter of selection (takhayyur) from among different madhahib of recognized schools of fiqh;[5] and second, modernization (tahdith) based on the principles of maslaha (public welfare). Those who worked on reforming and unifying the family law should have scientific knowledge, intellectual maturity, responsiveness, tolerance and flexibility.

Qadi Muhammad Faris compiled Abu Sardana's decrees in one booklet, in which Abu Sardana's legal and administrative concerns are manifested. On 29 August 1994, almost three months after his appointment, Abu Sardana issued his first decree, on the wali's role. It started with an introduction about the principles of the Shari'a, 'which should facilitate people's affairs when they approach the courts rather than complicate them, especially in matters related to marriage procedures'. The decree went on to explain,

> If the woman's wali is travelling, then the next agnate should take charge provided that two persons identify him. If there is no wali (close or remote), the qadi should act as her wali because guardianship of adult women (balig, rashid) is not obligatory.
>
> (Faris 2002)

Abu Sardana repeated the same concern after eight months. On 2 May 1995, he decreed: 'The wilaya (guardianship) in marriage is waliyat istihbab (preferable). . . . If none of the woman's walis is present, the qadi should take charge because the woman should not miss out on the qualified (kufu) groom' (Faris 2002: 21). This pronouncement on the role of the wali, over which the judges and the women's movement were at odds during the family law debate, touched upon a very sensitive subject. Its declaration that the presence of the wali should be viewed as preferable (rather than obligatory) represented a discourse and practice that were different from those of Shari'a court judges. We shall see later in this chapter that the new proposal for the unified family law drafted by Abu Sardana's successor as qadi al-qudah not only redefined the role of wali as obligatory but even specifically declared that the marriage would be invalid if the wali did not accept it.[6]

A decree on 29 August 1994 related to the filing of cases. Women used to combine several cases in one suit, but Abu Sardana required that each case in the suit be filed separately. Thus, suits concerning alimony (nafaqa), value of wife's furniture (tawabi), children's nafaqa, nursing fees (ujrat hadana), breast-feeding fees (ujrat ridaa) and so on could no longer be grouped together. Abu Sardana's explanation for this was that each element of a case has its own reasoning and legal action; for example, the wife's nafaqa may take a longer time to establish, depending on the nature of the dispute, in which case the children could suffer harm while waiting for their mother's case to be settled (Faris 2002).

Abu Sardana also decreed that the value of dower (mahr) should be given in the Jordanian dinar, changing the previous practice of using any of three currencies: the Jordanian dinar, Israeli shekel or US dollar. This not only standardized the currency used, but it was also an expression of Arab and Muslim identity in that it sidelined the currency of the occupier and that of the country perceived as being its main supporter.

One of the important decrees was that wives who were declared disobedient by a court and ordered to go to the house of obedience should not be forced to do so, nor should their nafaqa be cut off automatically. Instead, procedural action should be taken. The Shari'a courts should leave it to God to punish her for her disobedience on the Day of Judgment. Abu Sardana also clarified that filing of a case of disobedience by a husband was not sufficient ground to cut off his wife's nafaqa; there should be a clear declaration by the wife that she was not willing to abide by the court's order. Her signature, confirmed by the executive officer, was considered crucial for such a declaration, which would then allow the husband to file a case for stopping payment of the nafaqa.

Abu Sardana's major decree was one relating to the age of marriage, and the way he constructed his discourse around the meaning of early marriage was interesting. He prohibited the judges from concluding marriage contracts for females younger than the age of 15 lunar (14.7 Gregorian) years and for males younger than the age of 16 years. The decree explained:

> Marriage below the age of puberty, as practised in the Shari'a courts of Gaza Strip, has proved to be socially, clinically and humanly harmful to the females under the age of puberty. The Islamic Shari'a instructs us that avoiding damage is superior to bringing advantages. It also states that we have to employ the finest interpretation (ijtihad) of Muslim scholars to serve the best interests of Muslims.
>
> (Decree No. 78/1995 of 25 December 1995, in Faris 2002)

These were the main decrees and actions of Abu Sardana during his term of less than three years. The underlying principle of Abu Sardana's decrees remains in keeping with the asymmetrical gender power distribution. However, the qadi al-qudah's decrees responded to practical demands by lawyers and particular sectors of the women's movement.

The actions of the qadi al-qudah were driven by a vision of unifying family law in Gaza and the West Bank, Islamization of the project of state-building during the transitional period and modernization of the personal status law on the basis of serving the best interests of the public (maslaha). This vision of modernization is similar to that of Muhammad Abdu in the nineteenth century, during which the various needs of society and ambitions for change were viewed through religious spectacles. Abu Sardana attempted to bridge the gap between the past and future by employing the concept of maslaha and deriving reform from the teachings of a wide range of madhahib. He laid the ground for the unification process by setting up a committee to review the laws of Gaza and the West Bank. His view of takhayyur among the various madhahib and choice of the best to serve the interests of people in the contemporary era can be viewed as a moderate (though not new) approach towards codifying the Shari'a.

He also contributed to the incorporation of the Shari'a in the project of state-building in Palestine. While the draft Constitution neglected the issue of Shari'a courts, ifta and awqaf altogether, the mere invitation of Abu Sardana to Tunis and his appeal to the leadership of Fatah to incorporate these aspects in the future Palestine played a significant role in establishing the position of Shari'a courts as one of the main institutions in constructing the future family law of Palestine.

9.3 Deliberation within the women's movement

The most active sector of the women's movement during the debate on family law was driven by the equality strategy (Hammami and Johnson 1999; Jad et al. 2000), and that strategy was the dynamic force behind initiatives such as the creation of the Women's Charter (1994), the campaign for female candidates for the Palestinian Legislative Council, the various reviews of existing laws and the campaigns for family law reform (Johnson 2004: 147). In 1999 came the 'National Campaign for a Unified Palestinian Family Law', which was organized by a number of women's organizations, NGOs and human rights centres that defined themselves as a group of Palestinians 'seeking the participation of society in the legislation process for a Palestinian family law based on full equality in rights and duties within the family'.[7] The campaigners' main objectives, formulated at a meeting held in 1999, were:

1   to prepare a draft Palestinian family law on the basis of justice and equality;
2   to enable Palestinians from various sectors who believed in full equality to participate in discussing and proposing Palestinian family law;
3   to raise people's awareness of the importance of protecting human rights within the family;
4   to lobby for the proposed draft among legislators and decision-makers.

The campaigners emphasized the importance of viewing family law and reform as a subject of concern not only for women but for the whole society. Therefore, they proposed, communication with political groups should be broadened, legal experts should be involved, journalists should be encouraged to write about family law reform and the dialogue with the Legislative Council should be continued.[8] Above all, the law should be termed the 'family law' instead of the inappropriate 'personal status law'. This new strategy was born out of conflict between two approaches within the movement: the 'NGO' approach, which looked at the process of legal reform as a donor-driven 'project' with specific activities, and an (alternative) approach that regarded legal reform as part of a larger socio-political process (Johnson 2004: 157).

After several rounds of deliberation, the campaign's activities and objectives were updated, and the links between Palestinians' national tragedy and the existence of conflicting and paradoxical laws in Gaza and the West Bank were further elaborated. The elaboration provided a detailed account of the creation of Israel on part of Palestine in 1948, followed by Jordanian rule on the West Bank, Egyptian rule over the Gaza Strip and the occupation of the rest of Palestine in 1967, which subjected the people in Gaza and the West Bank to more than a thousand Israeli military rules. This situation was seen by the drafters as justification for urgently unifying the laws that governed Palestinians as a nation. The campaigners suggested that the 1996 election of the Legislative Council was an opportunity for Palestinians to propose laws that would meet the requirements of sustainable development. They called for reform of family law on the following bases:

1   Women's rights to be regarded as human rights
2   Elimination of all direct and indirect discriminatory measures against women reflected in laws, policies and the prevalent discriminatory culture
3   Equality and democracy in the family
4   Housework to be defined as productive and a contribution to family welfare

With regard to the frame of reference for the reform, the campaigners suggested three major sources, among others: the Declaration of Independence (1988), the draft of the Basic Law and the goals of the Shari'a (maqasid al-Shari'a).[9]

The campaigners stressed the need for popular participation in the debate and in the process of reform; they said the historical role of Palestinian women in the national struggle should be recognized and their voices should be heard; and they called for a 'democratic family' to be established to meet the challenges of the future and the building of a democratic society.

Johnson (2004: 159–60) suggests that reforming family law on the basis of gender equality is far more complicated than addressing it in the framework of an NGO project, since it 'requires a wide process of democratic participation'. However, viewing family law as merely a political initiative, whether perceived as an NGO project or as an element of a wider political process, could run the risk of ignoring the needs and interests of the vast majority of women, who do not claim representation or have no voice in the political process. In particular, the document prepared by the women's movement gave little consideration to how women experience the law or the kind of strategies they adopt in challenging or accommodating to the law. The areas of ambivalence in the existing law that provide a space for women to manœuvre were not explored. More importantly, the mere statement of participation of 'those who believe in full equality' was exclusionary, because neither 'equality' nor the meaning of 'full equality' was defined. The women's movement draft did not look into issues such as equality of whom, with whom and under what conditions. However, when the draft was written, this shortcoming was recovered. It specified that in terms of legal capacity, men and women should be treated as equals.

9.4 Draft of women's movement

The main points stressed in the women's movement draft were:

1   The age of marriage should be 18 years for both men and women.
2   The marriage contract should be viewed as a contract of rights and obligations between two equal partners.
3   Women should be viewed as equal to men in terms of their legal capacity, and thus no wali should make decisions about their marriage on their behalf, especially with the minimum age of marriage set at 18 years.
4   Divorce should be legally valid only when it is carried out in the court, with both husband and wife having equal right to request it.
5   The government should establish an alimony fund (sanduq al-nafaqat).
6   After divorce, wealth accumulated during the marriage should be divided between husband and wife, with housework being recognized as contributing to that accumulation.
7   Alimony should be paid in the case of arbitrary divorce.
8   Children's maintenance and custody should be the equal responsibility of both parents during marriage and after divorce.

When analysing the draft, one encounters serious problems in terms of outlook, conception and methodology. To begin with, the draft tacitly assumed that the upcoming state would be a welfare state that would be responsible for paying the nafaqa of unemployed spouses, providing dwellings to divorced mothers, paying for the care of children and so on. Additionally, the draft endorsed the same concepts of raji (revocable) and bain (irrevocable) divorce as defined in Islamic family law, but gave them different meanings and enacted them through different mechanisms. The draft stated that every divorce should be revocable, except when the wife had finished her idda period, in which case the divorce should be declared irrevocable. Islamic family law does not follow this logic; as shown in earlier chapters of this volume, there are different circumstances in which a divorce is declared revocable or irrevocable. Moreover, once the divorce is declared by the judge, the party injured by the termination of the marriage has the right to claim compensation, in which case the judge is responsible for estimating the amount of compensation.

Article 77 of the women's movement draft limited the nafaqa that a divorced wife could receive; it proposed that if the husband requested the divorce, his wife should receive nafaqat al-idda (maintenance costs given to a divorced wife to cover her expenses of food, shelter and clothing for three lunar months), but if the request for divorce came from the wife, she did not deserve the nafaqat al-idda, and the husband would have no further financial responsibilities for her well-being. Thus, the draft effectively cancelled the other nafaqa granted to wives under Islamic law. Moreover, even for the nafaqat al-idda, the draft did not specify how judges should measure the hurt sustained by the wife as a result of the divorce, how much the nafaqa should be and on what basis it should be calculated. In other words, it did not answer the following question: if nafaqa as a fundamental right of wives under Islamic family law were eliminated, then on what basis would injury be evaluated? Similarly, the draft endorsed the concepts of revocable and irrevocable divorce as well as of talaq with baynuna kubra (the 'greater finality' occasioned by the third talaq) and sughra (the 'lesser finality' occasioned by the first or second talaq); but it did not state under which circumstances the qadi, having become the arbiter of the marriage, would make the decision. The same applied to the endorsement of the concepts of irregular marriage (zawaj fasid) and void marriage (zawaj batil).

By recognizing the nafaqat al-idda as the only financial right of the wife when a marriage was terminated, and by leaving the compensation to be estimated by the qadi without any specification, the draft was a backward step in comparison with the Jordanian law, in which a man who abruptly divorces his wife is obliged to pay her compensation equivalent to nafaqa for up to one year. In sum, the drafters did not seem to understand the logic of Islamic law, nor did they know how to end the harmful measures in the family law by referring to the sources to which they adhered. It seems that, while setting up a legal framework for the spouses to be treated equally, the drafters ignored the reality that the couple have unequal power resources.

Interestingly, while the drafters advocated the equality discourse and asserted the economic responsibility of the state towards its citizens, they retained some Islamically arranged economic responsibilities, not only among members of the nuclear family but also beyond it to members of the 'extended family'. For example, a full chapter was dedicated to the relatives' maintenance. In articles 53–61, the drafters arranged for the nafaqa of the children, parents and grandparents on the basis of the same philosophy as Islamic law despite some modifications. Parents and their children were kept mutually dependent on each other. Grandparents were entitled to be economically looked after by their grandchildren. Even some relatives were given financial rights upon judicial request. These arrangements contrasted with the first page of the draft family law, which described the family as the fundamental unit of society (al-labina al-assasiyya li-l-mujtama), and then went on to focus on marital arrangements. It is not clear whether the drafters put more emphasis on the importance of the position of the nuclear family or on its responsibilities towards the wider network of kinship relations.

In article 92, the drafters made hadana the responsibility of both parents for as long as the marriage lasted. After dissolution of the marriage, the mother was designated as hadina (carer); next in line for the role was the children's father. If neither parent was alive, the hadana was transferred to the child's relatives. This transference, in contrast to Islamic law, was cited without any ordering arrangement. As discussed in Chapter 7, hadana is not transferred to the father immediately after the mother in the *Book of Personal Status Rulings* (*BPSR*). When a mother fails to qualify as a carer, her right to hadana is transferred to other females. In particular, article 384 of the *BPSR* states that if the mother dies or if she marries a stranger [non-muhram to the child] or if she is not eligible for hadana, her caring right is transferred to the maternal grandmother. If the latter is not alive or is ineligible, the hadana is conveyed to the paternal grandmother.

In this transference of hadana, the potential carer's proximity to the child's mother ranks higher than her proximity to the child's father. Moreover, regarding the issue of guardianship, it was not clear in the draft whether hadana conferred full decision-making powers with regard to the ward.

The drafters seemed to be either unaware of the meaning and implications of this order in Islamic law or had decided to ignore the issue altogether due to its problematic implications. Another interpretation might be that the drafters wanted to emphasize the notion of the nuclear family, in which children's affairs are the business of their close father and mother and nobody else.

An interesting element in the draft was the endorsement of housework as productive work, but it is a complex issue. It requires an entirely different definition of 'work' and major reforms in state policies, particularly the economic structure. The division of work into productive and reproductive is at the heart of modern gender asymmetry. To recognize housework as productive in Palestine would presuppose not only ideological commitment to gender symmetry but an entirely different economic system that does not suffer from the anomalies characterizing the economy of a country under occupation.[10]

Another new issue in the draft was that the spouses should divide the wealth accumulated during the marriage period between them, except that which came to either of them through inheritance or donation (hiba). This was a step forward in comparison with Islamic family law despite the difficulty of its application.[11]

The main issues in the draft produced by the women's movement were: ending the wali's right; banning polygyny; economic equality between partners in terms of household expenses; depriving dower of any legal or economic meaning; eliminating women's right to nafaqa from their husbands; and, finally, granting women the right to engage in the labour market without the husband's permission.

These proposals, while appearing to establish family relations on the basis of equality, ignore both the wider system of power distribution in Palestinian society and the various ways in which women use these legal dispositions. As we have seen in previous chapters, the right of women to nafaqa and dower are not always used straightforwardly; women have devised various strategies to claim these rights as well as socially acceptable power resources to negotiate others. The right to nafaqa is only an economic right, but women use it to negotiate fundamental aspects in their lives. The same applies to women's right to dower; women use it as their main economic resource. A woman can voluntarily transfer her dower (in the form of gold) to her husband to make a point and thus strengthen her position in the family. It may be used to help children in their studies. Various needs are fulfilled by the economic means, however limited, provided by the dower.

What is suggested by the women's movement is no less than elimination of the limited power resources provided by the legal system, however oppressive it is, without presenting a viable alternative. How would ordinary women benefit if they were granted the right to go out to work if there were very few jobs for them? Engagement in wage labour is not an objective in itself; it has to be placed in the broader framework of access to power resources and in the potential of such an amendment to transform marriage into a more egalitarian institution. How would ordinary women benefit from the elimination of dower with no alternative economic power being suggested, especially in the absence of social security, the prevailing political crisis and extremely restricted and gendered labour markets?

9.5 Disagreement within the religious establishment

This section highlights the disagreement within the religious establishment regarding the gender arrangements of the amended family law. The qadi al-qudah at that time, Taysir Al-timimi, voiced some of his views at a meeting attended by Muslim scholars, entitled 'The First Palestinian Forum for Islamic Fiqh and Issues Related to Personal Status', held in Ramallah on 12 November 2001. Al-timimi, who was the moderator, expressed the needs of broader segments of Palestinian society on the one hand, and his recognition of the 'gaps and weaknesses' in the existing legislation on the other. However, he was clear and firm that the 'ulama' (Islamic scholars), from whichever discipline they came, had the authority to decide personal status matters. Another point to note in his statement was his reference to the Legislative Council as the institution authorized to ratify the new family law.

Al-timimi identified the gaps and weaknesses he had observed in the application of the law. For example, he referred to court cases of niza wa shiqaq (discord and strife between spouses) as a source of pain and delay in the courts. In his view, there were difficulties in providing proof in such cases, a point on which the majority of lawyers and the judges agreed. To speed up the pace of such cases and minimize the difficulties of litigants (obviously women), he proposed that the judges should be encouraged to use their discretion more often. However, he also suggested that the decisions made by the judges in cases of discord and strife should be subject to the approval of the Court of Appeal.

Another example of his sensitivity regarding the problems of women in the court, and an indication of his practicality, was his position regarding compensation for arbitrary unilateral divorce. His view was that the current legislation, which provided women with nafaqa for up to one year as compensation for such a divorce, did not make up for the harm inflicted on them. Therefore, Al-timimi proposed that compensation should correspond to the degree of injury, no matter how much that was. However, later, in his proposed draft, Al-timimi suggested that the compensation should amount to nafaqa for a maximum of five years.

The rights and arrangements of divorced parents to visit their children were also sources of concern to Al-timimi. He expressed dissatisfaction over divorced parents having to visit their children in courts and police stations, which, in his view, led to psychological problems for the children. In his draft, he suggested that children should be visited in specialized centres.

Al-timimi also recommended that the age at which the mother's hadana ended be amended to bring it more 'in line with the Islamic Shari'a'. In addition, he proposed an increase in the minimum age of marriage to harmonize it with the age of financial capacity, which is 18 years. He contended that the onset of puberty was subject to climatic conditions and so was not a reliable measure of sexual maturity. Al-timimi repeatedly stated that, when amending the law, reference should be made to all the Islamic madhahib, which was another indication of his adherence to the principle of selection (takhayyur). Al-timimi's agenda for improving the functioning of Shari'a courts included founding a trust fund for orphans and another one for nafaqa (sanduq al-nafaqat), from which the state would pay nafaqa to wives whose entitlement was upheld by a Shari'a court. The state, through its agencies, would then pursue the man to repay the amount.

Al-timimi ended his speech with a general remark about the Shari'a being the sole reference for amendment of the personal status law.

The mufti of Jerusalem, Shaykh Ikrima Sabri, who had been invited to the forum, made the following points:

1   Women who work outside the home do not deserve nafaqa, whether their work is performed with the permission of their husbands or not.
2   Women who have not reached the age of maturity (sin al-rushd) have no right to file for mukhala'a. In this regard, the mufti criticized the Egyptian law on khul that had been ratified in January 2001.[12] In his view, legal space should not be given to women with regard to khul as in Egypt; instead, it should be decided by the qadi.
3   Regarding compensation to women for arbitrary divorce, the court should take into account how long the spouses have been married. A man who has been married for only one year should not be judged in the same way as one who has been married for 20 years.
4   There should be more restrictions on how mothers can become eligible for hadana. First, they should not work outside the home. Second, children should not go back to the mother even after her legal ineligibility for hadana has changed to eligibility. (According to the family law, if the mother marries a man who does not have a prohibited degree of kinship in relation to the children, the children should be taken from her. However, it also states that if the reason for taking the children no longer applies [that is, if she is divorced from that man], the children should go back to her.) The mufti argued that the children would have become used to their carer over time, and going back to their mother would inflict emotional conflict on them. He also called for an end to payment of caring fees (ujrat hadana) to mothers whose husbands had died; his reasoning was that the continuation of

children's care without being given money for it would 'prove their loyalty to their children, to their dead husbands and to their in-laws'.
5   The age of marriage should continue to be the age of puberty: 'If the daughter's family wants to get her married early or late, that is their business.'

It is clear that the mufti's views were more conservative than those of the qadi al-qudah: decisions regarding marriage, divorce, repudiation and mukhala'a should never be in the hands of females; women should continue to be treated as minors, with their families deciding on their marriage, husbands deciding on their divorce and judges deciding on their repudiation and mukhala'a; families should be free to marry off their daughters at the age of their choice. As far as the mufti was concerned, the law should not, under any circumstances, give women the right to make decisions. His view regarding the age of marriage is particularly alarming in the framework of the state-citizens relation.

The mufti's discourse regarding hadana was even more conservative than that in the classical fiqh (see Chapter 7). The sayings of Prophet Muhammad, the practice of his companions, and the fiqh about children's hadana do not take such an approach. Although children's rights are not much elaborated in the classical fiqh, hadana is clearly recognized as both the right and responsibility of the mother. Yet, citing potential psychological problems for the child, the mufti wanted to deprive the mother of her right to hadana.

Al-timimi responded to the mufti regarding the point on khul: 'If you suggest that underaged women have no right to mukhala'a, how then can we accept their marrying at that age?' He followed this up with a caution about early marriage: 'Early marriage is dangerous. The girl enters the marriage institution without knowledge about her rights; she does not know what is prompt dower and what is deferred dower.' To reach a compromise with the mufti, Al-timimi proposed that judges should be given the right to allow teenagers (murahiqat) to marry in some instances.

Unlike in pre-modern times, when the judges and muftis were arguing within the framework of different interpretations of the various madhahib, the current contestation is taking place in the context of the state attempting to codify the Shari'a, or, more precisely, to re-codify the existing laws. Thus, the dispute at the public forum can be seen as a conflict over whose interpretation should be dominant and whose views should constitute the state's codified law.

Gender relations and roles organized by family law will probably continue to be a disputed topic within the religious establishment as long as these roles and relations witness changes; thus, it will pose critical questions with regard to their organizing legal framework. Furthermore, the position of the mufti, unlike that of the qadi al-qudah, who has more practical views, reflects the ideological stance of those who are removed from the daily life of the Shari'a court (see Moors 2003: 6). In the final analysis, the religious establishment, like the women's movement, is far from being unified; this has important political implications in terms of how to engage in fruitful dialogue with those who have various degrees of sensitivity towards women, both as litigants and as political actors.

9.6 Al-timimi's draft[13]

While keeping the overall picture of gender roles and relations unchanged, Al-timimi's draft provides some practical solutions to the problems faced by female litigants in Shari'a courts. It focuses on issues relating to the age of marriage, the role of a wali, kafa (equivalent status of bride and groom), dwelling, nafaqa, women's engagement in wage labour, divorce and mukhala'a, compensation for arbitrary unilateral divorce, tafriq (divorce by judicial decision), inheritance and hadana. Let us now analyse the main points of the qadi al-qudah's draft further in the following sections.

9.6.1 On the age of marriage

The draft establishes an institutional and familial hierarchy for underaged girls to get married. Females under the legal age of marriage should get the permission of three authorities; two are from the religious hierarchy and the third is the male guardian in the family (the wali). Furthermore, the groom should be kafu' (equivalent). This proposal is less reformative than the Abu Sardana decree, derived from the Jordanian law, in which he totally forbids the judges from permitting the marriage of girls younger than age 15. Al-timimi's proposal would create the possibility of girls as young as nine being given legal permission to be married off by their guardians.

9.6.2 On the wife's return to her husband's house

Al-Timimi's draft replaces the following clause in article 37 of the Jordanian law: 'After getting her mahr, the wife moves to the shar'i house of her husband.' The new text reads: 'After getting her mahr, the wife is obliged (tulzam) . . . to move to her husband's house.' Using 'obliged to move' instead of 'moves' might lead to an interpretation that the wife can be moved to her husband's house forcibly. However, article 37 is cautious about that; it states clearly that if the wife does not move to her husband's house, she is considered nashiz, which (as explained in Chapter 6) may mean that force is not to be used.

9.6.3 On the role of the wali

The major regressive step in Al-timimi's draft is the strengthening of the wali's power to decide on marriage. A marriage without the wali's permission would be considered fasid (irregular), a condition that does not exist in the Jordanian law. This formulation is a step backward even from the *Book of Personal Status Rulings*, article 34 of which makes the agreement of the wali a condition for the validity of marriage between underaged males and females (al-saghir wa al-saghira) but not for the marriage of those who have crossed the age of puberty. It is also a step backward from Abu Sardana's decree that makes the mere acceptance of the marriage by the wali preferable instead of obligatory. The schools of Islamic law, too, do not support Al-timimi's position on irregular marriage. In his review of madhahib positions on regularity of marriages, Samara (1987: 140) finds that non-acceptance by the wali is only considered a reason for declaring a marriage irregular in cases where the male and female are under the age of puberty. Thus, the Al-timimi draft in this regard is a step backward even in comparison with the most conservative views in classical fiqh.

Another problem relating to Al-timimi's formulation is that of the disparity between legal and religious legitimation. (Chapter 2 discussed this point and referred to the possibility of such conflicts.) For example, marriages performed without the permission of the wali are considered irregular by Al-Timimi, but in the view of religion (or at least of some madhahib), they are legitimate.

9.6.4 On consulting women

Al-timimi's draft includes a new clause relating to a husband having to inform his wife of his intention to divorce her in order to marry another woman; however, that notification does not give her the right to object to the husband's decision. A step forward in the draft, which does not exist in the Jordanian law and fiqh schools, is that the proposed bride should be informed of his first marriage. It is probably a response to the women's movement's demand to restrict the freedom of men to have more than one wife, especially considering the historical tendency towards monogamous marriage. The inclusion of such a 'gender-sensitive' article may have been intended as compensation for strengthening the role of the wali. However, Al-timimi's draft is less innovative in this regard than some personal status codes in many other Arab countries.

9.6.5 On nafaqa

This was one of Al-timimi's innovations. While article 68 of the Jordanian law states that no nafaqa is to be paid to a woman engaged in wage labour without her husband's permission, in Al-timimi's draft, the articulation is different. A woman who works outside of the home is still able to claim her right to nafaqa if her husband accepted her work initially and changed his mind later, or if he has not carried out his duty of maintaining his wife, thus making her wage labour a necessity. Although the women's movement fought for women's civil rights, including wage employment, the issue requires further thought. Wage employment is not an objective in itself; it has to be placed in the broader framework of enabling women to have greater access to power resources and in the potentiality of such an amendment to transform the gender contract of the marriage itself.

9.6.6 On mukhala'a

While Al-timimi's draft gives the judges legal room to allow a wife to repudiate her husband if she has the financial resources to repay her dower or to pay reasonable badal or awad (compensation), the Jordanian law does not include such a possibility. Instead, mukhala'a has to be granted on the basis of an agreement between the two spouses. Arabi (2001: 188), cited in Welchman (2004: 6), regards this change as a 'radical break' from classical fiqh. Under 'classical' fiqh, as Welchman (2004: 6) observes, this type of divorce would need the consent of the husband. In addition, the Al-timimi draft does not permit children's rights to be bargained away in the negotiation between the parents. Their hadana, nafaqa and dwelling are immune from any arrangement between their parents.

9.6.7 On compensation for arbitrary unilateral divorce

In Al-timimi's draft, three articles elaborate the arrangement of and compensation for arbitrary unilateral divorce, while in the Jordanian law, one article is devoted to the issue. Al-timimi extends the compensation to five years of nafaqa, while in the Jordanian law the duration of compensation does not exceed one year. Furthermore, Al-timimi considers the dwelling and furniture in the house to be part of the belongings of an arbitrarily divorced wife; this is a major departure from the Jordanian law, which does not specify such a right. It resonates with Egyptian Law No. 44 of 1979, known as Jihan's Law, which grants the dwelling to an arbitrarily divorced wife. The compensation to the wife for arbitrary divorce is a major step forward because it does not feature in the 1954 *LFR* (which is implemented in Gaza). However, article 99 of the draft, which relieves a husband from compensating his wife if he can prove that there was reasonable cause for his arbitrary divorce, is a weak point because it might enable husbands to manipulate the law.

The right of wives to their share of the wealth accumulated during the marriage period is also not found in the Jordanian law. Section C of article 100 in Al-timimi's draft seems to have been a response to the women's movement's demands regarding division of the wealth accumulated during marriage. However, the women's movement also proposed that women's housework should be calculated as a contribution to the accumulated wealth, a point that Al-timimi does not include in his draft. Another obstacle that may appear if this draft is ratified is that, even when women contribute to the accumulation of wealth, the cultural practice is that these assets are registered in the name of the husband. Again, law and society might drive in two different directions, a point that was examined extensively in Chapter 5 (on nafaqa) and Chapter 6 (on the house of obedience provision).

9.6.8 On tafriq (judicial divorce)

The difference on this issue is the following: in article 114 of the Jordanian law, a wife who knew about her husband's 'medical' defect before the marriage, or who accepted it after marriage, is not allowed to request tafriq. In contrast, Al-timimi creates space for a wife who knew of her husband's defect or even accepted it before marriage to change her mind and ask for tafriq if there is proof that it is impossible for her to continue living with him on that basis. The draft allows wives to request tafriq if the husband has proved to be unable to procreate, which is not stated in the Jordanian law.

9.6.9 On hadana (care of children)

Al-timimi's reforms are progressive steps in comparison with the Jordanian law because they allow the mother to keep the children with her until they reach the age of puberty. Moreover, if she does not marry again, she can keep them with her until they reach the age of 18 years.

9.7 Gradual change in the new millennium

The aim of this section is to analyse the extent to which 20 years of Palestinian women's struggle for family law reform has brought about positive change in the implementation of Shari'a laws.[14] It is an update to the research done in the Gaza Shari'a courts in the first half of this decade. Because the draconian blockade of Gaza from 2007 onwards has made it impossible for me to travel there and carry out further ethnographic research, this section is based on my regular telephone contacts with Shari'a court judges and lawyers as well as activists in the women's movement and civil society organizations, in addition to relevant publications.

Among the publications consulted for this section are the decrees published by the Shari'a authorities. Given the changes that Hamas has effected in Gaza in terms of political liberties, civil law and social policies, it was logical to expect additional legal provisions that suggested attempts to mirror its tenets, but, to my surprise, I found none. Many activists lamented that there had been incidents of political nepotism, including appointment of members, or relatives of members, of Hamas to specific positions. However, from a legal perspective, and as published documents and communications with the concerned lawyers and personnel demonstrate, the 'independence' of the Shari'a courts has not changed. Or perhaps, as one feminist activist in Gaza commented, 'the Shari'a court is the ultimate locus of conservatism; Hamas can add no more.'

By the end of the Model Parliament campaign (1997–99), President Yasir Arafat formed a committee to draft a new family law. The committee was chaired by the head of the High Council of the Shari'a Judiciary and comprised 'Shari'a court judges, academics and professors of Islamic Shari'a law, and lawyers. Women were, however, absent' (Abu Hayya 2011: 6). The women's movement then formed the 'National Coalition on Family Law' in cooperation with a number of civil society organizations. As noted earlier, the most important priorities of the National Coalition were: raising the age of marriage for girls from 15 to 18; annulling guardianship for girls aged 18 and older; granting women the same rights as men for judicial divorce; linking custody rights with serving the best interests of the child; imposing restrictions on polygyny to make it extremely difficult; and dividing the common wealth equally between husbands and wives after the annulment of marriage (Abu Hayya 2011: 6).

However, due to the outbreak of the second intifada in 2000,[15] the debate on family reform plummeted to the bottom of the list of priorities, not only of the Palestinian Authority but also of the women's movement and civil society organizations in general.[16] In 2006, Palestinians elected their representatives to the Palestinian Legislative Council (PLC), and Hamas legitimately won the majority of the seats. However, due to the Israeli blockade and arrest of many of its members, the PLC was not able to convene; thus, not a single law was passed by it. This legal vacuum led the president to use a provision in article 43 of the Basic Law of 2003 that empowered him to issue decrees that had the power of laws (Aby Hayya 2011: 7). That led civil society organizations to doubt the wisdom of submitting a new family law to be imposed by presidential decree.

In 2007, the Hamas cabinet minister of women's affairs, Amal Siam, made a joint decision with the head of the High Council of the Shari'a Judiciary to forward the draft personal status law to the president for his approval. This step was not welcomed by the National Coalition on Family Law, and it called on its members to send protest letters to the president, the minister of women's affairs and the head of the High Council of the Shari'a Judiciary. They asked for a 'chance to comment on the draft, and have those comments appropriately discussed and incorporated' (Abu Hayya 2011: 7). Their request was accepted and their members met with the president, who promised them that nothing would be passed without their agreement.

From 2007 until now, due to the takeover of Gaza by Hamas and the ensuing political complications, there has been no major discussion of family law. With Hamas in power, Palestinians became subject to two different governments led by two different political factions. The judiciary was also split. As stated earlier, the project of state-building in Palestine witnessed the emergence of competing discourses related to the question of family law reform, recodification and unification. The debate on these issues went so far as to address larger questions related to the identity of the state, the location of Islam, the meaning/definition of citizenship and the epistemological and political basis upon which codification should be based. The weakness and authoritarianism of the Palestinian Authority (representing the upcoming state) and its unwillingness, or perhaps inability, to rely on constituency-based politics (Hammami 2004) made it improbable that comprehensive and gender-sensitive family law reform could be achieved.

Faced with having to operate within the framework of a weak and authoritarian government, and with the mufti of Jerusalem constantly denigrating his proposals, the qadi al-qudah allied himself with the 'enlightened 'ulama' inside the Shari'a courts to achieve his vision of gradual reform on a low-key basis. He started with modernization of the administration apparatus and issued the following decrees:

1   Clarification of the relations between the three hierarchical bodies in the Shari'a court: the judges of first instance, the Court of Appeal and the qadi al-qudah.

172 *Change, a step at a time*

2   Establishment, for the first time in the history of Palestine, of a Shari'a High Court comprising the qadi al-qudah as the president and a number of the judges of the Court of Appeal as members. This court was to be the highest authority at the national level to which citizens could appeal if they were not satisfied with the decisions of the courts in their districts.
3   Creation of an implementation department in the Shari'a courts, which freed the courts from dependence on the civil legal system for implementation of their decisions.
4   Two bills, one relating to investment of the financial resources of orphans and the other relating to the setting up of an alimony fund (sanduq al-nafaqat), were presented to the president for ratification and issued as decrees.

The qadi al-qudah's approach was to introduce reformative actions gradually through decrees instead of waiting for the family law to be unified and ratified by the PLC. This approach became the standard method of legal change in the Palestinian territories after the national election of 2006 and the ensuing arrests of the members of the Legislative Council by Israel, as well as the impossibility of convening the PLC due to the blockade of Gaza. For example, President Abbas issued 120 decrees between 2006 and 2016, a number that exceeds the number of Palestinian laws passed by the PLC during the 10 years of its life. In Al-timimi's view, reform based on public campaigns and discussions draws exaggerated responses from different political parties and groups, since each group has its own agenda and interests. Many issues can be resolved by decrees, which, he argues, are less provocative.

The qadi al-qudah made two other significant changes: upgrading of judges' skills and strengthening of relations between the Shari'a court, as an institution, and the community. Upgrading of skills was done in two ways. The first was by exposing judges to the latest developments in the codification and application of personal status law in other Arab and Muslim countries, through exchange of experiences and by attending conferences and workshops in other parts of the Muslim world. The second was by building a national centre to train Palestinian Shari'a judges. To raise the community's awareness about the content of Islamic family law in general, and particularly about the duties and responsibilities of couples before, during and after marriage, the qadi al-qudah initiated a major programme to bring the Shari'a court, as an institution, closer to the community. For example, awareness-raising events were designed to increase public knowledge about the entitlement of women (and men) to insert conditions into the marriage contract.

Substantive changes in the family law itself were proposed and defended by Al-timimi, but many of them were issued as decrees by the president or the next qadi al-qudah. For example, prolonging the period of female widows' hadana was issued as Law No. 1 of 2009 by the president of the Palestinian Authority. It authorizes judges to permit 'female widows' to continue the hadana of their children as long as they keep 'imprisoning' themselves to do so. 'Imprisonment' in this context means total dedication to the children, which may entail the widowed mother not working outside the home and not marrying again because that would reduce her attention to the children. Widows who get the right to exercise hadana are also required to allow the asaba (a relative of the children from their father's side) to see and monitor the children. Following the issuing of this law, many women's organizations requested the Palestinian Authority to extend the law to cover divorced women who were proved appropriate to carry out their right of 'hadana'.

Employing women in the Shari'a court was a priority for Al-timimi. To begin with, he advocated appointing women as family counsellors, who would make their recommendations directly to the qadi al-qudah. The social counsellors are recommended by the judge to couples involved in a dispute, to mediate between them and help them reach an agreeable solution. Once that is achieved, the solution is accepted in writing by both spouses and then ratified by the qadi al-qudah, after which no court (including the Court of Appeal) can overrule it. This mechanism seems to work to a certain extent outside of the courtroom. According to Al-timimi, 'This route of conflict resolution is meant to establish the Shari'a court as an alternative to the customary law mechanisms (al-hilul al-'asha'riyya).'

The qadi al-qudah also recommended the appointment of women as attorneys-general, as a first step towards their later being appointed as judges in the Shari'a courts. Another innovation was the appointment of female mathouns (marriage notaries) in the West Bank. This role has historically been assigned to men. In April 2015, Tahrir Hammad became the first woman to be appointed mathoun in Palestine and to take up her formal role of concluding marriage contracts. Few Muslim-majority countries allow women to take up this job.[17]

In 2009, the qadi al-qudah took the appointment of women to public office a big step forward by naming two women as Shari'a court judges, a step that most Muslim-majority states did not dare to take. Justifying the appointments, al-Tamimi said, 'I teach in Shari'a and law schools in many universities, and I often find female students smarter and more dedicated than male students. I also rely on previous fatwas and I have not read any fatwa that forbids appointment of women as Shari'a court judges.'[18]

Despite these innovative steps, the representation of women in the Shari'a courts (as employees in all ranks) is still quite low. For example, women hold only 1% of clerical jobs and 6% of Shari'a judiciary and prosecuting magistrate jobs. These percentages are far below the international norm of at least 12%.[19]

In April 2017, at a ceremony to appoint a number of male and female Shari'a court judges, the newly appointed qadi al-qudah, Mahmoud al-Habbash, said,

> There is no difference between women and men in taking up public duty, including ultimate general mandate (alwilaya al-amma) positions. It is women's right to take up such positions as long as they have the required knowledge and capability and as long as they meet the legal requirement to occupy such posts.[20]

In my view, unless this statement was made only for public consumption, it contributes to the already established controversy in the Islamic literature regarding women's taking up a general mandate position. The four Sunni madahib as well as the Shias reject such a position for women, following the hadith, 'A people who make a woman their ruler will never be successful' [reported by al-Bukhari]. Women were first appointed as judges in the 'modern' Shari'a court in Indonesia in 1989 after almost two decades of deliberation (Nurlaelawati and Arskal 2017: 102).

By April 2017, four female Shari'a court judges had been appointed in the West Bank. There was no such appointment in Gaza even though, in contrast to recurrent criticism of various political and legal decisions taken by the West Bank government, no one had objected to the decision to appoint female judges in the West Bank. According to Sonneveld and Lindbekk (2017), appointment of women as judges in other parts of the Muslim world came as a result of international pressure on the one hand and availability of funds on the other. That was not the case in Palestine. It only needed long-term campaigning by the women's movement, civil society support and advocacy, continuous negotiation with the concerned institutions (using power resources, including political networks, to put pressure on the qadi al-qudah, but also acceptance of compromises in certain fields) and perhaps wise leadership in the Shari'a court.

Decrees have been used to improve the legal position of Palestinian women to some extent in other ways, too. According to lawyer Halima Abu Sulb, Decree No. 42 of 2010 nullified the requirement that wives should take the family name of their husbands; they now have the right to keep their own natal family name (Abu Sulb 2012). The decree also gave women over the age of 18 years, whether they be daughters or wives, the right to apply for passports without their father's or husband's permission. Widows who have not been divorced have the right to apply for passports for their children provided they have proof from a Shari'a court that the children are under their care. Palestinian women who are married to non-Palestinian men are allowed to transmit their citizenship to their children and register them in their ID cards until they become 16 (at which age they get their own independent IDs). The same right is given to Palestinian men who are married to non-Palestinian women.

In 2010 and 2011, the qadi al-qudah in the West Bank issued three decrees. The first, mentioned earlier, required a man who intended to marry a second time to inform his first wife of his intention and the proposed bride of his current marital status. The second decree made divorce outside the Shari'a court illegal, with violators liable to a fine of NIS [New Israeli Shekels] 500. The third decree concerned inheritance claims; it forbade filing of cases to determine shares of inheritance until four months after the death of the bequeather.

In Gaza, the only change that was disappointing to the Palestinian women's movement was a decree issued by the Hamas-appointed qadi al-qudah on 7 February 2016, which extended the existing right of wives to file suits for divorce due to discord and strife (niza wa shiqaq) to husbands. The decree increased men's ability to divorce their wives without paying them prompt and deferred dower.

Until then, only wives could file for judicial divorce due to discord and strife because, unlike husbands, they could not divorce at will (Abou Jalal 2016).[21]

In March 2009, the president of the Palestinian Authority signed CEDAW, the Convention on the Elimination of all forms of Discrimination Against Women.[22] This signing was more symbolic than practical, since eliminating all forms of discrimination requires a free and unified nation, unoccupied land, political stability and powerful authority; all these elements and many more (for example, democracy and rule of law, respect of human rights) are lacking in Palestine. Whether CEDAW will be incorporated into the Palestinian legal framework is unclear. In a study published in 2012, Palestinian lawyer Halima Abu Sulb provides interesting information about recent developments in the Palestinian territories regarding legal change through presidential and ministerial decrees. She unwittingly shows that, while piecemeal reforms have been made, they are quite remarkable in terms of their influence on gender justice in Palestine.

According to Abu Sulb, in 2010, Decree No. 42 of the ministry of the interior did away with the requirement that wives should take the family name of their husbands; they are now permitted to keep their own natal family name. The decree also stated that women older than 18 years, whether daughters or wives, would no longer be required to get the father's or husband's permission to obtain passports. Widows (not divorced) have the right to obtain passports for their children if they have proof from the Shari'a court that they have custody over the children. Another change is that a Palestinian woman who is married to a non-Palestinian man is allowed to transmit her citizenship to her children and register them in her ID card until they reach the age of 16 years (when they get their own independent IDs anyway). The same right is given to Palestinian men married to non-Palestinian women.

9.8 Conclusion

This chapter was partially concerned with the way two legal proposals were articulated; the long-lived legal framework of the religious establishment, derived from a number of codified laws, particularly from Egypt and Jordan, but claiming Islamic authenticity and arterial connection with the Shari'a, and the newly constructed framework of the women's movement, derived from hybrid sources and frames of reference including the fiqh, codified laws and Shari'a (though proclaimed as objectives of the Shari'a). The chapter also looked at the process of constructing the identity of the upcoming state of Palestine as an Islamic state through the initiatives of Shaykh Abu Sardana. Although the process of recodification in post-Oslo Palestine bears a remarkable resemblance to the process at the turn of the twentieth century over issues related to claims, aspirations and, to some extent, methodology, it occurred in a totally different political and social context. In Palestine, different actors used different styles of articulation, sharing the same objective of social change pronounced with the idioms of reform and unification of the family law, though the meaning of social change might be significantly different for each of them. Thus, the translation of these desires into legal texts brought conflicts over the meaning of citizenship, the role of Islam and the Shari'a, gender roles and relations, and the ideal future state.

In countries that have been liberated from long-lasting colonial occupation, law is viewed as a tool for social engineering and state-building. It is believed by the women's movement and other actors that changing legislation is one of the main ways of state-building. In Palestine, the situation is complex because the Oslo Accords did not provide sovereignty from Israeli rule. Using law for social change in Palestine is made more challenging by the fact that the legal systems in Gaza and the West Bank are different, and there are few precedents to draw on for unification of two different legal systems (Robinson 1997: 52). The few steps taken by the Palestinian Authority to unify the legislation in Gaza and the West Bank pose political and procedural problems:

> In both areas [the West Bank and the Gaza Strip], the inability to build consensus has led to the proliferation of laws by decree; the absence of an enforceable and codified rule of law has led to the emergence of personality-driven and often secretive decision making.
>
> (ibid.)

The situation is worsened by the fact that neither area 'possessed any mechanism for legal development or for adopting new laws; in neither area did the law in any way reflect the changing needs of the society it served' (ibid.: 53). Yet another factor to take into account is that when the subject for reform is Islamic family law, the competition between political actors becomes an exercise in identity politics (Hammami 2004: 125).

However, if one looks back at 1997 and the demands put forward by the Model Parliament, one sees a number of undeniable achievements. For example, the demand to create a nafaqa fund has been met, as have some other demands, among them: protection of existing women's inheritance rights; a man intending to marry a second wife having to inform his current wife of his intention and the proposed second wife of his marital status; divorce outside the court being made illegal; and custody rights of widowed mothers over their children until adulthood. What is yet to be done is: raising the age of marriage to 18 years for girls (it is still 17 lunar years in Gaza and 18 Gregorian years in the West Bank, with the judge being authorized to make exceptions in both regions); women being permitted to marry without a guardian's permission; equal division of assets acquired after marriage; and an end to forcing mothers to renounce their custody rights.

The Model Parliament made no demand for the government to sign the Convention on the Elimination of all Forms of Discrimination Against Women, but that has been done (unlike in Morocco, Syria and many other Muslim-majority countries). For the first time ever in Palestine, women have been appointed as Shari'a court judges. They have also been appointed as prosecutors in both Shari'a courts and civil courts. These achievements, when viewed historically, comparatively and contextually, are unequivocally remarkable. From a historical perspective, Palestinian women have taken big steps towards gender justice in 20 years. In terms of comparison, women in many Muslim countries, in the Middle East and elsewhere, have yet to attain the same level of achievement, for example, in appointments as Shari'a court judges. In terms of context, Palestinians live under occupation, have been split geographically and politically, are strangled economically, and yet have been able to take significant steps towards gender justice.

The above achievements should inspire cautious optimism. They are the fruit of the struggle of social agents for change, on the one hand, and enabling context on the other. The persistence of the women's movement and Palestinian civil society organizations as social agents for change deserves recognition. Equally, so does the degree of flexibility shown by the Shari'a authorities and courts in incorporating a good proportion of the women's demands and issuing new decrees to reduce gender inequality. Were it not for the split between Gaza and the West Bank, and the deterioration of the living standards of the people resulting from the ongoing blockade of Gaza, there would probably have been even more advancement. As it is, the current situation forces Palestinians in Gaza to focus more on meeting their daily needs for food, shelter, electricity and clean water than on organizing for more legal change to achieve gender justice. In this light, permission is prevalent, especially if one widens the callipers to comprehend the extremely negative transformation of global politics and the depressing situation in Syria, Yemen, Iraq, Libya and other parts of the Middle East.

Notes

1 It is worth noting that the women's movement in the West Bank used lawyer Asma Khadr's (1998) book *Law and the Future of Palestinian Women* as a manual for its activities before and during the Model Parliament campaign. In the Gaza Strip, the campaigners designed their activities without reference to Khadr. This chapter does not analyse Khadr's work for two reasons: first, it has been dealt with extensively by Welchman (2000, 2003); second, this chapter addresses a different historical period, namely that which followed the completion of the Model Parliament's activities.
2 The document that will be analysed in this chapter was produced by the movement's activists in the West Bank during the years following the conclusion of the MP campaign.
3 The Constitution (or Basic Law) drafted by al-Qasem stated that 'the Palestinian people are the source of all authority', which is in line with the 'spirit of the secular and nationalist discourse historically used by the Palestine Liberation Organization' (Johnson 2004: 118–19). Johnson also refers to what Hilal (2000) terms the 'secular outlook' of the Palestinian Basic Law. However, when the Basic Law drafted by al-Qasem was reviewed by the Palestinian Legislative Council, an additional article was added, which stated clearly that: (i) Islam is the official religion of Palestine with respect accorded to the sanctity of all other religions; and (ii) the principles of the Islamic Shari'a are a principal source of legislation (The Basic Law 2002). In this formulation, the Palestinian Basic Law is replicating the general trend in the Constitutions of other Arab countries in which idioms of Islam and the Shari'a are used as tools of legitimation (Johnson 2004: 119).
4 Shari'a court personnel were not affected by Abu Sardana's action. The replacement of 'previous Israeli personnel' was restricted to those who had worked directly under the Israeli administrator, who had been the highest authority in Gaza. They numbered only three to five employees.

5 Abu Sardana made it clear that the four madhahib should be recognized, in addition to other 'non-dominant' schools of thought in the Islamic fiqh.
6 Even after Abu Sardana's decrees, the judges' and litigants' practice with regard to the wali issue did not change. During my research in the court archives, which covered the years between 1918 and 2001, I came across only three cases of women appealing to the qadi to act as their wali because of refusal by their fathers to do so (adl al-wali).
7 Miswaddat wathiqat al-mabadi ('Draft of Document of Principles') for the National Campaign for the Palestinian Family Law, document for internal circulation, 2 October 1999, p. 1.
8 Minutes of the meeting of the Preparatory Committee for Family Law, 11 September 2001.
9 The following documents were also listed: the Women's Movement Charter of 1994, the International Declaration of Human Rights, the UN Convention on the Elimination of All Forms of Discrimination Against Women, the International Accord for the Minimum Age of Marriage, the Declaration of the Rights of the Child, and the International Declaration of Rejection of All Kinds of Violence Against Women.
10 In post-Islamic-revolution Iran, an innovative approach was adopted in 1993, in which women were able, in cases of divorce initiated by their husbands, to claim compensation for their housework. This is elaborated by Kar and Hoodfar (1996: 31): 'A man who intends to divorce his wife without legally accepted grounds must pay her nafaqa according to Shari'a as well as wages for housework determined by the court before the divorce can be registered.' The authors recognize that this is one of the few occasions when women have gained economic rights. The authors acknowledge that although the law provided women with compensation for housework, neither women nor courts were sure of the conditions under which divorced women could apply for such payment. Because of this confusion, in 1995, Parliament passed a law granting women compensation, along with their mahr and nafaqa, before the divorce is registered (Kar and Hoodfar 1996: 32–3; see also Hoodfar 2000).
11 Again, in post-Islamic-revolution Iranian law, when divorce is initiated by the husband, the court may divide the wealth accumulated during marital life between the two spouses (Kar and Hoodfar 1996: 16).
12 Khul (the act of mukhala'a) is a divorce settlement that involves an agreement between husband and wife that the wife would relinquish her financial rights or compensate the husband financially, in return for which the husband would pronounce a final talaq (talaq bain baynuna sughra). The major step forward in the new Egyptian law was that the wife could petition the court for khul regardless of (or against) the will of the husband.
13 The Al-timimi draft needs to be approved by the Palestinian Legislative Council before it becomes law. However, the Legislative Council has not met for a long time because of the split between Gaza and the West Bank, the second intifada and the Israeli blockade of Gaza, among other factors, so the contents of the draft remain proposals.
14 The terms 'family law' and 'personal status law' are used in this section interchangeably. Although this is not totally correct conceptually and historically (see Cuno 2015), it reflects the use of the terms by my sources. Interchangeable use of the terms is common in many circles, including political and legal ones, in Palestine.
15 The second intifada (2000–2005) was the uprising of Palestinians in the West Bank and Gaza against Israeli occupation following a provocative visit to the al-Aqsa Mosque in the Old City of Jerusalem in September 2000 by the leader of the

Israeli opposition Likud party, General Ariel Sharon, accompanied by hundreds of soldiers and supporters. For background and analysis, see Baroud (2006), Pressman (2006) and Ajluni (2003).
16 The level of violence against Palestinian civilians during the second intifada was unprecedented, and many civil society organizations made a strategic decision to suspend their 'development' programmes and focus instead on humanitarian aid.
17 Among the many news sources that reported this is www.thenational.ae/world/meet-the-first-palestinian-woman-to-marry-couples-in-the-west-bank-1.57049, accessed on 23 August 2017.
18 Announcement by the qadi al-qudah on 9 June 2009. https://goo.gl/QjA4Ev, accessed 20 July 2017.
19 These statistics are from the 'Guiding Document on the Integration of Human Rights in Palestinian National Development Plans' (2014), p. 31. https://goo.gl/S9juwx, accessed 23 July 2017.
20 Al-Habbash's speech was published on April 2017 by Ma'an news agency. www.maannews.net/Content.aspx?id=902164, accessed 23 July 2017.
21 <http://www.al-monitor.com/pulse/originals/2016/03/gaza-husbands-file-divorce-abuse-by-women.html>, accessed 23 August 2017.
22 'National Strategy to Combat Violence against Women'. (2011–2019). *No Date, No Author.* https://goo.gl/L52iti., accessed 25 July 2017.

Bibliography

Abu Hayya, A. (2011) *The Experience of Personal Status Law in the Occupied Palestinian Territories.* Ramallah: WCLAC publications.

Abou Jalal, Rasha (2016), 'How this new divorce law further marginalizes Gaza's women', in <www.al-monitor.com/pulse/originals/2016/03/gaza-husbands-file-divorce-abuse-by-women.html>, accessed 23 August 2017.

Abu Sardana, M. (n.d.) *Al-qada' al-shar'i fi 'ahd al-sulta al-wataniyya al-filastiniyya (The Shar'i Judiciary Under the Palestinian Authority).* Gaza: Sharakat Fanun.

Abu Sulb, H. (2012) 'Analytical Study of the Role of the Judiciary Institution in Empowering Women', *Ramallah: WCLAC.* <www.wclac.org/atemplate.php?id=177> accessed 15 July 2017.

Ajluni, S. (2003) 'The Palestinian Economy and the Second Intifada', *Journal of Palestine Studies* 32(3): 64–73.

Al-Qasem, A. (1992, 1994) 'Commentary on the Draft Basic Law for the Palestinian National Authority', in *IV Yearbook of Islamic and Middle Eastern Law*, pp. 187–211. London and The Hague: University of London, School of Oriental and African Studies, Centre of Islamic and Middle Eastern Law and Kluwer Law International.

Anleu, S. L. R. (2000) *Law and Social Change.* London and New Delhi: Sage.

Baroud, R. (2006) *The Second Palestinian Intifada: A Chronicle of a People's Struggle.* London: Pluto Press.

Bourdieu, P. (1987) 'The Force of Law: Toward a Sociology of Juridical Field', *Hastings Law Journal* 38: 814–53.

Celis, K., J. Kantola, G. Waylen and S. L. Weldon (2013) 'Introduction: Gender and Politics in a Gendered World, a Gendered Discipline', in G. Waylen, K. Celis, J. Kantola and S. Laurel Weldon (eds) *The Oxford Handbook of Gender and Politics*, pp. 1–19. New York: Oxford University Press.

Cuno, K. M. (2015) *Modernizing Marriage: Family, Ideology, and Law in Nineteenth- and Early Twentieth-Century Egypt.* Syracuse, NY: Syracuse University Press.

Faris, M. (2002) *Ta'amim qadi al-qudah khilal saba' sanawat (Decrees of qadi al-qudah Over Seven Years)*. Gaza: No publisher.
Fraser, N. (1997) *Justice Interruptus*. New York: Routledge.
Frohmann, L. and E. Mertz (1994) 'Legal Reform and Social Construction: Violence, Gender and the Law', *Law and Social Inquiry* 19: 829–51.
Hammami, R. (2004) 'Attitudes Towards Legal Reform of Personal Status Law in Palestine', in L. Welchman (ed.) *Women's Rights & Islamic Family Law: Perspectives on Reform*, pp. 125–44. London and New York: Zed Books.
Hammami, R. and P. Johnson (1999) 'Equality With a Difference: Gender and Citizenship in Transitional Palestine', *Social Politics* 6(3): 314–43.
Hilal, J. (2000) 'Secularism in Palestinian Political Culture', *Background Paper for Palestine Case Study for the Comparative Islamic Family Law Project*. Ramallah: Institute of Women's Studies.
Hoodfar, H. (2000) 'Iranian Women, Citizenship, and the Family Code', in S. Joseph (ed.) *Gender and Citizenship in the Middle East*, pp. 287–314. Syracuse, NY: Syracuse University Press.
Htun, M. and L. Weldon (2010) 'When Do Governments Promote Women's Rights? A Framework for the Comparative Analysis of Sex Equality Policy', *Perspectives on Politics* 8(1): 207–16.
Jad, I., P. Johnson and R. Giacaman (2000) 'Transit Citizens: Gender and Citizenship Under the Palestinian Authority', in S. Joseph (ed.) *Gender and Citizenship in the Middle East*, pp. 137–57. Syracuse, NY: Syracuse University Press.
Jamal, A. (2001) 'Engendering State-Building: The Women's Movement in Palestine', *The Middle East Journal* 55(2): 256–77.
Johnson, P. (2004) 'Agents for Reform: The Women's Movement, Social Politics and Family Law Reform', in L. Welchman (ed.) *Women's Rights & Islamic Family Law: Perspectives for Reform*, pp. 144–64. London and New York: Zed Books.
Kar, M. and H. Hoodfar (1996) 'Personal Status Law as Defined by the Islamic Republic of Iran: An Appraisal', in *Women & Law in the Muslim World Programme: Special Dossier, Shifting Boundaries in Marriage and Divorce in Muslim Communities*, 1(Fall): 7–37.
Khadr, A. (1998) *Al-qanun wa mustaqbal al-mar'a al-filastiniyya (Law and the Future of Palestinian Women)*. Jerusalem: WCLAC and UNDP.
Moors, A. (2003) 'Introduction: Public Debates on Family Law Reform: Participants, Positions, and Styles of Argumentation in the 1990s', *Islamic Law and Society* 10(1): 1–12.
Nurlaelawati, E. and A. Salim (2017) 'Female Judges at Indonesian Religious Courtrooms: Opportunities and Challenges to Gender Equality', in N. Sonneveld and M. Lindbekk (eds) *Women Judges in the Muslim World: A Comparative Study of Discourse and Practice*. Leiden. Brill.
Pressman, J. (2006) 'The Second Intifada: Background and Causes of the Israeli-Palestinian Conflict', *Journal of Conflict Studies* 23(2).
Robinson, G. (1997) 'The Politics of Legal Reform in Palestine', *Journal of Palestine Studies* 27(1): 51–60.
Samara, M. (1987) *Ahkam wa athar al-zawjiyya: sharh muqaran li-qanun al-ahwal al-shakhsiyya (Rules and Consequences of Marriage: Comparative Commentary on the Law of Personal Status)*. Jerusalem: (No publisher).
Singh, I. P. (1989) *Women, Law and Social Change in India*. London: Sangam Books.

Smart, C. (1986) 'Feminism and Law: Some Problems of Analysis and Strategy', *International Journal of the Sociology of Law* 14: 109–23.

Sonneveld, N. and M. Lindbekk (eds). (2017) *Women Judges in the Muslim World. A Comparative Study of Discourse and Practice*. Leiden: Brill.

Weber, M. (1968) *Economy and Society. An Outline of Interpretive Sociology* (Vol. 1). New York: Bedminster Press.

Weedon, C. (1987) *Feminist Practice and Poststructuralist Theory*. New York: Basil Blackwell.

Welchman, L. (2003) 'In the Interim: Civil Society, the Shari'a Judiciary and Palestinian Personal Status Law in the Transitional Period', *Islamic Law and Society* 10(1): 34–70.

Welchman, L. (2000) *Beyond the Code: Muslim Family Law and the Shar'i Judiciary in the Palestinian West Bank*. The Hague: Kluwer Law International.

Welchman, L. (ed.) (2004) *Women's Rights and Islamic Family Law: Perspectives on Reform*. London and New York: Zed Press.

Legislation

'The Palestinian Basic Law (2002)', published in the *Palestinian Gazette* on 7 July 2002. <http://muqtafi.birzeit.edu/pg/>, accessed 22 August 2017. The full text can be accessed at <http://muqtafi.birzeit.edu/pg/getleg.asp?id=14094>.

'National Strategy to Combat Violence against Women (2011–2019)'. *No Date, No Author*. <https://goo.gl/L52iti.>, accessed 25 July 2017.

10 Epilogue

The twenty-first century is witnessing an unprecedented focus on Islam and Muslims. Quite often, terrorism is joined to Islam to keep painting Muslims essentially as terrorists. This study is concerned with Palestinians, but instead of working towards an alternative political representation/formal political perspective on Palestinians, it has explored issues from within the society, taking into account the diverse perspectives of ordinary people in their interaction within the legal sphere. Therefore, it provides a different perspective from that in mainstream representations.

The establishment of Israel in 1948 on the land of Palestine and the subsequent atrocities committed against the people there led some Palestinians to regard themselves as a 'completely unique' nation, with an unparalleled historical experience that made many theoretical paradigms irrelevant (Tamari 1997: 18). This study combined ethnographic rigour and textual analysis to examine a particular reality of Palestinian people: negotiating legal rights in the Shari'a courts. Furthermore, when scholarly research has been conducted in the Palestinian context in the past, it has often centred on the West Bank due to the latter's greater historical, political, religious and geographical significance. Gaza has been rarely researched, perhaps because it is smaller, poorer and isolated. Gaza is frequently treated as an extension of the West Bank, simply by virtue of being part of Palestine and having been occupied by Israeli forces at the same time as the West Bank. However, the differences between the two regions in terms of their legal framework, and political and social milieu, though commonly overlooked, are significant (see Roy 1995). This book has focused on this neglected geographical area, revealing the dynamics of its people's interaction with law, including their coping strategies, their daily interaction with the legal system and their persistent attempts to influence its application.

Among the many issues that this study investigated was the experience of Palestinian women. Here, the literature often passionately focuses only on one aspect of their role. Palestinian women's roles have been analysed mostly with reference either to their impact on the national struggle or vice versa (see, for example, Hasso 2005; Khalili 2007; Taraki 1989; Peteet 1991; Jad 1995; Hiltermann 1991; Abdulhadi 1998; Hammami 1990; 1993, 1995; Segal 2015; Kuttab 2010). In contrast, the focus of this book has been on the experience of ordinary

Palestinian women (and men) and their legal initiatives in the Shariʻa court, an area that has rarely been explored in Gaza. This study looked at family law, a field that is often seen as concerning the private sphere; the field research showed not only that familial issues are political but also that by studying familial disputes in the legal field, one may develop a broader and more nuanced vision of the interrelated issues of politics, law and social change. In this sense, the research filled a gap in both sociology of law and the study of legal settlement in societies beset by a high degree of political and social tension.

The study analysed the debate on family law in Palestine. Its exploration might be considered an empirical and analytical contribution to the broader, more passionate debate on the reform of personal status law in the Arab world and thus addresses one of the major fields of contention between advocates and opponents of gender rights in contemporary Arab societies. In the Palestinian context, not only is the question of who may claim the right to interpret the sources of law at issue, but there is also a clash between appeals for reinforcing equal citizenship rights and claims of cultural and religious specificities in the context of the national struggle for liberation and state-building since the signing of the Oslo Accords in 1993 (which will be summarized later in this chapter).

Nevertheless, the family law debate in Palestine shares certain similarities with that in other Arab countries, in that it masked a struggle for power and legitimacy between various Palestinian political actors. The debate appeared to be both open and controlled. It was open in terms of its inclusion of new participants and publics; yet various control mechanisms were imposed by powerful actors to silence certain identities, prohibit given subjects or impose chosen methods of deliberation (see Moors 2003). The communication of arguments, the process of exclusion or inclusion of subjects and identities and the shifting domains of articulation were just indicators of how the power structure was able to compromise the course of deliberation, even in the absence of formal acts of prohibition (Fraser 1993). The Palestinian public sphere, while experiencing one of its most intense debates, hosted conflicting and competing publics (see Fraser 1993; Eley 1993).

Family law reform was a political project in which diverging assumptions about the role of the Shariʻa, Islam and gender were put forward as an expression of the 'social will' (Hammami 2004: 126) that each group claimed to represent. Moreover, although there was an undeniable difference between opponents and supporters of reform, the actors were not so unified within each group. Close examination revealed internal heterogeneity in world views and objectives regarding the ideal legislation for the Palestinian Muslim family. This conclusion runs against the widespread categorization of these actors as being inherently unified. It may provide political and theoretical insights into how to strategize for reform while remaining open to the multiplicity of voices and ideologies within each camp.

Exploring the debate on family law was crucial to understanding the gulf between how Islamic law is ideologically conceptualized and how it is concretely implemented. The study revealed major discrepancies between the political conceptualization of the law in the public sphere and its highly differentiated and contextually determined implementation. In particular, the observation and analysis of court practice provided new insight into the reciprocal determination of jurisprudence, gender asymmetries and personal strategies; thus, while the realm of politics falls short of recognizing these complexities, this research might contribute to better understanding of the application of the law.

The major focus of the study was on how family law is applied. The experience of doing fieldwork in the court was an eye-opener, for it permitted me to observe how family law is experienced by lay people and how their socio-economic and political experiences influence their legal actions. This indicates the importance of studying family law not only from the perspective of how it is formulated from above but also how it is remade from below.

This study has shown some variance between the application and the text of family law. In the Shari'a court, application was characterized by pluralism, whereas the text was characterized by rigidity, restriction, stability and, in some respects, superficial clarity. Despite this, the text had specific gaps and ambiguities that provided actors in the courts with some space to manœuvre. What is particularly significant is the behaviour of the judges, who, contrary to my previous assumption, were acting in accordance with multiple references derived from various sources instead of using the codified text as a point of departure. Observing the application of family law in situ exposed the gulf between the richness of the application and the dryness of the legal text. Thus far, the legal perspective adopted in the literature has focused on only one aspect; it needs to be supplemented by looking at the articulation of the law through the eyes of the people involved in and affected by implementation of the law (see Dwyer 1990).

Another dimension highlighted was the interplay of social norms and values on the one hand, and the actions of judges on the other. Judges are not detached from the values embraced by their community. Judges do more than share the locality of their litigants; they are well informed about 'who is who' and 'what is what' in the community and have strong contacts with community members. Judges' decisions thus depend not only on the history of cases filed but, more importantly, on the potential consequences of their judgments on the individual litigants and the larger community behind them (Rosen 1989). Such observations are rarely found in the literature.

Women, indeed people in general, are less responsive to 'fixed' texts than to their concrete needs, no matter how they perceive or articulate them, if and when they decide to take an issue to court. Moreover, the 'fixed' law itself contains areas of indeterminacy, ambiguity and uncertainty. People often search for such gaps in the interplay of codified law, social customs and the multi-referential frameworks of judges and thus find space to express and materialize their needs and interests. In the course of their attempts to obtain justice, women often manœuvre and manipulate these elements and sometimes succeed in turning them to their benefit. People's interaction with the legal framework is both manipulative and instrumental. They exploit the law's fixity when it suits them and utilize its indeterminacy when it serves their interest.

The study has also brought a new perspective to the debate in the literature about the impact of codification. The re-evaluation of classical (uncodified) Islamic law as a highly flexible and fluid system has led to an emphasis on the purported inflexibility and rigidity of codified family law (see Messick 1993; Tucker 1998; Sonbol 1996; Sanadjian 1996). However, the findings of this study indicate that codified family law is not applied in a vacuum, but is bound by a context in which the judges' world view, state structure and people's agency jointly affect the outcome. The field data demonstrated that codification of Islamic family law is not synonymous with an end to the traditional flexibility and fluidity of Islamic jurisprudence. The concrete functioning of Islamic family law needs to be observed where lawsuits are negotiated. The law is manipulated by people, and the judges often act as mediators. Contrary to some historians' assumption that today's judges have lost their subjectivity, Gaza judges are still loyal to the heritage of Islamic law that asserts concepts of fairness, consideration of the context and protection of the weak. The fieldwork revealed the extent to which codification has impacted on judges' subjectivity.

The study shows that the judges, who represent the legal institution, act as 'protectors' of the female litigants, shielding them from the harm that their male kin might inflict upon them. In light of this, the study concludes that constructing dichotomies between two distinct voices in Islam – one ethical and the other technical (Ahmed 1992) – is refuted by empirical evidence. The boundaries between the two voices and those who articulate them are blurred. Nonetheless, the study sounds a note of caution. While acknowledging the judges' protective behaviour, it does not overlook their gendered views. Judges, as members of society, are bound to be influenced by the dominant gender discourse, which legitimizes unequal division of rights and duties within the family. Yet, their daily encounters with the unfairness, oppression and injustices inflicted on women by their kinsmen enhance their sensitivity towards women's plight. The study has tried to capture the complexity of the operation of Islamic family law in this nuanced approach.

The conventional notion of ijtihad is that of engagement with the original sources in an interpretative enterprise to devise shar'i measures. This study has used its empirical data as a point of departure to explore the literature on ijtihad, a theme around which the debate is still vibrant in many parts of the Islamic world. It concludes that ijtihad has been a feature of Islamic jurisprudence throughout Islamic history and continues to be practised today. This runs counter to the dominant claim in the mainstream literature that the gates of ijtihad have been closed.

Codification created a vacuum in the legal system. In order to solve the problems posed by this awkward development, the judges exercise ijtihad by implementing the codified law in the wider framework of principles of fairness, protection of the weak and preservation of the social order. This observation led the study to conclude that there is a need to re-conceptualize ijtihad to acknowledge the contemporary practice of judges, who, unlike their predecessors, are forced to deal with the challenges of 'modern' life armed with a limited and insufficient legal text.

The process of codification produced a written legal corpus that is poorer than those of the four madhahib, in which contradictions are a built-in aspect of jurisprudence and thus allow for the tuning of the legal judgments with the existing needs of society. The movement towards codification confronted the judges with an unresolvable problem: if, on the one hand, they apply the codified law as it is, they inevitably injure both litigants and the moral principles of the Shari'a by issuing 'unjust' judgments. On the other hand, if they go beyond the scope of the codified statutes, they can be accused of violating the law. To resolve this dilemma, judges rely on orality. Most of their actions, reactions, interventions and 'violations' of codified law are, understandably, not recorded anywhere. The fact that judges have the authority to dictate the written record allows them to decide on the exclusion or inclusion of certain material: for example, oral negotiations, the devices of certain judgments, out-of-court solutions and in-court propositions appear nowhere in the court record. Thus, no one can trace the judges' exercise of ijtihad. Codification forces jurisprudence to resort to orality, which means that there is no way to reconstitute the entire picture unless the researcher adopts an appropriate methodology based on the observation and recording of the daily practice of ijtihad. Another consequence of orality is the judges' inability to rely on precedents. The lack of written precedents makes every case 'new' and to be dealt with not on the basis of what has been accumulated through court history, but on the basis of the accumulated experience of the individual qadi alone. Unfortunately, contemporary ijtihad is obscured by the recourse to orality. Innovations are covered up and changes in the system concealed. Every qadi, therefore, is a single universe whose judgments are subjectively made and orally transmitted. Ra'y (subjective reasoning), which is one of the foundations of ijtihad, is obscured through orality, and thus no legacy (turath) is allowed to accumulate. This leads to stagnation of the text on the one hand, and proliferation of oral ijtihad on the other.

The analysis of judges' actions also took into consideration their background. They are not trained in a law school. Their background is in usul al-din (theology) or Shari'a studies. This educational background influences their views and the judgments they reach. Judges have to find a way out of the contradictions between the morally inspired Shari'a they have studied and the restricted codified law at their disposal. This triggers a further dilemma: how can they provide justice (haqq) by using the nass (text) of the law and abandoning other rich resources? How can they arrive at a hukm shar'i (religiously legitimate judgment) that accomplishes God's will within the framework of codified law, while their daily experience reminds them repeatedly of the imperfection of the codified law in comparison with the haqq provided by the Shari'a? This dilemma, which I often observed, is overcome by shifting to a wider frame of reference that helps them to make haqq prevail.

The study analysed the judges' supportive actions towards women within this framework. It provided a profile of the variety of interventions by judges to protect women from the abuse inflicted upon them by their male relatives, in order to promote Islamic justice as they view it. Elements related to judges' sense of justice, protecting the weak, membership of the community and the overall gender ideology can be viewed as the framework in which to interpret their conduct.

Within this multiplicity of texts and rules, the ethics of religiously educated (rather than legally educated) judges, their membership in the semi-autonomous community and their embeddedness in the multiplex relations within the community, the judges have to tread the road of intersectionality quite cautiously. Any misrecognition of a specific intersection may lead to a highly undesirable result. The research that is incorporated in this book makes it clear that we need to carry out more observation and analysis in the courtroom when trying to understand the implementation of family law in Shari'a courts.

Bibliography

Abdulhadi, R. (1998) 'The Palestinian Women's Autonomous Movement: Emergence, Dynamics, and Challenges', *Gender and Society* 12(6): 649–73.

Ahmed, L. (1992) *Women and Gender in Islam: Historical Roots of a Modern Debate*. New Haven, CT: Yale University Press.

Dwyer, D. H. (1990) 'Law and Islam in the Middle East: An Introduction', in D. H. Dwyer (ed.) *Law and Islam in the Middle East*, pp. 1–15. New York: Bergin & Garvey.

Eley, G. (1993) 'Nations. Publics, and Political Cultures: Placing Habermas in the Nineteenth Century', in C. Calhoun (ed.) *Habermas and the Public Sphere*, pp. 289–339. Cambridge: MIT Press.

Fraser, N. (1993) 'Rethinking the Public Sphere: A Contribution to the Critique of Actually Existing Democracy', in C. Calhoun (ed.) *Habermas and the Public Sphere*, pp. 109–43. Cambridge, MA and London: MIT Press.

Hammami, R. (1990) 'Women, the Hijab and the Intifada', *Middle East Report* 20(3&4): 24–8.

Hammami, R. (1993) 'Women in Palestinian Society', in M. Heiberg and G. Ovensen (eds) *Palestinian Society in Gaza, West Bank and Arab Jerusalem: A Survey of Living Conditions*, pp. 283–312. Oslo: FAFO Publications.

Hammami, R. (2004) 'Attitudes Towards Legal Reform of Personal Status Law in Palestine', in L. Welchman (ed.) *Women's Rights & Islamic Family Law: Perspectives on Reform*, pp. 125–44. London and New York: Zed Books.

Hasso, F. S. (2005) 'Discursive and Political Deployments by/of the 2002 Palestinian Women Suicide Bombers/Martyrs', *Feminist Review* 81(1): 23–51.

Hiltermann, J. (1991) *Behind the Intifada*. Princeton: Princeton University Press.

Jad, I. (1995) 'Claiming Feminism, Claiming Nationalism: Women's Activism in the Occupied Territories', in Amrita Basu (ed.) *The Challenge of Local Feminisms*, pp. 226–48. Boulder, CO: Westview Press.

Khalili, L. (2007) *Heroes and Martyrs of Palestine: The Politics of National Commemoration* (Vol. 27). Cambridge: Cambridge University Press.

Kuttab, E. (2010) 'Empowerment as Resistance: Conceptualizing Palestinian Women's Empowerment', *Development* 53(2): 247–53.

Messick, B. (1993) *The Calligraphic State: Textual Domination and History in a Muslim Society*. Berkeley, CA: University of California Press.

Moors, A. (2003) 'Introduction: Public Debates on Family Law Reform: Participants, Positions, and Styles of Argumentation in the 1990s', *Islamic Law and Society* 10(1): 1–12.

Peteet, J. (1991) *Gender in Crisis: Women and the Palestinian Resistance Movement*. New York: Columbia University Press.

Rosen, L. (1989) *The Anthropology of Justice: Law as Culture in Islamic Society*. Cambridge: Cambridge University Press.
Roy, S. (1995) *The Gaza Strip: The Political Economy of De-development*. Washington, DC and London: I. B. Tauris, for Institute of Palestine Studies.
Sanadjian, M. (1996) 'A Public Flogging in South-Western Iran: Juridical Rule, Abolition of Legality and Local Resistance', in O. Harris (ed.) *Inside and Outside the Law: Anthropological Studies of Authority and Ambiguity*, pp. 157–84. London: Routledge.
Segal, L. B. (2015) 'The Burden of Being Exemplary: National Sentiments, Awkward Witnessing, and Womanhood in Occupied Palestine', *Journal of the Royal Anthropological Institute* 21(S1): 30–46.
Sonbol, A. (1996) 'Adults and Minors in Ottoman Shari'a Courts and Modern Law', in A. Sonbol (ed.) *Women, the Family and Divorce Laws in Islamic History*, pp. 236–59. Syracuse, NY: Syracuse University Press.
Tamari, S. (1997) 'Social Science Research in Palestine: A Review of Trends and Issues', in R. Bocco and J. Hannoyer (eds) *Palestine, Palestinian: National Territory, Community Spaces*, pp. 17–37. Beirut: Beirut Center of Studies and Research into the Contemporary Middle East.
Taraki, L. (1989) 'The Islamic Resistance Movement in the Palestinian Uprising', *Middle East Report* 19(156): 30–2.
Tucker, J. (1998) *In the House of Law: Gender and Islamic Law in Ottoman Syria and Palestine*. Berkeley, CA: University of California Press.

Glossary

'adat (see *'urf*)	social customs
ahkam shar'iyya	legitimate judgments (Islamically legitimate judgements)
ahl al-dhimma	non-Muslims living in Muslim countries during the Caliphate period
ahl al-ikhtisas	religious specialists
'aqd	contract
asala	authenticity
'asaba (pl. *'asabat*)	agnate(s)
asl	nature, root, source, principle
'awad (see *badal*)	*compensation*
awqaf	Islamic endowment
'ayb	biological defect in the husband
badal	compensation
baligh	person who has reached puberty (see *bulugh*)
ba'in	for divorce (final)
batil (*zawaj batil*)	invalid, void (of contract of marriage)
baynuna kubra	the 'greater finality' occasioned by the third *talaq*
baynuna sughra	the 'lesser finality' occasioned by the first or second *talaq*
bayt al-ta'a	house of obedience
bikr	virgin, unmarried woman
bulugh	puberty, adulthood, sexual maturity (see *baligh*)
dar al-'ifta'	the institution that issues fatwa(s)
damm	'annexation,' taking into one's protective custody
darar	harm (injury)
dukhul	consummation (of marriage)
faqih (pl. *fuqaha'*)	jurist, expert in Islamic law (*fiqh*)
fasad	corruption
fasid (*zawaj fasid*)	irregular (of a contract of marriage)
faskh	judicial dissolution, annulment (of marriage)
fatwa (pl. *fatawa* but in the study, I use *fatwas*)	non-binding legal opinion; authoritative or accepted view of the jurists in a school of law

fasiq	dissolute
fiqh	Islamic jurisprudence, legal doctrine(s)
fuqaha'	grand thinkers
hadana	care (of children); inadequately translated as custody
hadith (pl. *ahadith*)	narrative of the Prophet Muhammad
hijja (pl. *hijaj*)	court record(s), deed(s)
hajr	desertion; sexual abandonment
halal	religiously allowed, permitted, permissible
hamula (pl. *hamayil*)	clan
haram	religiously forbidden
hardana	the wife who leaves her house in a state of anger
hukm shar'i	religiously legitimate judgment (pl. *ahkam shar'iyya*)
'ibadat	ritual practices, e.g. ablutions, prayers, tithes, fasting and pilgrimage
ibra'	renunciation, waiving (of rights)
'idda	waiting period of the woman after the end of her marriage by divorce or widowhood, during which she may not remarry (three menstruations, a period equivalent to three months)
'ifta'	the act of issuing *fatwa*
ijbar	compulsion
ijma'	the consensus of Muslim scholars
ijtihad	independent reasoning; authentic scholarly endeavour
'ilm	knowledge (of religious science)
imam	the person who leads a prayer
islah	reform
'isma	'protection' or authority, e.g. being under husband's *'isma* means under his authority
istislah	seeking solutions that best serve the public interest
istihsan	juristic preference (seeking the most equitable solution)
jihaz	bride's trousseau
jilbab	modern Islamic dress: long, wide coat with long sleeves
kafa'a (in marriage)	equivalence of groom's status with that of the bride
kafu'	the groom who is equivalent to his bride
kashf	investigation, examination
katib (pl. *kuttab*)	court recorder, scribe.
khul'	(the act of *mukhala'a*) divorce settlement involving a final *talaq* by the husband in return for a consideration (usually the waiving of the wife's financial rights)
khutba	betrothal
la darar wala dirar	no one should be injured
laji'in	refugees
lijan al-zakat	committees to collect *zakat* (see *zakat*)
lilat al-dukhla	the first night of consummation

madhahib (sg. *madhhab*)	schools of interpretation in Islamic law
mafqud	missing husbands (at times of war)
mag'ad	a place where clan members meet
mahjura	abandoned
mahr	dower
Majalla	digest (of commercial and civil laws known as the Majalla in 1869–76)
maskan shar'i	(religiously) legal dwelling
maslaha (pl. *masalih*)	public interest(s)
ma'thun	official marriage notary
mu'amalat	transaction between human beings, including issuing of marriage contract
mu'asara	modernization (see also *tahdith*). In many settings it implies modernizing education system, cultural practices and cultural production and reproduction.
mubah	religiously permissible matters
mufasirin	exegetists
mufti (pl. *rijal al-ifta'*)	person who is authorized to practise '*ifta*' (see *fatwa*)
muhram (pl. *maharim*)	person outside the prohibited degree of kinship (for marriage)
mujbar	obliged
mujtahid (pl. *mujtahidin*)	scholar qualified to exercise independent reasoning (*ijtihad*)
mukhala'a	mutually agreed divorce
mukhtar (pl. *makhatir*)	clan or community leader (representative of the collectivity)
mu'minin	believers
murahiq	male teenager
murahiqa	female teenager
murtadd	male apostate
murtadda	female apostate
muwatinin	indigenous Palestinians, as opposed to refugees (*laji'in*)
nafaqa	maintenance (for the wife)
nafaqat al-'idda	maintenance paid to wife during the waiting period
nakba	Arabic word for the catastrophe of 1948
nasab	lineage
nashiz	disobedient
nushuz	disobedience
nass (pl. *nusus*)	text; primary source, i.e. Quran or *hadith*
niza' wa shiqaq	discord and strife (as grounds for husband and wife to seek judicial divorce)
qadi p. *qudah*	judge, judges

192 Glossary

qadi al-qudah	chief judge
qiyas	analogical reasoning
ra'aya	Muslim and non-Muslim residents in the country (during the Caliphate periods)
raj'i	revocable *talaq*
ra'y	opinion
rushd	legal maturity
shaqiq	sanguine brothers
shaqiqa	sanguine sisters
shari'a/shar'i	(inadequately translated) Islamic law
sijil (pl. *sijillat*)	court record
shaykh	elder, chief; often to refers to religious scholars and imams
silat al-rahim	blood relations (through the wombs of mothers)
siyasa shari'yya	governmental legislation
sum'a and sharaf	moral reputation
sunna	The Prophet's conduct and actions as represented in the *hadith*
ta'a/bayt al-ta'a	obedience/house of obedience
tafriq	the act of *iftiraq*, judicial divorce
tafriq lil niza' wa al-shiqaq	judicial divorce for 'strife and discord'
tafsir	exegesis, explanation, interpretation
tahdith	modernization (see also *mu'asara*). The general understanding of Tahdith is that it relates to infrastructure, industrialization, building roads and bridges, etc.
takhayyur	selection from different schools of *fiqh*
talaq	divorce
talaq lil darar	judicial divorce for injury
talaq raj'i	revocable divorce
talfiq	fabrication
ta'mim	regulation or decree
taqnin	codification
tajdid	renovation
tatwir	development
tawabi'	(sg. *tabi'*) attached to; connotes value of wife's furniture, sometimes replaced by the term *'afsh al-bayt* (house furniture)
thayyib	not a virgin
'ulama'	religious scholars
'ujrat hadana	nursing fees
'ujrat rida'a	breast-feeding fees
'urfi marriage	unregistered marriage (in the court)
'urf (pl. *'araf*)	social norms and customs
usul al-fiqh	legal theories

usul al-din	theology
wali	guardian (in marriage or custody issues)
wikala (pl. *wikalat*)	to authorize someone to act as a proxy
wakil (pl. *wukala'*)	proxy
wilaya	guardianship of a minor (involving authority of father or agnate to marry his ward)
wudu'	ablutions (before prayer)
zakat	alms tax
zawaj batil	void marriage
zawaj fasid	irregular marriage

Index

age of marriage 21, 155, 158, 161, 165, 166, 167, 170, 178n9
Anis al-Qasem 156

Book of Personal Status Rulings According to the School of Abu Hanifa 5, 12, 53, 103, 107, 108, 117, 138n2, 143, 163, 167

Code of Islamic Jurisprudence 125
codification 3–4, 18–23, 27n3, 57–60, 71, 111, 140–1, 185–6; approaches to 19–23
Court of Appeal 33, 46, 47, 48, 125, 136
custody 117–18, 124–5, 145; *see also* 'guardianship'
customary practice 8–9, 13–14, 17, 16–18, 128–9

deputy qadi al-qudah 35, 37
diaspora returnees 73–8; cultural friction 75–7; permits nightmare 74
divorce 12; arbitrary 20–1, 54–5, 164, 169; before consummation 52, 54, 100–1; compensation for arbitrary unilateral divorce 162, 164, 165, 169; division of assets after divorce 161, 169, 178n11; due to disappearance of husband 22; in exchange for giving up financial rights 108–9, 165, 178n12; for husband's physical defect 22; increase in cases 73–4, 75, 78–80; for 'strife and discord' 23, 164; wife's and potential bride's information rights 168; women's movement proposals 161

Family Law debate in Palestine 140, 141–6, 147, 148, 149, 150n10, 154; political context of 142–5; *see also* 'Model Parliament for Women and Legislation'
family/social counselling 54, 55, 173

Gaza Shari'a courts 32–5, 38–9, 48n4; archives 33–5; the courtroom arena 38–43; gender in the legal profession 35; hierarchical relations in the legal system 46–8; networking in women's waiting room 35–8; procedure for appointing judges 45–6; role of scribes 32; role of ushers 32–3
gender in parenthood 117–25, 126–7
guardianship (wilaya) 64, 65, 117, 122, 156–7

hadana (physical care of children) 117–20, 120, 122, 126–7, 137n1, 162–3, 165, 170; eligibility to be a carer 118–20, 122; transference of hadana 118–20, 162–3
'house of obedience' order 53, 103–7, 111, 112, 158, 167; consequences for the husband 105–7; criteria for a shar'i house 105–7; difference between Gaza and the West Bank 80; effect of refugee influx 111; *see also* 'wifely obedience'

implementation of Islamic law 9, 63–5, 66–7, 70–1; flexibility of judges 3, 9, 70; incorporation of customary law 13–14, 16–18; judges' frame of reference 2–3, 26, 7; non-recorded proceedings 69, 186; preservation of social order 3, 17, 111, 112–13; protection of children 169; protection of women 3, 48

Islamic jurisprudence, elements of 12–25; contemporary itjihad (independent reasoning) 23–5; fiqh (legal doctrines) 14–15, 21; ijma' (consensus of the community) 14, 28n9; ijtihad (independent reasoning) 15–16, 23–6; istihsan (seeking the most equitable solution) 14, 50, 61, 65, 66, 70; istislah (seeking the solution that will best serve the public interest) 13, 65; maslaha (public welfare) 17, 50; methodologies of jurists 13, 14–15, 16, 19–20; Quran 3, 13, 38, 40, 58, 69, 88, 98; sunna (words and actions of Prophet Mohammed) 13, 14, 18; urf (customary law) 16–18

Islamic schools of interpretation 15; Hanafi 15, 18, 19, 20, 21, 22, 23, 25, 29n23, 29n28, 48n4, 102, 115n10; Hanbali 13, 15, 17, 20, 22, 23, 29n27, 109; Maliki 13, 15, 17, 19, 20, 22, 23, 102; Shafi' 15, 23, 102, 109, 115n10

Judges: appointment procedure 44–6; background 43–4; ethical stance 50–7; multifaceted identity 70; training 26–7; use of discretion 57–65; *see also* Implementation of Islamic law

Law of Family Rights (applied in Gaza 1954) 5–6, 21, 53, 80, 81, 93, 101, 102–3, 108, 118, 125, 127, 169; *Egyptian* 21, 26; *Ottoman* 19, 21, 22
Law of Personal Status (Jordanian) 53, 103, 137n1

mahr (dower) 17, 54, 80, 81, 85, 86, 99, 101, 102, 106, 109, 158, 163, 164, 174, 178n10
Majalla 18, 20, 28n19, 28n22
mediation 17, 55, 61, 129
Model Parliament for Women and Legislation 145–7, 148–9, 150n10, 154; attempts to control debate 146; differences within the religious establishment 146, 148, 164–6; differences within the women's movement 144, 146, 148; proposals for family law reform 145
multiplex relationships 8, 50, 63, 137, 187

nafaqa (alimony, maintenance) 9, 22, 46, 63, 66–7, 73–4, 75, 80–3, 88–93, 115n16; children's nafaqa 84, 124; increase in nafaqa cases 73–4; innovative use of 88–93; as proportion of total Shari'a court cases 74
nakba 49n6, 79, 104

Qadi al-qudah 33, 46; Abu Sardana 33, 64, 71n2, 73, 156–9, 178n5; Mahmoud al-Habbash 173; Taysir Al-timimi 74, 164–5, 166, 167–70, 171–3

reformists *vs.* conservatives in Egypt 20, 29n26

Shari'a 3, 12–15, 16, 18, 19, 21, 27n3, 50
Shaykh Ikrima Sabri (mufti of Jerusalem) 165–6
Sultan Sulayman al-Qanuni 18

tawabi' (value of wife's furniture) 84–8; evolution of 84–5, 96n14; frequency of suits 85; as a tool for negotiation 87

wali (a woman's guardian in marriage or custody issues) 64, 65–6, 118, 157–8, 167–8
wifely obedience 80, 93, 98–112, 114n1, 158; chastisement for disobedience 101–2, 107, 114n5, 114n7, 114n10; court handling of obedience cases 107–9; roots of obedience concept 98–100
women's movement 141, 144–7, 159–64, 170–1; proposals on marriage and divorce 161; successes 126, 149, 151–2, 153, 154–5, 174, 175, 176; *see also* Model Parliament for Women and Legislation